T0271182

The Lean, Smart, Digital Supply Chain

Technology plays a key role in enabling lean and agile supply chain operations. For example, connecting to suppliers in real-time facilitates re-supplying parts and materials for a just-in-time production environment. But choosing the wrong technology can create waste in terms of the time, effort, and money spent evaluating, selecting, implementing, and using it.

Furthermore, lean has been traditionally thought of as a "pen and pencil" technique as they were mostly confined to a single facility. As a consequence, while there are many books written on lean manufacturing, lean office, and, to a lesser degree, lean global supply chain, most if not all barely discuss the role and impact of technology in process improvement, and there aren't many books that combine the topics of a lean and agile supply chain and technology (smart and otherwise) in this way.

This book makes the case that technology is a key enabler of a lean supply chain and is unique in that it links lean and agile thinking with available and affordable technologies to get the most out of improved processes.

Essentially, this book details various supply chain and logistics management areas where lean and agile thinking in combination with existing and emerging technologies such as the Internet, e-commerce, Enterprise Resource Planning (ERP) systems, Robotics, IoT, AI, and Data Analytics can take an organization to the next level through increased speed, accuracy, integration, and collaboration among all parties in the supply chain.

Paul Myerson is currently an adjunct Professor of Supply Chain Management at Kean University. He holds a BS in business logistics from Pennsylvania State University and an MBA in physical distribution from Temple University.

Myerson has an extensive background as a Supply Chain and Logistics professional, consultant, and teacher (both full- time at Monmouth and Lehigh Universities and at various times as an adjunct at Kean University and New Jersey City University).

As an industry professional, trainer, and consultant, Myerson has been a successful change catalyst for a variety of clients and organizations of all sizes. His 40 plus years of experience in Supply Chain Management, Logistics Strategies, and Operations Systems have resulted in bottom-line improvements for companies such as General Electric (GE), Unilever, and Church & Dwight (Arm & Hammer).

Myerson created and marketed a Supply Chain Planning software tool for Windows® in 1998 and more recently in 2024, with a technology partner, created a multi-platform Supply Chain Planning app for small businesses (www.forecisely.com).

He is also the author of seven books on Supply Chain & Logistics Management and has written a column on Lean Supply Chain for *Inbound Logistics* magazine, both since 2012.

The Lean, Smart, Digital Supply Chain

How to Enable a Lean and Agile Global Supply Chain with the Help of Technology

Paul Myerson

Routledge
Taylor & Francis Group

A PRODUCTIVITY PRESS BOOK

First published 2025
by Routledge
605 Third Avenue, New York, NY 10158

and by Routledge
4 Park Square, Milton Park, Abingdon, Oxon, OX14 4RN

Routledge is an imprint of the Taylor & Francis Group, an informa business

ISBN: 978-1-032-44534-2 (hbk)
ISBN: 978-1-032-44533-5 (pbk)
ISBN: 978-1-003-37263-9 (ebk)

DOI: 10.4324/9781003372639

Typeset in Garamond
by SPi Technologies India Pvt Ltd (Straive)

Contents

INTRODUCTION

1

Chapter 1

Supply Chain and Technology: A Very Smart Combination

In recent times, supply chains have been in a state of transition partially due to the pandemic as well as a stream of other seemingly never-ending man-made and natural disruptions. Not surprisingly, many leading firms have been attempting to change their supply chain strategies to become more resilient, sustainable, and collaborative with customers, suppliers, and other stakeholders. To avoid future backlogs, shortages, and disruptions, many solutions are being explored including a switch from just-in-time inventory to just-in-case, as well as near-shoring, on-shoring, redundancy, omni channel retail, etc.

Technology can play a significant role in securing global supply chains via automation, software, and connectivity. New technology developments can be utilized from production to storage, delivery, and reverse logistics. There has been increasing investment in supply chain technologies like artificial intelligence (AI) and analytics, robotic process automation, and control towers while retraining workers.

Time for Action

Now that vulnerabilities in supply chains have been fully exposed, it is time for organizations to take lessons from supply chain disruptions and adjust their operations to become more flexible and responsive. Organizations

DOI: 10.4324/9781003372639-2

need to embrace digitalization and technology more broadly throughout the supply chain in an integrated, holistic model.

From robotics in manufacturing and automated guided vehicles in warehouses, new technologies in the production area of the economy can help to automate processes, increase productivity, and lower costs. In the transportation sector, technology can help decrease delivery times and novel transportation solutions can lower delivery costs. New technology such as AI and machine learning can help companies bring products to market faster and more efficiently and digitization can help keep supply chains running smoothly.

The Lean, Agile Supply Chain and Technology

Technology plays a key role in enabling and creating resiliency in lean, agile supply chain operations, but businesses must be careful when selecting and applying it. For example, connecting to suppliers in real-time facilitates re-supplying parts and materials to enable a just-in-time production environment. However, choosing the wrong technology can create waste in terms of the time, effort, and money spent evaluating, selecting, implementing, and using it.

Furthermore, lean thinking has been traditionally thought of as a "pen and pencil" technique as it was mostly confined to a single facility. Consequently, while much has been written on lean manufacturing, lean office, and, to a lesser degree, lean (global) supply chain, most if not all barely discuss the role and impact of technology in process improvement and there aren't many books that combine the topics of a lean, agile supply chain and (smart and otherwise) technology in this way.

This book makes the case that technology is, in fact, a key enabler of a lean, agile, and smart supply chain and can lead to a competitive advantage, in that it links lean and agile thinking with available and affordable technologies to get the most out of improved, resilient processes.

Specifically, it details various supply chain and logistics management areas where lean and agile thinking, in combination with existing and emerging technologies such as the internet, e-commerce, enterprise resource planning (ERP) systems, robotics, internet of things (IoT), AI, data analytics, etc., can take an organization to the next level through increased speed, accuracy, integration, and collaboration among all parties in the supply chain.

This new way of thinking is presented in an easy-to-understand format and includes tools, methodologies, best practices, examples, and cases of how, when, and where technology can be combined with a lean and agile philosophy to "turbo charge" a supply chain to give a company a distinct competitive advantage.

Unfortunately for the practitioner, there really isn't much out there currently written on the lean, agile, and smart supply chain, creating a "gap" between existing material and the great interest on the topic; especially with the growth of the global supply chain (and its inherent problems magnified by the pandemic) enabled by an assortment of technology such as supply chain planning systems, control towers, IoT, AI, data analytics, and omni channel retail, to name a few.

Supply chain professionals, executives, consultants, and even everyday businesspeople need or want to know more about this topic as supply chain costs can represent as much as 50–70% of a company's revenues.

Technology for a "Smart" Supply Chain

Traditional supply chains are increasingly becoming intelligent with more objects embedded with sensors and better communication, intelligent decision-making, and automation capabilities. The new "smart" supply chain presents huge opportunities for achieving cost reduction and enhancing efficiency improvement.

Some people refer to this concept as "supply chain 4.0", meaning the application of the IoT, the use of advanced robotics, and the application of advanced analytics (including AI) of big data in supply chain management: place sensors in everything, create networks everywhere, automate anything, and analyze everything to significantly improve performance and customer satisfaction.

Companies expect their supply chains to deliver more … to be responsive to demand and resilient to change, to optimize costs and do good for society. To achieve all this, supply chain leaders must reimagine their supply chains for tomorrow.

Future-ready supply chains are intelligent, self-driving networks of growth. They're built on a foundation of digital, data, and AI to provide the visibility, agility, and new ways of working needed to create 360° value, enterprise wide.

These intelligent supply networks deliver across some key priorities:

Improved modeling – It is critical to develop contingency plans to identify, prepare for, and mitigate supply chain risk exposure. Additionally, the supply chain network itself needs to be constantly evaluated and optimized to enable a lean and agile supply chain.

Agility and resiliency – A supply chain that is agile and customer-centric, addressing demand changes, is critical in today's volatile environment. Clothing retailers such as H&M and Zara developed some of these techniques in the early 2000s for a quicker response to changing consumer trends. They invested in sorting and material-handling technologies to expedite newly designed products through distribution while companies like Dell and Nokia gained an advantage in crises by working on contingency plans and relationships with backup vendors in advance of floods and fires hitting their supply chains.

Real-time data – Despite the growing use of radio frequency identification or "RFID", a technology used in supply chains to track and manage assets since the 1990s, end-to-end supply chain visibility has remained a pipe dream because of data limitations. Today, companies are starting to use technologies such as sensors and the IoT to gain added visibility on their shipments, beginning with the highest-value, most sensitive items.

So how can we make it happen? The following are some areas to consider:

Artificial intelligence – Transform data-driven decision-making across the supply chain using AI, analytics, and intelligent automation. The most advanced companies understand that while the cloud sets you up with next-level computing power and access to new kinds of data in the right quantity and quality, AI is the bridge to convert that data into business value.

Cloud – Change through custom cloud services and solutions that accelerate innovation, intelligence, and value across the supply chain.

Ecosystem to support an intelligent enterprise – Navigate a complex partner ecosystem across the supply chain, accelerate digital transformation, and enhance the digital core. The supply chain ecosystem refers to a network of interlinked companies, such as suppliers and distributors, who interact with each other, primarily complementing or supplying key components of the value propositions within their products or services.

Industry X.0 (and supply chain 4.0) – A term coined by consultant Accenture meaning to reimagine the way products, services, and experiences get designed and built in the age of digital disruption to speed up operational efficiency and enterprise-wide growth. Think in terms of how products are designed and engineered, sourced and supplied, manufactured, serviced, returned, and renewed. Industry X.0 and supply chain 4.0, while generalized concepts, will be critical in the ongoing transformations.

Sustainability – Become responsible by design by building sustainable value chains that positively impact business, society, and the planet. For organizations to meet their customers' expectations and be truly sustainable, they must ensure responsible business practices inside their own organization and across their entire value chain.

The supply chain is continually evolving. As it becomes smarter, more sustainable, and lean, supply chain and logistics will continue to be transformed.

By starting down this path now rather than waiting, the lean, smart supply chain can help you manage day-to-day operations as well as handle global disruptions, visualize the full picture, and respond in real-time. Isn't that the "smart" thing to do? (Myerson, 2022)

Before we delve into what exactly a lean, agile, and smart supply chain is, let's first look at how we've arrived at this point and time where we can finally achieve what many have long dreamed about.

Chapter 2

Supply Chain, Technology, and Their Growing Importance to Business and Society

Supply Chain Defined

The terms "supply chain" and "supply chain management" (SCM) should be separately defined as they are sometimes (mistakenly) used interchangeably.

The supply chain itself is a system of organizations, people, activities, information, and resources involved in the planning, moving, or storage of a product or service from supplier to customer (actually more like a "web" than a "chain"). Supply chain activities transform natural resources, raw materials, and components into a finished product that is delivered to the end customer.

SCM, as defined by the Council of Supply Chain Management Professionals (CSCMP),

> encompasses the planning and management of all activities involved in sourcing, procurement, conversion, and logistics management.
>
> It also includes the crucial components of coordination and collaboration with channel partners, which can be suppliers, intermediaries, third-party service providers, and customers.

DOI: 10.4324/9781003372639-3

SCM integrates supply and demand management within and across companies and typically "includes all of the logistics management activities noted above, as well as manufacturing operations, and it drives coordination of processes and activities with and across marketing, sales, product design, finance and information technology" (www.cscmp.org, 2023).

Some people take a narrower view of the supply chain and in many cases think of it as focused more on the supply end (i.e., purchasing) and ignore the logistics side (*as defined as the part of the supply chain that plans, implements, and controls the efficient movement and storage of goods, services, and information from the point of use or consumption to meet customer requirements*). In other cases, many just assume that logistics is included but don't state it. Still others, while including both areas above, ignore the planning aspects of the supply chain. Personally, I tend to refer to the field as "supply chain and logistics management" when teaching to make clear what is included.

In fact, according to an article titled "Continuing Education – Making the Right Selection" (Trunick, 2011), "Some of the most passionate debates in academic circles still center on what constitutes supply chain management and its place in the academic structure. Not surprisingly, that same debate rages in the commercial world". The article goes on to say that some people use the terms "logistics" and "supply chain" interchangeably, while others feel that it's important for logistics to still have its own place.

As we will see in this book, it is very important to understand the similarities and differences between more functional areas like logistics, which includes transportation and distribution, versus the broader concept of SCM which is cross-functional and cross-organizational. This can have a major impact on decision-making, structure, staffing, and technology requirements in an organization, so it needs to be understood and examined carefully.

Depending on one's view, some of the functions below may be included within the supply chain and logistics organization:

- Procurement – The acquisition of goods or services from an outside external source.
- Demand forecasting – Estimating the quantity of a product or service that customers will purchase.
- Customer service and order management – Tasks associated with fulfilling an order for goods or services placed by a customer.
- Inventory – Planning and management.
- Transportation – For hire and private.

- Warehousing – Public and private.
- Materials handling and packaging – Movement, protection, storage, and control of materials and products using manual, semi-automated, and automated equipment.
- Facility network – Location decision in an organization's supply chain network.
- Information management (including generating and sharing customer, supplier, forecasting, inventory, and production information) – This includes all of the information required to ensure that supply matches demand throughout the supply chain.

SCM is also intertwined with operations management which consists of activities that create value by transforming inputs (i.e., raw materials) into outputs (i.e., goods and services), which is where we sometimes use the term "supply chain and operations management" and thus will be covered under the "Supply Chain Software Systems: Make" section of this book. Both activities support the manufacturing process.

History of Supply Chain and Logistics Management

What is now known as "supply chain management" (a term which wasn't even coined until the early 1980s) has a long history. Starting with a focus on cost minimization to now encompassing interconnected, complex global networks.

The first major steps were aimed at using scientific management operations research techniques created by Frederick Taylor on military logistics processes in World War II.

After World War II, businesses began to understand the relationships and trade-offs involved such as inventory costs vs. transportation costs and logistics gained an important place in the business world as well.

In the 1960s physical distribution, a more integrated concept that included activities such as transportation, inventory control, warehousing, and facility location had become an area of study and practice in education and industry. Physical distribution involved the coordination of more than one activity associated with supplying products to the marketplace (i.e., more focused on the "outbound" side of manufacturing).

In the mid-1960s, the scope of physical distribution was expanded to include the supply side including inbound transportation and warehousing

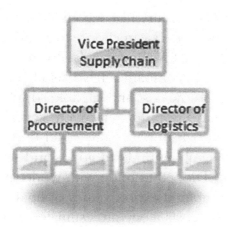

Figure 2.1   Supply chain organizational chart.

and was referred to as business logistics. In many cases, purchasing was not included and went under the heading of "materials management" or "procurement".

In the early 1980s as American manufacturing had been hammered by overseas competitors for over a decade and began actively outsourcing materials, labor, and manufacturing overseas, the term "supply chain management" entered the common business lexicon. It defined the new, complex global world we now live and do business in, as well as an understanding of the integration and importance of all activities involved in sourcing and procurement, conversion, and logistics management. This includes coordination and collaboration with channel partners, which can be suppliers, intermediaries, third-party service providers, and customers.

As opposed to the past, where physical distribution, logistics, purchasing, etc. were all fragmented, many of today's organizations feature in integrated supply chain organizations in most cases led by a senior-level executive (Figure 2.1).

Increasing Use of Technology in Supply Chain Management

Technology has helped to drive the concept of an integrated supply chain starting with the development of electronic data interchange (EDI) systems as a standardized format for the electronic transfer of data between business enterprises (which really took off in the 1980s), as well as the introduction of "off the shelf" enterprise resource planning (ERP) software systems which featured integrated core business processes in a common database.

Furthering this into the 21st century has been the expansion of internet-based collaborative systems where users can choose to "rent" instead of "buy" software they want using what is known as "software as a service" or SaaS.

Since the mid-1960s, U.S. companies have also been slicing up their supply chains in search of low-cost and capable suppliers offshore. In the 1980s, there was a move from "producer-driven" supply chains to "buyer-driven" chains. Today, global supply chains cover finished goods as well as components and sub-assemblies, in both goods and service industries with more than 28% of U.S. GDP tied to trade with world exports of intermediate goods exceeding the combined export values of final and capital goods. Total annual U.S. logistics costs alone are estimated to be well over $1 trillion, with over 50% of that spent on transportation costs and 33% on inventory carrying costs.

Intricate supply networks require interaction with hundreds – or even thousands – of outsourced resources, partners, suppliers, and customers around the world. That's why innovative manufacturers are embracing new collaboration and automation technologies to help overcome inefficient, error-prone, manual processes.

Specifically, the benefits of supply chain technology can include:

- Added competitive advantage
- Increased visibility
- Increased efficiency
- Better customer relationships
- Optimized operations
- Improved responsiveness
- Better decision-making
- Supply chain operations optimization

This supply chain evolution has resulted in both increasing value added and cost reductions through integration and collaboration with a wide range of technologies enabling this to occur efficiently.

An emphasis on low-cost thinking made sense through the early 2000s when the focus was mainly on cost reduction (which helped to rein in inflation for 30+ years). However, since around 2010, there has been a shift in thinking from an emphasis on an efficient supply chain to a more responsive one requiring flexibility. This has led to many companies applying a "hybrid" supply chain strategy which utilizes a combination of efficiency and responsiveness (which is discussed in some detail in Chapter 4).

To be truly successful in a lean and agile endeavor, not only do your processes need to have these characteristics, but so do your people with the technologies to support the strategy.

Supply Chain Technology Today and Tomorrow

As previously mentioned, the term "supply chain management" first entered the lexicon in 1983, but by then it was a better term for an already well-developed concept. By the early 1980s, with the arrival of the first IBM PC computers were widely available which made it easier for businesses to monitor and optimize their supply chains.

By the late 1980s software developers were providing better systems for SCM, and soon after, ERP systems helped to automate supply chains further.

ERP systems centralized many business processes into a single suite of software on a shared database, integrating SCM with other business functions. This also enabled businesses to manage their costs and operations better.

Today, most supply chains are run using ERP systems, which have moved to the cloud and many now have technologies such as artificial intelligence (AI), machine learning, and predictive analytics. AI-powered systems make it possible for businesses to oversee supply chains with less human oversight, and perhaps to become the brains of tomorrow's autonomous supply chains.

Robotics and self-driving vehicles are moving toward widespread adoption in supply chains worldwide as well. Amazon, for example, is currently making use of robots to prepare products for shipment (rtslabs.com, 2020).

The Technology-Enabled Supply Chain

When we talk about a technology-enabled supply chain, we are looking at the points of interaction between your suppliers and customers. These suppliers may be new or existing suppliers; they may be local or international, or from diverse backgrounds.

A technology-enabled supply chain makes communication, engagement, and fulfillment as easy as possible for stakeholders with the help of the latest tools and tech.

A system like this supports and connects many departments including asset, management, engineering, HR, logistics, and finance. For supply chain professionals, this interconnectedness is an opportunity. The tech-enabled supply chain serves as a hub by which organizations can access broad data and make strategic decisions that can impact their organizations and their bottom lines.

The Latest Supply Chain Technology

The pace of technological growth and innovation is accelerating and can make it a challenge to know all the ways that our systems are starting to change, and then adapt to that change. The supply chain is constantly transforming using technologies such as the following:

The Internet of Things (IoT) – Refers to the global network of inter-connected devices, with its most important output being data. There are projections of over 21 billion connected devices globally by 2025, where always-on data streams will provide deep insight and optimization opportunities for supply chain managers.

Data, machine learning (ML), and AI – Planning, scheduling, spend analytics, logistics optimization, and forecasting are all areas where AI could eventually have a large impact.

eProcurement and digitization – Cutting costs, reducing opportunities for errors, increasing collaboration, speeding up processes, and accumulating data for improved insight and decision-making.

Drones – As of 2019, the Federal Aviation Administration (FAA) has given the green light to Amazon, UPS, and Google to deliver to homes (subject to unique rules for drone delivery usage, known as exemptions, for each operator). Walmart, for example, which works with multiple drone-delivery startups, completed around 6,000 U.S. deliveries in 2022. This is gradually changing last-mile delivery.

LIDAR and driverless – LIDAR (light detection and ranging) is a remote sensing technology that uses light in the form of a pulsed laser to measure ranges (variable distances) to the earth, which has been steadily improving in recent years. For the supply chain, its largest impact may be on the improvement and continued implementation of driverless vehicle technology which eventually should dramatically impact long-distance shipping rates as well as logistics for last-mile delivery.

Warehouse automation – The continued automation of warehouses has shown efficiencies in time and reliability, while cutting labor costs (Shaffer, August 2021).

The Role of Information Technology in the Supply Chain

There really isn't any aspect of supply chain and logistics that isn't touched by technology in today's world. Today, thanks to both advances in software and hardware technologies and the internet, companies of all sizes can automate and integrate internal processes and connect with customers and suppliers with ease.

Supply Chain Information

Information provides the foundation on which supply chain processes execute transactions and managers make decisions. Hardware, software, and people throughout a supply chain gather, analyze, and execute utilizing the information. The information must be accurate, accessible in a timely manner, of the right kind, and shared.

Information is used when making decisions about facilities, inventory, transportation, sourcing, and even pricing and revenue management (more of a sales and marketing responsibility impacted by supply chain structure and efficiency).

Interactive View of Information

There are subtle differences between data and information. Data are the facts from which information is derived to make decisions. Pieces of data are rarely useful alone as for data to become information; it needs to be put into context. That is the purpose of information systems.

> An interactive view of information enables people to define the level of information they need to solve problems or make decisions. Depending on the decisions, some people can use data to answer the questions, but others need to extract information from the same data to solve their problems. This interactive view also enables people to trace the source of knowledge from the available data, or to specify the required data based on their explicit knowledge (Figure 2.2).
> An information system is used to collect, process and disseminate information to make it available for decision makers at the right time. Traditionally, an information system deals with transferable data through plain media of communication such as EDI and

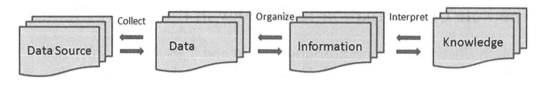

Figure 2.2   Interactive view of information.

the internet. The recent advance of information technology offers a rich variety of media such as video conferencing and online decision support systems that enable decision-makers to convert tacit knowledge into explicit knowledge and to share explicit knowledge.

(Simatupang & Sridharan, 2001)

An organization's information requirements in general are that it needs to be easy to access, relevant to them, accurate, and timely.

Thus, the information technology (IT) used will have a direct impact on a company's performance, both internal and external through integration, which will enable collaboration (Figure 2.3).

A phenomenon known as the bullwhip effect (Figure 2.4) occurs where demand variability increases moving up the supply chain away from the consumer, and small changes in consumer demand can result in large variations in orders placed upstream. It is largely the result of poor information management in the supply chain and therefore can lead to excess inventory levels. By having greater demand visibility throughout the supply chain, inventory levels can be reduced. Therefore, at least in theory, it is possible to substitute information for excess inventory using information systems.

SCM information systems use technology to more effectively manage supply chains.

In terms of the supply chain itself, Fawcett and Magnan (2002) identified four levels or steps of integration:

1. Internal cross-functional integration.
2. Backward integration with first-tier suppliers.
3. Forward integration with first-tier customers.
4. Complete backward and forward integration (from the supplier's supplier to the customer's customer).

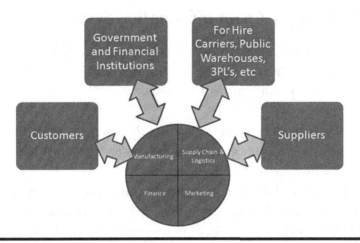

Figure 2.3   Internal and external supply chain information flows.

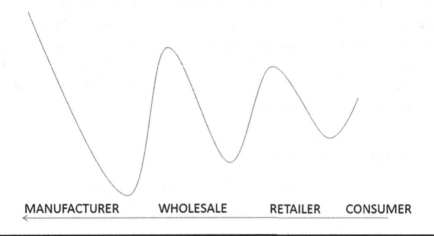

Figure 2.4   The bullwhip effect.

To move from the traditional, fragmented to a more integrated internal and external supply chain requires changes to the ways in which both customer and supplier relationships are established and managed.

In order for a supply chain to achieve its maximum level of effectiveness and efficiency, material, money, and information flows throughout (internal and external) must be integrated and managed in its entirety, within overall service and cost objectives. To accomplish this, IT must play a major role.

Viewpoints of Supply Chain Information Systems

Since there are so many applications in today's global supply chain, it is best to look at information needs from strategic, tactical, and execution viewpoints. The viewpoints are as follows:

Strategic – Develop long-term decisions that help to meet the organization's mission and focus on strategic plans for new products or markets as well as facility capacity decisions.

Tactical – Develop plans that coordinate the actions of key supply chain areas, customers, and suppliers across the tactical time horizon. They focus on tactical decisions, such as inventory or workforce levels. They plan, but don't carry out, the actual physical flows.

Routine – Support rules-based decision-making. Usually in short time frames where accuracy and timeliness are important to the user.

Execution – Typically more transactional oriented where they record and retrieve transaction processing data and execute control of physical and financial information flow. These systems usually have very short time frames, are highly automated, and use standardized business practices (Bozarth & Handfield, 2018).

Supply Chain Macro Processes

One way to look at the supply chain and its functional technology needs, at least at a high level, is by breaking it into macro processes. They are:

1. Supplier management (SM) – To ensure that supplies are at the best cost and terms. This can be for a strategic buy, a tactical negotiated purchase, or a heavily engineered item.
2. Internal supply chain management (ISCM) – Includes a number of activities with respect to receiving, conversion, and movement of finished goods.
3. Distribution channel management (DCM) – The links in a distribution network that has multi-tier arrangements. Will depend upon the industry and type of products shipped and can also include service providers such as transportation, distribution, and third-party logistics (3PL) companies.
4. Customer relationship management (CRM) – Practices, strategies, and technologies that companies use to manage and analyze customer

interactions and data throughout the customer lifecycle, with the goal of improving business relationships with customers, assisting in customer retention, and driving sales growth.

5. Transactional management (TM) – The base transactional data such as order and inventory information to run the "day to day" aspects of a business.

Processes 1–4 above (Figure 2.5) provide access and reporting of supply chain transaction data. Advanced systems use analytics based on transaction data to improve supply chain performance and ERP systems form the foundation of a supply chain IT system.

Supply Chain Information Technologies

Today, most companies have implemented at least some components of supply chain systems, such as warehouse management or forecasting. The organizations that have taken an integrated, extended supply chain approach to these systems are the ones who get the greatest benefit.

The general category of SCM software also benefits from what is known as supplier relationship management (SRM) software, CRM, and product lifecycle management (PLM) software.

SRM software is a subsystem of SCM software that helps to automate, simplify, and accelerate the procurement-to-pay processes for goods and services.

CRM software originally was a stand-alone system directed at sales force automation, marketing, and customer service. More recently, it has become more integrated with supply chain software such as ERP systems.

PLM software helps companies to collaborate and manage the entire lifecycle of a product efficiently and cost-effectively, from ideation, to

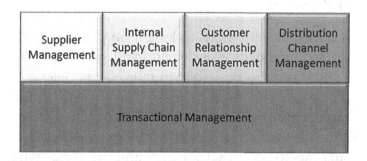

Figure 2.5 Supply chain macro processes.

design and manufacture, through service and disposal. It is where applications such as computer aided design (CAD), computer aided manufacturing (CAM), computer aided engineering (CAE), and product data management (PDM) come together.

According to marketresearch.biz, the global SCM software market size accounted for USD $14.3 billion in 2022. It is projected to surpass around USD $35.3 billion by 2032 and is poised to reach a CAGR of 9.7% from 2023 to 2032.

Furthermore, some key takeaways from the report were:

- By type, in 2022, the SCM software market was dominated by the large enterprises segment.
- By component, the solution segment dominated the market with a significant share.
- By deployment mode, the SCM software market is dominated by the cloud segment.
- In 2022, North America dominated the market with the highest revenue share of 34%.
- Asia-Pacific is expected to be the fastest-growing region in the SCM software market (marketresearch.biz, 2023).

SCM systems can be viewed in terms of supply chain planning (SCP) and supply chain execution (SCE).

In general, SCP applications apply algorithms to predict future requirements of various kinds and help to balance supply and demand.

SCE software applications usually monitor the physical movement and status of goods as well as the management of materials and financial information of all participants in the supply chain.

Supply Chain Planning

SCP software vendors address short- to long-term planning and focus on demand, supply, and the balance of demand and supply together usually in the form of an S&OP process described in more detail below.

Demand management – There are three main functions of demand management software which are: (1) predicting demand, (2) using "what-if" analysis to create sales plans, and (3) using "what-if" analysis to shape demand. Forecasts are typically a rolling 24–36 months.

Modern supply chain systems have moved toward a demand "pull" driven model, so demand management has moved from a purely forecasting tool to one that optimizes and shapes demand to some extent.

Supply management – This area helps meet demand with minimal resources at the lowest cost. Software functionality typically found in this area includes supply network planning or optimization (SNP), production scheduling (sometimes referred to as advanced planning systems or APS), distribution requirements planning (DRP), replenishment, and procurement.

Sales & Operational Planning (S&OP) – Facilitates monthly executive planning meetings to tie together sales, operation, and financial plans on an aggregate level, along with the related tasks to make sure supply adequately meets demand at the lowest cost. Input is collected from demand, capacity, and financial plans culminating in a consolidated sales and operational plan.

Supply Chain Execution

SCE systems primarily include warehouse management software (WMS) and transportation management software (TMS) and feature planning, scheduling, optimizing, tracking, and performance monitoring as described below.

Warehouse management systems – WMS controls the flow of goods through the warehouse and interfaces to the material handling equipment. They also typically include automated processing of inbound and outbound shipments and the storage of goods. Administrative features can include processing of EDI transactions, planning shipments, resource management, and performance tracking.

Transportation management systems – A TMS helps to manage global transportation needs including air, sea, ground, and carrier shipments. In terms of transportation acquisition and dispatching, a TMS may also handle the planning, scheduling, and optimizing of shipments. They also provide tracking of vehicles including exception management, constraints, collaborating with partners, and monitoring of freight. Administrative features can include cost allocations, freight auditing and payment, and contract management.

Enterprise resource systems (ERP) – While some may not include ERP systems as SCM tools, a great deal of the functionality is supply chain and logistics related. ERP systems are an extension of an MRP system to tie in all internal processes as well as customers and suppliers. It allows for the automation and integration of many business processes including finance, accounting, human resources, sales and order entry, raw materials, inventory, purchasing, short-term scheduling, shipping, resource and production planning and CRM. An ERP shares common databases and business practices and produces information in real time and coordinates business from supplier evaluation to customer invoicing.

E-businesses must also keep track of and process a tremendous amount of information and as such have realized that much of the information they need to run an e-business such as stock levels at various warehouses, cost of parts, and projected shipping dates can already be found in their ERP system databases. As a result, a significant part of the online efforts of many e-businesses involve adding Web access to an existing ERP system.

ERP systems have the potential to reduce transaction costs and increase the speed and accuracy of information but can also be expensive and time-consuming to install.

Other Supply Chain Technologies

There are other categories of software often used in the supply chain including:

Supply chain event management – These are software applications that allow companies to track orders across the supply chain in real time between trading partners providing managers with a clear picture of how their supply chain is performing. The information provided by these systems allows a company to sense and respond to unanticipated changes to planned supply chain operations. This breed of systems conveys information regarding supply chain processes at a specific event level, such as a hand-off from one supply chain entity to another, the commitment of a product to an order, the movement of a shipment between two logistics network nodes, or the placement of a product into storage.

Business intelligence (BI) – This category is made up of applications, infrastructure, tools, and best practices providing analysis of information to improve and optimize decisions and performance. BI tools help to sort through the vast amount of data that has become available through the continuing adoption of SCM technologies.

Additionally, there are related tools for supply chain collaboration, data synchronization, and spreadsheets and database software.

In fact, there are many smaller companies today that still operate their primary planning functions using spreadsheets and run their day-to-day operations with accounting systems such as QuickBooks and Peachtree rather than spend the resources on a full-blown ERP system.

Supply Chain Integration Tools

As information links all parts of the supply chain, other hardware and software tools are used for this purpose including:

- **Internet** – Allows companies to communicate with suppliers, customers, shippers, and other businesses around the world instantaneously.
- **e-Business** – Gradual replacement of physical business processes with electronic ones. It comes in two general forms, the largest being business-to-business (B2B) and business-to-consumer (B2C).
- **Electronic data interchange (EDI)** – The computer-to-computer exchange of standardized business documents. Today, EDI may also come through the internet.
- **Bar code and point-of-sale data** – Creates an instantaneous computer record of a sale.
- **Radio frequency identification (RFID)** – Technology that can send product data from an item (containing an RFID chip) to a reader via radio waves.

Supply Chain Technology Trends

The supply chain and logistics management software landscape is already mature and is being redefined to align with businesses' needs for more agility, resiliency, and intelligent operations. SCM applications are diverse – from large-scale suite providers offering portfolios of solutions to niche providers specializing in specific industry verticals. Applications are further evolving with innovative providers offering functionality such as advanced analytics (AA) and AI.

According to a recent Gartner SCM software market guide (2022), in the post-pandemic climate, the net investment of businesses in logistics and

SCM software appears to be positive. Over 56% of survey respondents say they have increased spending (permanently or temporarily) on logistics and SCM applications in the past two years.

The SCM software market can be broken down into three segments: SCP, sourcing and procurement, and SCE. The planning segment includes applications that deal with developing demand forecasts, establishing supplier relationships, scheduling manufacturing and developing metrics to ensure cost-effective operations. Sourcing and procurement applications help users improve the mechanics of purchasing through timely payments and by improving the terms of trade. Execution applications cater to delivery and distribution processes, such as creating purchase orders, updating the inventory, moving products, and delivering goods to customers.

Trends shaping SCM software adoption include:

- The rise in online retail sales is boosting the demand for effective warehouse, inventory, and transportation control.
- New supply chain tech investments are favoring SaaS providers that deliver innovative solutions. Software is being prioritized that is easy to use; cost-friendly, and quick to deploy in an existing application ecosystem and offers better collaboration between teams.
- SCM software providers are integrating advanced analytics, AI, and data science capabilities in their applications. By 2026, over 75% of supply chain software providers will embed these technologies to improve decision-making for users, according to Gartner.

By 2026 over 75% of SCM software providers will deliver embedded advanced analytics (AA), AI, and data science.

Top Reasons to Digitalize Supply Chains

Over half of the survey respondents say they purchased logistics and SCM software for productivity improvements. Market competition (43%) and the need for advanced SCM technology (40%) are the next top triggers for logistics and SCM software investment.

Business disruptions due to events such as the global pandemic drove nearly 19% of respondents to invest in logistics and SCM technology to improve operations and supply chain resilience (Gartner Digital Markets, 2022).

Recently Emerging Supply Chain Technology Trends

While the types of software applications in the supply chain probably won't drastically change, the methods for gathering, analyzing, using, and sharing data and applications will.

There are many "technology trends" lists compiled every year in the supply chain field, but here are some that seem to have the best chance of having a lasting impact:

AI, IoT, RPA, AR/VR, cloud technology – The next generation of supply chain trends will also be supported by advanced technologies including computing and machine learning (AI/ML), the IoT, robotic process automation (RPA), autonomous vehicles (drones, self-driving vehicles, etc.), and digital twins and augmented/virtual reality (AR/VR). Companies will find new technological ways for supporting end-to-end SCM, execution, predictive analysis, and data analysis. The AI/ML, IoT, AR, and cloud platforms are expected to assist in identifying patterns, errors, and supply chain data issues in real-time.

Digital supply chain twins create realistic digital settings that are exact replicas of physical assets and operations. They can simulate multiple scenarios, thereby helping to optimize logistics processes and minimize risks. VR takes it one step further by providing immersive experiences for training purposes, reducing the hazards involved in manual processes, and boosting productivity.

Advanced data analytics and automation to be preferred – These two factors will keep accelerating, helping organizations mitigate disruption via digital, agile SCM. The implementation of predictive and prescriptive analytics, similarly as advances in big data, algorithms, and robotics, will have broad-reaching effects. Enterprises will choose greater visibility, data-driven decision-making, execution efficiency, predictability, and profitability. Further, effective data security, reskilling employees, and governance are going to be given more importance in the coming years.

Supply chain agility is critical – It is now important to form flexible networks that cater to dynamic customer demand and ever-increasing uncertainty. It'll be important to proactively identify ways to extend responsiveness through variable cost structures using tools such as lean supply chain combined with technology. However, as there's no one-size-fits-all approach, organizations must also foster continuously innovative cultures. The lean and agile supply chains of the longer term are those that can react quickly to changes, delays, and unexpected events to satisfy customer expectations, outpace the competition, and drive growth.

Visibility into supply chains will remain essential – Supply chain visibility has always been important for organizations and will be equivalently vital in the future. Visibility is going to be a key objective for organizations besieged to realize true transformation, satisfy customers, and capture new markets.

The supply chain is constantly moving, and inventory levels and demand shift frequently (and sometimes unexpectedly).

Real-time monitoring enables business owners and their teams the ability to stay on top of operations with an extra layer of transparency without being involved every minute of the day.

Real-time monitoring is also crucial when it comes to managing inventory. Accessing real-time inventory data provides an accurate and transparent view of inventory levels at any given period of time. It also displays deep insights into past and future demand, as well as SKU (stock keeping unit) and channel performance.

Furthermore, blockchain can also significantly improve supply chain visibility, which often lacks traceability and transparency. Blockchain provides a decentralized and secure database that records every transaction along the supply chain. Picture real-time tracking and traceability of products, with regularized updates on each stated leg of a journey.

More focus on last-mile delivery – Demand for last-mile is growing rapidly and is anticipated to grow by 78% globally by 2030, as per the economic forum. This is partially a result of the fact that since the COVID-19 pandemic, an enormous inflow of home deliveries has resulted in businesses adding more emphasis to their last-mile deliveries. As last-mile delivery costs contribute to over 50% of total shipping costs, the increase in home delivery can cause logistics inefficiencies. So many businesses have started to adopt last-mile delivery technologies such as autonomous delivery, lockers, delivery from local stores, etc. into their logistics operations and this trend will continue to increase.

Rise of omni channel fulfillment and e-commerce systems – The rise of e-commerce and omni channel, accelerated by the pandemic, is one of the largest forces affecting today's supply chains. E-commerce and omni channel fulfillment will help shape the way organizations identify and establish key priorities, creating challenges concerning scale and network efficiency while producing new opportunities and technology to realize a competitive advantage. A McKinsey survey of consumers shows that 15% of consumers value delivery speed and value. As a result, omni channel retail will drive more innovation and simplification of existing technology.

Optimization and automation of shipments – Optimizing shipments and loads by selecting the optimal mode will help manage and improve delivery times and costs. For example, shippers can move freight with trucks instead of rail if loads are more time-sensitive or switch from a full truckload (TL) to a less-than-truckload (LTL) choice to make the most of existing routes that fit their needs. This will ensure paying the correct price supported by the amount of service needed and can be where cloud-based systems will be beneficial for door, slot and vehicle management alongside enhancing warehouse management.

Increased cybersecurity for data protection – Cybersecurity is critical to protecting networks from cyberattacks, which be a significant threat to global supply chains now and in the future. The significant increase in information and data-driven organizations is creating more vulnerability which means supply chain partners can accidentally expose one another and their customers to privacy breaches, fraud, ransomware, etc. As a result, there will need to be greater collaboration when safeguarding networks, devices, people, programs and beyond in their corporate IT systems and their factories and warehouses' operational technology environments. Additionally, many organizations will tend to invest in redundancy, firewalls, advanced anti-hacking technologies, and employee training.

Increased automation to cut back manual tasks – Almost every link within the supply chain can enjoy some sort of automation within the system. In general, automating manual tasks allows companies to reduce manpower, freeing up teams to specialize in high-level strategic work and productivity instead of repetitive tasks. Specifically, time-consuming methods including setting appointments, checking shipment status, and generating invoices will be automated, which will allow companies to handle the increased number of shipments more efficiently. Finally, manual errors will be avoided if repetitive, tedious yet crucial operations are automated.

Focus on customer-centricity – Customer-centricity is important to supply chain professionals today, as consumer expectations demand ethical, sustainable business practices. Managing a successful supply chain would force upskilling talent with greater cross-functional and analytical skills so people have the training to support these new levels of customer-centricity (cargoflash.com, 2022).

Integrate circular and sustainable supply chain practices – Consumers across the globe are demanding more sustainable products, and companies must respond by embedding end-to-end sustainability into their supply chain processes. Building circularity into supply chain processes means not only trying to reduce a negative footprint but also creating a positive one. This can be accomplished by using renewable energy in manufacturing and delivery and aiming for zero waste along the value chain. Enterprises are also looking for ways to reduce carbon emissions in the supply chain, and this means they must reconsider things like the materials used in manufacturing and packaging, the markets they compete in and optimizing supply chains. While this might not seem like a technological trend, we are, for example, starting to see a shift in IoT investment on the plant floor away from things like predictive maintenance toward energy tracking.

While the growth and importance of the global supply chain has at least partially been enabled by technology, it has created a much more complex environment in which to operate. That is why the concept of a digital supply chain, covered in the next chapter, has gained momentum.

Chapter 3

The Smart, Digital Supply Chain

We have entered the digital supply chain age with the application of electronic technologies being applied to every aspect of the extended supply chain.

Electronic connectivity is at the basis of the digital supply chain and is enabled by a range of technologies such as internet of things (IoT), end-to-end digital connectivity, cloud computing, blockchain, big data, predictive analytics, artificial intelligence (AI), machine learning, virtual and augmented reality, voice activated technology, wearable devices, control towers, robotics, 3D printing, on demand additive manufacturing, cyber security, autonomous vehicles, drones, software as a service (SaaS), and much more.

What these technologies all have in common is that they are all electronics and/or use digital forms of communication.

Digital supply chain technologies could eventually replace all uses of paper, eliminate all manual data entry, and updates and eliminate the need to request information as you would already have it available to you.

The implementation of electronic sensors and supply chain visibility software with advanced tracking capabilities will allow for the real-time tracking of the movement of all goods throughout every aspect of the manufacturing, transportation, and logistics processes found in the supply chain.

It also means the extended supply chain is fully integrated from the customer to all levels of suppliers with transparency and visibility throughout, as well as supply chain performance management and optimization.

DOI: 10.4324/9781003372639-4

Using tools such as AI, big data, predictive analytics, and digital control towers can even support an electronically directed and managed supply chain with minimal human action required.

This means that a digital supply chain, and its underlying processes, can be managed with the optimal availability of information on performance, requirements, and dynamics.

Today, supply chain management software is a baseline rather than an option for businesses to optimize costs, speed up operations, and access statistics. Consumers now routinely track the delivery, availability, and popularity of items they purchase, requiring companies to adopt new workflows to create the best experience.

Process management, material flow, supply and demand planning, resource planning, inventory levels, cash flow, and strategy can all be managed dynamically in a digital world with real-time, global information that is available in the digital supply chain (www.supplychaingamechanger. com, 2022).

What is So Smart about the Digital Supply Chain?

The use of the many emerging technologies previously mentioned along with their people, process, and decision support systems allows organizations to cut costs, shorten delivery times, increase flexibility, reduce negative environmental impact, and achieve greater levels of automation.

A 'smart' supply chain is a self-improving and resilient system that can function in an unpredictable environment and involves seamless sharing of information, partial reliance on automation, and continuous optimization of workflows based on real-time data.

This smart supply chain has recently become a major trend due to the following factors:

- The increasing accessibility of modern technologies exposes the obsolescence of some current supply chain practices.
- Customer expectations have grown rapidly, forcing companies to figure out how to manufacture products faster and simplify SKU management.
- Growing environmental concerns, increasingly stringent transportation regulations, and travel and transportation restrictions caused by the pandemic create the need for new ways of managing supply chains.

In summary, the current business environment has forced companies to have more agile, digitalized, resource-efficient, and resilient supply chains.

Now, let's get into a bit more detail as to what a smart supply chain is and compare it with a conventional supply chain.

Conventional versus Smart Supply Chains

A conventional supply chain involves a limited number of different parties that proactively communicate with each other and exchange assets. But since these supply chains took shape way before the internet and digital technologies, they are somewhat static and linear (Figure 3.1).

For example, think of a simplified version of the bicycle supply chain. Raw materials are supplied to original equipment manufacturers (OEMs), where they are turned into bicycle parts. Then these parts are shipped to bicycle manufacturing facilities, where they are assembled into bicycles. Finally, bicycles are distributed to retailers and finally sold to consumers. Today, this form of supply chain simplicity is usually found in small-scale, more local businesses.

Advances in commerce have caused modern consumers to raise their minimum expectations. The arrival of next- and same-day delivery has created a standard of demand that puts a new kind of pressure on businesses.

This network between companies and suppliers includes beginning stages like sourcing and procurement to final delivery and involves all activities, employees, technologies, a multitude of organizations, data, resources, processes, and components involved with getting goods or services to the users.

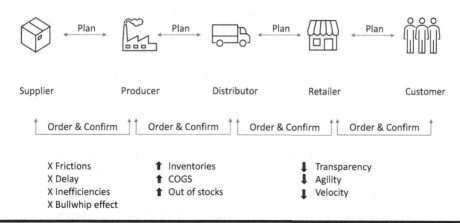

Figure 3.1 Traditional supply chain ecosystem.

In today's global marketplace with supply chains that are increasingly intertwined, the supply and demand function has become extremely complex.

Because of this increase in demand, the entire supply chain is rapidly evolving from having a functional orientation to a global and interconnected network of data and processes.

Now let's discuss some of the important components of a smart supply chain.

A Digital Backbone

It is important to have your supply chain ecosystem digitized first in order to gain the potential of advanced supply chain technologies like AI, IoT, and blockchain. All of the technologies that comprise a smart supply chain require real-time access to data. So, the benefits of integrating smart supply chain technologies will likely be reduced if even a small part of your supply chain network is dependent on paper-based information sharing.

In addition to that, a cloud-based approach to data storage and exchange is also critical to scaling up your supply chain operations. Many activities in your supply chain, such as reacting to sudden market changes or expanding into new sectors, can be managed much more rapidly in the cloud.

Internet of Things

For the supply chain, IoT facilitates remote identification of equipment performance and gives decision-makers granular data on a devices' state and their environment. IoT sensors on a freight vehicle, for example, inform a company if it needs immediate maintenance as well as other information about vehicle location for determining alternative routes.

Similarly, IoT sensors used with environment-sensitive goods in storage or in transit such as drugs or food can notify managers when the temperature, humidity, or light intensity exceeds allowed levels to help companies reduce waste and ensure product quality.

Example of IoT in Supply Chain

Maersk, a Danish industrial container transportation provider, uses IoT sensors and Microsoft Azure cloud computing to adjust certain parameters on the fly to ensure that products are delivered to customers in good condition. For example, for fruit and vegetables, employees can adjust oxygen and dioxide levels in containers to speed up or slow down fruit ripening.

Artificial Intelligence

AI enables supply chain organizations to improve planning and minimize disruptions caused by unpredictable events. Gartner, the provider of research and consulting services, predicts that half of supply chain organizations will invest in AI and advanced analytics capabilities by 2025.

It seems that demand forecasting is one of the most important uses for AI in the supply chain as planners must assess many data sources to make predictions about the demand. Demand forecasting typically has a low level of accuracy and a tendency for human mistakes. The use of AI can automatically process data from all network participants to a unified data location and help make evidence-based resource planning decisions.

AI is even more valuable when paired with IoT as AI can automatically analyze data streaming from IoT sensors and suggest maintenance activities or route and inventory optimization decisions that can further be analyzed and approved by employees.

Blockchain

A smart supply chain is the ideal location for blockchain to be implemented as blockchains (described in more detail in Chapter 16) provide a supply chain network with an immutable ledger, guaranteeing companies that data will be reliable and remain secure. It creates a reliable and transparent environment for both companies and consumers, allowing companies to be confident in their decisions and the AI model output.

An example of its use would be to track products using IoT sensors and record the data on the blockchain, which provides distributors with accurate data on product conditions to help identify spoiled products quickly and accurately.

Also, with the help of programmable electronic protocols referred to as "smart contracts", companies can automate contract execution with blockchain. This technology allows for completing contracts faster, minimizes the risk of human error, and eliminates mediator costs. With smart contracts in place, blockchain can be a robust record-keeping system and an automated transaction platform.

An example of relying on smart contracts would allow companies to automatically transfer funds between each other when certain contract conditions are met; with AI added into the mix, smart contracts can also automatically adjust prices based on delivery times or other factors to help companies streamline the reconciliation of accounts and shorten settlement periods.

A Supply Control Tower

One of the most common criticisms of conventional supply chain ecosystems is the lack of integration and connectivity between the participants which was made even more apparent during the pandemic. Streamlined access to information is an important element of a smart and resilient supply chain.

A way to make this happen is to implement a "supply chain control tower", a term originally coined by Gartner. Instead of sharing data linearly, from party to party, supply chain network participants send all relevant data to a unified data repository, where the information can be accessed by relevant partners. Control towers allow companies to analyze operational data in real-time, allowing for proactive risk management, and more detailed control over operations as well (see drug supply chain example in Figure 3.2).

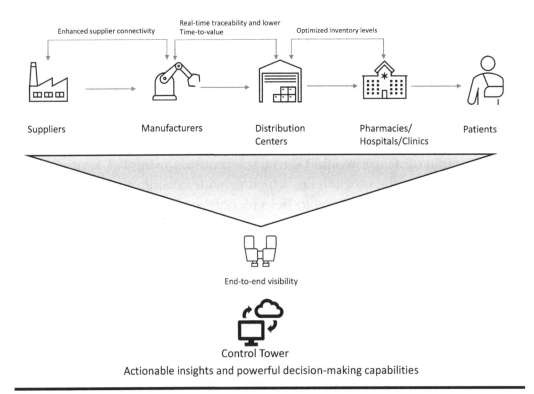

Figure 3.2 Example: Supply chain tower in a drug supply chain.

A Holistic Transformation Approach

Historically, most companies implement digital initiatives in a step-by-step manner, which implies gradual implementation of emerging technologies. However, for a supply chain to become truly smart and autonomous, a company needs to take a more holistic approach to integrating technologies, since AI, blockchain, and IoT are interconnected and complement each other in many ways:

- IoT sensors embedded in transportation and cargo allow companies to gather important data.
- AI allows companies to process data coming from a multitude of partners and IoT sensors to make evidence-based decisions daily.
- Blockchain enables organizations to ensure that the data remains secure and accurate at all times, while smart contracts allow companies to increase operational efficiency by automating essential supply chain processes like invoice payment.

So, implementing these and other emerging technologies companies can bring their extended supply chains closer to becoming self-sufficient, efficient, and increasingly automated.

Conclusion

The importance of a smart supply chain in today's constantly changing business environment can't be underestimated. In just the last few years alone, economic, environmental, and other events have disrupted many businesses and their supply chains.

Recent global events have created new levels of digital supply chain disruption, highlighting a lack of visibility into business and operations. In the face of disruption, organizations were left unable to forecast demand, predict supply, and meet delivery schedules.

Ultimately, there are two main ingredients to make a supply chain smart: emerging technologies and collaboration between supply chain network participants.

Organizations with mature, collaborative, resilient, and increasingly digitized ecosystems have been able not only to overcome the challenges but also thrive on them (Davydov, 2022).

Organizations of all sizes need to speed up their transformation initiatives to digitize their supply chains for flexibility, agility, and increased supply chain visibility into all trading partner activity.

Digitizing supply chains through modern integration, automation, and secure and connected ecosystems makes it easy to manage information flows and uncover insights to ensure continued operations, even in the face of major disruptions.

It's one thing to have all this great technology throughout your global supply chain, but technology is only an enabler of a good process. To accomplish that, we need to create a lean and agile supply chain to survive and thrive in this uncertain environment and to take advantage of all of the technological advances mentioned in this chapter. That is the topic of our next chapter.

Chapter 4

Lean Concepts and Their Applications in the Supply Chain

In today's volatile and constantly changing business environment, technology plays a critical role in driving innovation and growth. However, before investing in technology, it is important to evaluate and optimize the underlying business processes to ensure that the technology is implemented effectively. This is where process improvement comes into play.

Process improvement involves the identification and analysis of existing business processes to identify areas for improvement. This can include streamlining workflows, eliminating bottlenecks, and reducing waste. By improving processes before implementing new technology, organizations can maximize the value of their technology investments and achieve better outcomes.

Process Improvement Is Essential Before Technology Implementations

Below are some reasons that process improvement initiatives should be completed before technology implementations in your supply chain (and other areas):

DOI: 10.4324/9781003372639-5

1. Avoiding costly mistakes: Implementing new technology can be a significant investment for organizations. So, if business processes are not optimized, it can lead to costly mistakes and less than optimal outcomes.
2. Maximizing the value of technology: Technology is only as effective as the processes it supports. By optimizing processes first, organizations can ensure that the technology is aligned with their business goals and can deliver the desired outcomes, leading to increased efficiency, reduced costs, and improved customer satisfaction.
3. Identifying automation opportunities: Process improvement can help identify areas that can be automated using technology by identifying opportunities to automate repetitive tasks and reduce manual effort. This can lead to increased efficiency, reduced costs, and improved accuracy.
4. Enabling change management: Implementing new technology can represent a significant change for organizations. So by improving processes first, organizations can prepare their teams for the change and ensure that they are ready to adopt the new technology, leading to a smoother transition and better outcomes.

By taking a process-first approach, organizations can ensure that their technology investments are aligned with their business goals and can deliver the desired outcomes (Salazar, 2023).

The concept of a process-first approach is applicable in any area in the global supply chain as lead times are longer and inventory levels higher when compared to domestic examples. Longer supply chains are also associated with poor sales-forecasting accuracy and significant delays in resolving technical problems. Managers may underestimate these costs because they tend to plan for a relatively stable chain and do not fully appreciate the complex, dynamic way in which various disruptions affect a geographically dispersed supply chain.

As a result, while having a global supply chain that is lean and agile (or using another frequently used term "responsive") through process improvement used to be an option, in today's volatile environment it has now become a requirement.

The Journey to Continuous Supply Chain Improvement

Applying lean manufacturing principles to supply chain and logistics operations is one way that businesses have reduced their costs. Lean is a team-based form of continuous improvement that focuses on identifying and eliminating waste – activities that do not add value for the customer. After all, customers are ultimately paying for the end product or service, which to them is the value-added effort of transforming raw materials into finished goods. By this definition, activities that don't add value to the customer – such as products being stored, inspected, or delayed – are 100% waste.

In most supply chains, the full cycle time – when material or information enters the supply chain until it is delivered to the customer – primarily consists of waste. Little of this processing time is value-added from the customer's viewpoint.

Many lean manufacturing professionals refer to this cycle time as dock-to-dock time. The shorter the dock-to-dock time, the leaner the manufacturing process. The same can be said of your supply – and demand – chain.

In lean terms, supply chain and logistics areas are frequently viewed as a box (one activity, such as warehousing) or a line (transportation) on a value stream map, which is a form of process flow mapping unique to lean. Value stream mapping (VSM) separates value-added and non-value-added activities starting at the customer and working its way through the system back to the supplier.

Many concepts and tools in the lean practitioner's toolkit can be applied to your supply chain and logistics function. Some are relatively simple and easy to understand, such as 5S-workplace organization, visual workplace, and layout. Others, such as batch size reduction, quick changeover, and total productive maintenance or TPM (equipment-related waste), are more complex. All require ongoing training, support, and commitment from both management and the rank and file.

To get started requires a fundamental understanding of what is non-value-added or waste in the eyes of both the ultimate customer and the parties downstream who you are giving material or information to.

Taiichi Ohno of Toyota defines the seven wastes as transportation, inventory, motion, waiting, overproduction, overprocessing, and defects.

A good way to remember these wastes is the acronym "TIM WOOD". Many lean practitioners add an eighth waste: underutilized employees, or behavioral waste.

Lean principles can be a competitive weapon and a great advantage in tough economic times. Once you and your team start considering the opportunities to reduce waste, you'll wish you had started on the lean journey sooner (Myerson, 2012).

Using a tool like lean in a global supply chain environment can be challenging as in the past it was thought of as more of a "pen and pencil" activity in a single location such as a production facility or distribution center.

While that can still be useful, in the case of today's extended, complex supply chains, it doesn't prove to be nearly as effective as taking a more "holistic" approach.

So, what exactly is a "lean and agile" supply chain and how do you implement it?

A Lean and Agile (or "Hybrid") Supply Chain Strategy

In today's global, dynamic economy, it is beneficial for companies to operate a supply chain that is both lean and agile. Using lean and agile in combination is known as having a hybrid supply chain strategy.

A lean and agile or "hybrid" supply chain strategy may be appropriate for a company that chooses to segment its supply chain based on the characteristics of its different product lines. For example, for some of its product lines, they may be attempting to become a "mass customizer", using make-to-stock (MTS)/lean strategies for high volume, stable demand products, and make-to-order (MTO)/agile for smaller batch sizes (sometimes as little as one item) specific to customers' sometimes unique needs.

A lean supply chain focuses on adding value for customers, while identifying and eliminating waste – anything that doesn't add that value, often through standardization of processes and systems (e.g., standard operating procedures and ERP systems).

Being agile and responsive, on the other hand, implies that your supply chain can handle unpredictability – and a constant stream of new, innovative products – with speed and flexibility.

An agile strategy uses a wait-and-see approach to customer demand by not committing to the final product until actual demand becomes known (also referred to as postponement). For example, this might involve the subassembly of components into modules in a lower-cost process, with final assembly done close to the point of demand in order to localize the product.

An agile supply chain must be responsive to actual demand and capable of using information as a substitute (to some degree) for inventory through collaboration and integration with key customers and suppliers.

Either or Both

On some occasions, either an agile or a lean strategy might be appropriate for a supply chain. But many companies will probably face situations where a hybrid strategy is a better fit. If so, they need to carefully plan and execute the combined strategy with excellence, which is often easier said than done because it involves a lot of moving parts. As in so many aspects of supply chain and operations management, there is more than one way to accomplish this goal.

One example of a company using a hybrid strategy in its supply chain is Zara, a Spanish fashion designer and retailer. Zara directly manufactures most of the products it designs and sells and performs activities such as cutting, dying, labeling, and packaging in-house to gain economies of scale. A network of dedicated subcontractors performs other finishing operations that cannot be completed in-house.

As a result, Zara has a supply chain that not only is agile and flexible but also incorporates many lean characteristics into its processes.

Some semiconductor manufacturers incorporate a hybrid strategy using a flexible manufacturing and distribution model. Subcontractors perform distinct manufacturing processes at separate physical locations. This hybrid approach taps a virtual network of manufacturing partners and requires responsive, flexible, and information-driven sourcing, manufacturing, and distribution functions – in many ways, the opposite of Zara's strategy of shifting processes in-house.

Many organizations can find some form of hybrid supply chain that works well for them. In today's ever-changing, volatile, and competitive global economy, it may often be in a company's best interest to operate a supply chain that is both lean and agile (Myerson, 2014).

Lean Isn't Mean and Agile Isn't Cheap

While there are many benefits of a lean and agile supply chain, also known as a hybrid strategy, as mentioned above, depending on your product or service, your supply chain may tilt more one way or the other (or it might be segmented based upon products, customers, etc.), but still exhibit characteristics of both. For example, if you sell commodities, you will focus more on efficiency. If you were in fashion, you'd tend to be more responsive.

Also, because the supply chain consists of suppliers, customers, and producers, companies can achieve competitive advantage by aligning the entire extended supply chain to a competitive hybrid strategy.

To illustrate how important a hybrid supply chain strategy is, companies that took this approach to heart appear to have performed the best through the pandemic.

The fact is that many companies I have visited over the years have misinterpreted the idea of lean entirely. They thought they were already lean because they laid off a significant part of the workforce, had minimal levels of inventory, or had single-sourced suppliers.

This kind of thinking missed the point, dangerously as it turned out. Having a lean philosophy means getting to the root cause of your variabilities first and then lowering inventory levels.

Low-cost thinking made sense through the early 2000s when the focus was mainly on cost reduction (which helped to rein in inflation for 30+ years). However, since around 2010, there has been a shift in thinking from an emphasis on an efficient supply chain to a more responsive one requiring flexibility.

Furthermore, being lean means that you are flexible and agile to some degree anyway. A primary example of this is the conceptual idea of one-piece flow, where batch size reductions are enabled through quicker changeovers in manufacturing. As most activities in a factory, warehouse, or office involve batching and changeovers of some kind, it is really a universal concept.

Lean and Agile Success

To be truly successful in a lean and agile endeavor, not only do your processes need to have these characteristics, but so do your people. You also need the technologies to support the strategy.

Agility is all about customer responsiveness, flexibility, people, available information, collaboration within and between firms, and readying a company for change.

Your supply chain needs to take a hybrid approach structurally, as well as organizationally, which refers to the way decisions are made about how to schedule and utilize supply chain resources. This requires capabilities such as team alignment, end-to-end visibility, and cross-training.

Strategically, the hybrid supply chain professional of the future needs:

• To generate and manage large volumes of data and analyze and model it to support more frequent decision-making.
• A deep understanding of complex supply chain dynamics and how to plan or react.
• A better understanding of business objectives and how any daily individual decision or action can impact those objectives.

- The ability to communicate, often remotely, clearly and concisely with partners, other functions, senior management, and stakeholders.
- The ability to bring together dispersed and diverse teams through technology to solve problems.
- Up-to-date communication skills using new collaboration technologies (Myerson, 2022).

To implement a lean supply chain philosophy with its rather unique culture in today's omni-channel retail environment, you first need to understand what it's all about.

Lean History

Lean thinking has been around for a long time in one form or another. Its origins stem from a management philosophy used by the Japanese automobile manufacturer soon after World War II known today as the "Toyota Production System" (TPS) which shifted the focus of manufacturing from individual machines and their utilization to the flow of the product through the entire process.

In fact, it is only since the 1990s that it has been identified as "lean". At that time, Womack and Jones (1996), who helped make the term "lean" part of the popular lexicon, distilled these principles further to include:

1. Specify the value desired by the customer.
2. Identify the value stream for each product providing that value and challenge all the wasted steps (generally nine out of ten) currently necessary to provide it.
3. Make the product flow continuously through the remaining value-added steps.
4. Introduce pull between all steps where continuous flow is possible.
5. Manage toward perfection so that the number of steps and the amount of time and information needed to serve the customer continually falls.

Essentially, lean is a team-based form of continuous improvement which identifies and eliminates non-value-added activities or waste through a relentless focus on exactly what the customer wants.

While it was originally used in the automobile and other repetitive manufacturing industries, in recent years, the easy to understand and implement concepts and tools have spread to other forms of manufacturing and into supply chain and logistics, services, retail, healthcare, construction, maintenance, and government.

Toyota Production System

TPS focused on having appropriately sized machines for the volume required as well as machines that in essence were self-monitoring to ensure quality and in-process sequence. They also originated the idea of quicker equipment setups to enable production of small volumes of a variety of items, as well as the concept today known as a "kanban" where each downstream process lets upstream processes know of its need for materials. As a result of this type of philosophy, Toyota was able to have low cost and high variety production along with high quality and quick throughput times enabling them to respond to changing customer demand which is referred to today as demand "pull" manufacturing. This is in stark contrast to the concept of "push" manufacturing based upon the concept of economies of scale where large quantities of single items are produced to spread fixed costs over many units to keep the cost per unit low.

Value-Added versus Non-Value-Added Activities

To understand the lean concept of "waste", it is first important to understand the meaning of value-added versus non-value-added activities.

Any process entails a set of activities. The activities in total are known as "cycle" or "lead time". Lead time required for a product to move through a process from start to finish includes queues/waiting time and processing time.

The individual activities or work elements that transform inputs (e.g., raw materials) into outputs (e.g., finished goods) are known as "processing" time. In general, processing adds value from the customer's standpoint. Processing time is the time that it takes an employee to go through all their work elements before repeating them. It is measured from the beginning of a process step to the end of that process step.

If we think of a simple example such as taking raw lumber and making it into a pallet of 2 × 4's, the value added to the customer is the actual processing that transforms the raw lumber into the final pallet of 2 × 4's. This would include activities such as washing, trimming, cutting, etc. and

Figure 4.1 Value-added vs. non-value-added activities.

are a relatively small part of the cycle time (i.e., it may only take one hour to process the raw material into a finished pallet, but the entire cycle time may be one week).

In lean terms, the non-value-added time is much greater than just the lead time. We include the current inventory "on the floor" (i.e., raw, WIP, and finished goods) and, using a calculated takt time for a specific "value stream" (a single or family of products or services which will be discussed later in this chapter), convert those quantities to days of supply. Doing so can expand the non-value-added time from days to weeks (or even months).

It is very common for many processes (or value streams) to only have 5–10% value-added activities (Figure 4.1). However, there are some non-value-added necessary activities such as regulatory, customer required, and legal requirements that, while they don't add value, are waste. As they are necessary, we can't eliminate them, but should try to apply them as efficiently as possible.

It is normal for management to focus primarily on speeding up processes; often value-added ones such as the stamping speed on a press. From a lean perspective, the focus moves to non-value-added activities which in some cases may even result in slowing down the entire process to balance it, remove bottlenecks, and increase flow.

Waste

In lean terms, non-value-added activities are referred to as "waste". Typically, when a product or information is being stored, inspected, delayed, waiting in line or is defective, it is not adding value and is 100% waste.

These wastes can be found in any process, whether it's manufacturing, administrative, supply chain and logistics, or elsewhere in your organization.

Below are listed the eight wastes (Figure 4.2). One easy way to remember them is that they spell "TIM WOODS":

Transportation – Excessive movement of people, products, and information. This may include out-of-route stops, excessive backhaul, and locating fast moving inventory in the back of a warehouse which may cause unnecessary material handling distances.

Inventory – Storing material or documentation ahead of requirements. Excess inventory often covers variations in processes as a result of high scrap or rework levels, long setup times, late deliveries, process downtime, and quality problems. This can include early deliveries, receipt of orders for a quantity greater than required, and inventory in the wrong warehouse.

Figure 4.2 The eight wastes of lean.

Motion – Unnecessary bending, turning, reaching, and lifting and may include excess travel or reaching due to poor storage arrangement or poor design of work areas.

Waiting – For parts, information, instructions, and equipment. This may include the time between the arrival of a truck for a pick-up and the loading of the trailer, or the delay between receiving the customer's order information and beginning to pick the order.

Overproduction – Making more than is immediately required. This causes excess inventory or paperwork, potentially resulting in an increase in any or all of the other wastes.

Overprocessing – Tighter tolerances or higher-grade materials than are necessary. In the supply chain, for example, the longer the time required to process orders, the longer time to ship the product and get paid.

Defects – Rework, scrap, and incorrect documentation (i.e. errors). This does not only include product quality issues, but in the supply chain, data errors can result in shipping orders late, incorrect, and at greater expense, for example. It can also result in higher inventory costs to try to compensate for these inaccuracies.

Skills – Underutilizing capabilities of employees, delegating tasks with inadequate training. Perhaps the greatest waste of all, as employees are a company's greatest asset and source of ideas.

In addition to the eight wastes, there are other wastes to consider in your supply chain and logistics functions as mentioned by Robert Trent in his book "End-to-End Lean Management: A Guide to Complete Supply Chain Improvement". They include:

- Too many bits and bytes – The digital age produces less paper – at least in theory. However, technological advances guarantee plenty of data to go around. It is important to understand the difference between data and useful information. You can waste a lot of valuable time sifting through useless information, such as emails, reports, and analyses.
- Untapped creativity – People often take the path of least resistance, but that's not usually the optimal route. Creative skills take time to develop, but organizations can do their part by establishing a culture of lean thinking, which includes training, support, and a motivational reward system.

- Poor measurement – If you can't measure it, you can't improve it. In terms of lean, build your organization's supply chain function to support overall strategies, which can range from responsive to low cost, each strategy having its own type of metrics.

    In today's world, it is easier to gather measurements through technological solutions, aided by bar-code scanning and RFID. But make sure you measure, compare, and benchmark the right things. One source of standardized supply chain metrics is the Supply Chain Operations Resource model, which features more than 150 individual measurements.

- Excessive overhead – The financial impact of an inefficient supply chain goes right to the bottom line. This can be a result of unnecessarily high inventory levels to cover variability in a process, or underutilized assets such as forklift trucks, private fleets, and distribution centers.

- Overdesign – Overdesign can result in the waste of overprocessing. Minimize overdesign by developing a lean, collaborative product lifecycle management process that encompasses a product from inception to disposal of manufactured products. This strategy must also integrate people, data, processes, and business systems.

- Duplication of effort – Duplicated effort across sites or geographic locations means they don't communicate and understand each other's processes well. VSM is one way to visualize duplicated efforts and come up with solutions that leverage collaboration between organizations.

- Poor planning – Many companies do too much reacting, and not enough planning. A solid sales and operations planning process at both the grassroots and executive levels can help organizations shift the balance toward planning while monitoring lean performance metrics.

By focusing on adding value to the customer, you can significantly affect the financial bottom line, which is something that you must not lose sight of. As a result, identifying and eliminating all kinds of waste is a long-term battle worth fighting in today's ultra-competitive global economy (Myerson, 2015).

In addition to identifying the above eight wastes in your supply chain, below are some other ideas or principles laid out by Martichenko (Inbound Logistics, 2013) which are useful to consider:

- Make customer consumption visible to all members of the supply chain – Flow in the supply chain begins with customer consumption. Visibility to customer consumption for all supply chain partners is critical for acting as the "pacemaker" of the supply chain.
- Reduce lead time – Reducing inbound and outbound logistics gets us closer to customer demand which results in reduced reliance on forecasting, increased flexibility and reduced waste of "overproduction".
- Create level flow – Leveling the flow of material and information results in a supply chain with significantly less waste at all nodes in the system.
- Use pull systems – Pull systems reduce wasteful complexity in planning and overproduction that can occur with computer-based software programs such as material resource planning (MRP), and they permit visual control of material flow in the supply chain.
- Increase velocity and reduce variation – Fulfilling customer demand through delivery of smaller shipments more frequently increases velocity. This in turn helps to reduce inventories and lead times and allows you to more easily adjust delivery to meet actual customer consumption.
- Collaborate and use process discipline – When all members of the supply chain can see if they are operating in takt (i.e. demand rate) with customer consumption, they can more easily collaborate to identify problems, determine root causes, and develop appropriate countermeasures.
- Focus on total cost of fulfillment – Make decisions that will meet customer expectations at the lowest possible total cost – no matter where they occur in the supply chain. This means eliminating decisions that benefit only one part of the stream at the expense of others. This is the real challenge but can be achieved when all members of the supply chain share in operational and financial benefits when waste is eliminated.

Furthermore, Thompson, Mankrodt, et al (Jones, Lang LaSalle, 2008) identified six attributes of a lean supply chain from a survey of lean practices in the supply chain (Figure 4.3).

In general, they found that lean supply chain adopters reported improved collaboration, displayed an increased use of standards in processes and materials, reduced SKU counts and inventory levels, and had a general reduction in cost of goods sold compared with non-adopters. A lean supply chain is contributing to the bottom line.

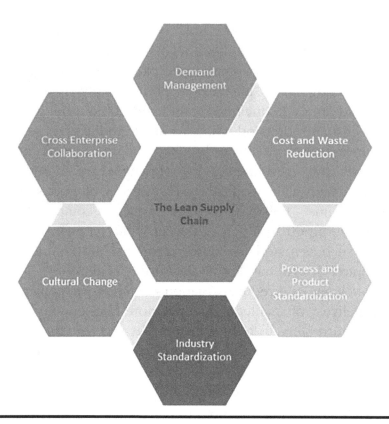

Figure 4.3 Six attributes of lean and effective supply chains.

The six attributes of a lean and effective supply chain found as a result of the survey were:

1. Improved demand management – Move as much as possible to the pull system, in which products or services are pulled (work initiated, services performed, products delivered) only when requested by the final customer. To minimize the bullwhip effect described in Chapter 2, a lean supply chain will work to have products pulled through the channel using customer demand from the point of sale in real time.

2. Cost and waste reduction – In a lean supply chain, partners have to work, together and individually, to eliminate wasteful processes and excess inventory across the channel. In general, a reduction in waste will result in a reduction in cost for the supply chain. Identification of non-value-added activities from end to end in the supply chain using VSM.

3. Process (and product) standardization – This enables a continuous, consistent flow of materials, products, and information to occur throughout the supply chain. As businesses become more collaborative, they will see where tasks are duplicated and linked and make improvements. Standardization of the products themselves can also help to reduce the number of different components and suppliers and support postponement efforts to reduce inventory levels of finished goods and can also help suppliers stabilize their own product lines. Today, companies can share intellectual property, metrics, and best practices for many activities and use (standardized) metrics to drive product and process standardization.

4. Industry standardization – The lean supply chain needs information to be exchanged and available in a standardized format between all trading partners to better communicate and collaborate. Industry product and process standardization can have cost benefits but reduces the proprietary nature of the products themselves, making areas like the supply chain that much more important from a competitive aspect.

5. Cultural change – To successfully implement lean may require a change in a company's culture. Survey leaders emphasized the importance of lean and TQM (total quality management) training as part of their new employees' training.

6. Cross-enterprise collaboration – An enabler of cross-enterprise collaboration is the use of teams. In a lean supply chain, these teams aren't functionally oriented or internally focused on their organization and tend to have a broader perspective.

Lean Culture and Teamwork

While there are a variety of tools and methods used in lean, a house always needs a foundation. In this case, the foundation is a lean culture that permeates throughout an organization (Figure 4.4).

To be successful, there must be top-down leadership as well as a support (and reward) system to create a bottom-up effect as well. As lean is about teams working on continuously improving processes and activities, everyone in the organization must be "rowing" in the same direction. To do so not only need executive leadership but also the necessary tools, training, and rewards available to everyone in the organization.

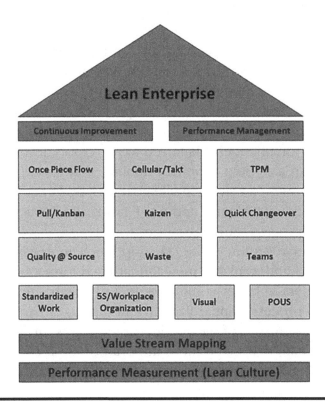

Figure 4.4   House of lean.

Key Success Factors

As many lean initiatives are not totally successful, it is instructive to understand some key success factors (KSF):

- Train the entire organization and make sure everyone understands the lean philosophy.
- Ensure that top management actively drives and supports the change with strong leadership.
- Everyone in the organization should commit to make it work.
- Find a good, experienced change agent as the "champion".
- Set a kaizen (improvement events) agenda and communicate it and involve operators through empowered teams.
- Start value streams mapping right away to identify value-added and non-value-added activities and an improvement plan using lean tools as soon as possible with an important and visible activity.
- Integrate the supporting functions and build internal customer and supplier relationships.

Elements of a Lean Supply Chain Strategy

Before getting into some of the major tools for the lean supply chain, it's useful to think about, at least on a high level, some of the elements required in establishing a lean supply chain. These can include:

- Identify and eliminate all waste in the supply chain so that only value remains using a collaborative, cross-functional, and interorganizational approach to ensure the smooth flow of materials, products, and information.
- Consider advancements in technology as will be described throughout this book to help enable a lean supply chain that is flexible and efficient.
- Strive for visibility of actual customer demand throughout the supply chain to minimize the bullwhip effects described earlier.
- Focus on lead time reduction using various lean tools that we will get to shortly to reduce "dock to dock" time, which is a great measurement of how lean you really are.
- Keep material flowing to ensure speed and flexibility in the supply chain.
- Move the point in your supply chain where you go from "pushing" large quantities to gain economies of scale, to demand "pull" of smaller demand-based quantities as far upstream in the supply chain as possible.

There are a variety of tools that exist to make sure that your supply chain is always striving to attain the critical elements which we will describe now.

Lean Tools and the Supply Chain

The lean toolkit really is an "umbrella" of ideas, new and old. It can include basic, general concepts such as standardized work, visual workplace, and layout as well as somewhat more complex concepts such as just-in-time (JIT), kanban, and work cells. We will discuss some of the more important ones and their applications in the supply chain below.

Basic Tools

Basic tools used in lean may include any or all of the following.

Standardized Work

Standardized work refers to how work is routinely done in the workplace. The idea is to make operations repeatable, ensuring consistently high productivity, and reduced variability of output, as variability inevitably contributes to waste.

To establish standardized work, one must collect and record data on a form. These forms are used to design the process as well as by operators to make improvements in their own jobs. They can include operation charts which analyze body movement, activity charts which are used to study and improve the utilization of an operator(s) and machines, and process charts (see Figure 4.5) which use symbols to document the movement of people and materials so that non-value-added activities can be identified and eliminated.

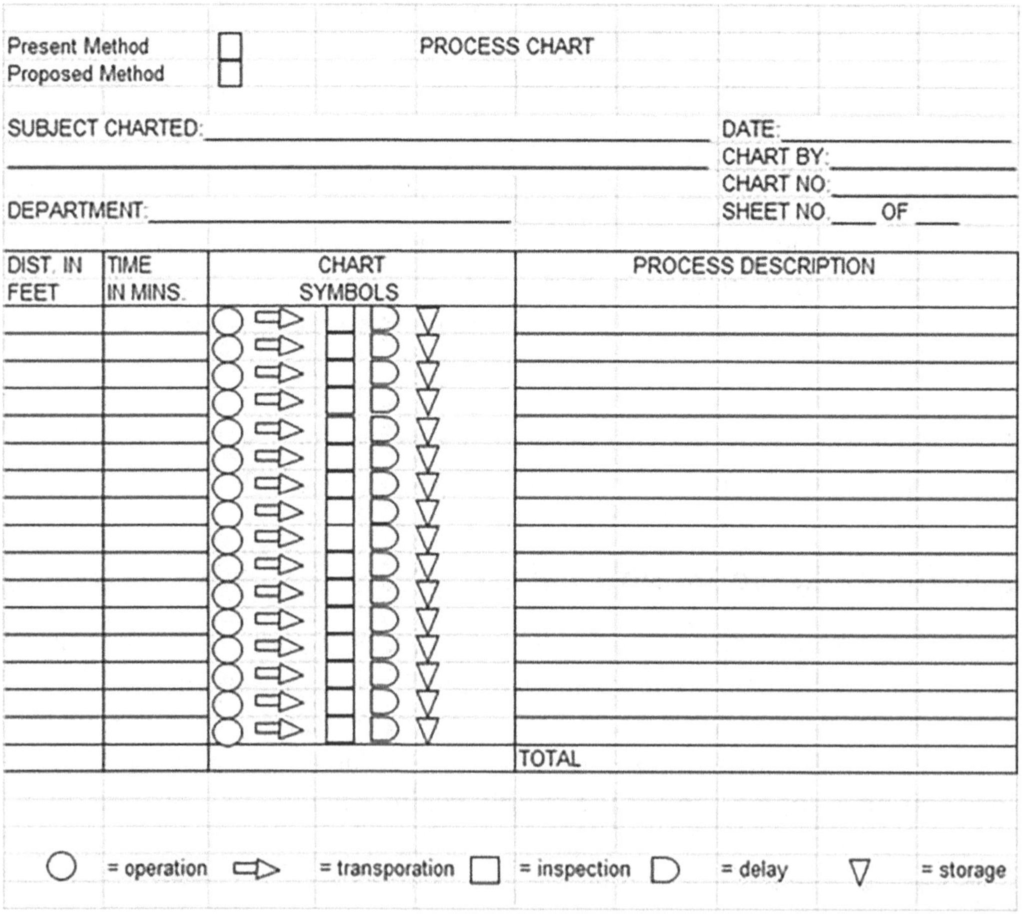

| Present Method ☐ | PROCESS CHART | | | | | | |
| Proposed Method ☐ | | | | | | | |

SUBJECT CHARTED:_____ DATE:_____

_____ CHART BY:_____
CHART NO:_____
DEPARTMENT:_____ SHEET NO.____ OF ____

DIST. IN FEET	TIME IN MINS.	CHART SYMBOLS	PROCESS DESCRIPTION
		○ ⇨ ☐ D ▽	
		○ ⇨ ☐ D ▽	
		○ ⇨ ☐ D ▽	
		○ ⇨ ☐ D ▽	
		○ ⇨ ☐ D ▽	
		○ ⇨ ☐ D ▽	
		○ ⇨ ☐ D ▽	
		○ ⇨ ☐ D ▽	
		○ ⇨ ☐ D ▽	
		○ ⇨ ☐ D ▽	
		○ ⇨ ☐ D ▽	
		○ ⇨ ☐ D ▽	
		TOTAL	

○ = operation   ⇨ = transporation   ☐ = inspection   D = delay   ▽ = storage

Figure 4.5   Process chart.

Visual Workplace

Visual workplace, which is also known as visual factory, is a lean concept that emphasizes putting important information at the point of use. Visual systems and devices play an important part in standard work as well as many lean tools which we will discuss shortly, including 5S, TPM, quick changeover, and kanban (pull production).

It is also a very important way to sustain these lean initiatives because it ensures that lean improvements remain visible, easily understood, and consistently adhered to well after a kaizen event or process improvement event is finished.

Specific areas include:

Visual order (or organization) – Creates a clearly identified place for everything, and for everything to be kept in its place. This may include location identifiers for tools, parts, materials, products, and equipment and the benefits may include reduced inventory, efficient space utilization, enhanced productivity, and reduced operational variability.

Visual standards – Used in standard work, quick changeover, and poka yoke (a mechanism that helps operators avoid mistakes). The visual standards are procedures and technical information shown at the point of use to ensure that best practices are followed consistently by all employees and are used in setup, operating, inspection, and maintenance instructions (see example in Figure 4.6). Benefits may include shorter cycle times, improved quality, better safety awareness, and simplified training and scheduling.

Visual equipment – Used in lean tools such as total productive maintenance (TPM; equipment-related waste), standard work, and quick changeovers. Visual equipment helps to speed proper setup, ensure correct equipment usage, and easily detect operating abnormalities. These can include operator control labels, gauge indicators, inspection and service labels, and hazard warning labels. Benefits may include faster changeovers, fewer operator errors, simplified autonomous (operator controlled) maintenance, and fewer defects.

Visual production/inventory control (supported by technology) – kanban/ demand pull production and just-in-time (JIT; strategy of receiving materials only as they are needed). Visual inventory controls material flow throughout the supply chain to ensure the right product is in the right quantity, at the right place, at the right time. It is also used to

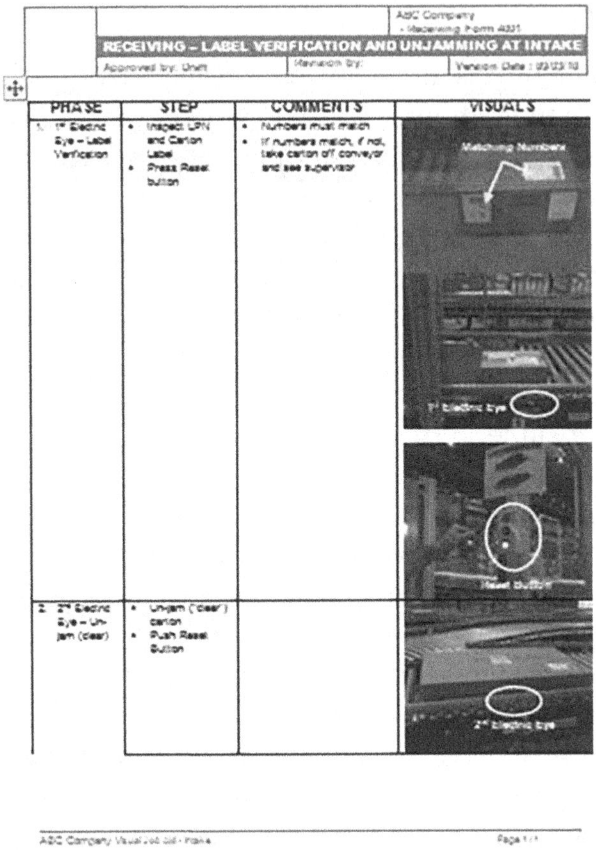
ABC Company

RECEIVING – LABEL VERIFICATION AND UNJAMMING AT INTAKE

Approved by: Unit

PHASE	STEP	COMMENTS	VISUALS
1. 1st Electric Eye – Label Verification	• Inspect LPN and Carton Label • Press Reset button	• Numbers must match • If numbers match, if not, take carton off conveyor and see supervisor	
2. 2nd Electric Eye – Un-jam (clear)	• Un-jam ("clear") carton • Push Reset Button		

Figure 4.6 Visual job aid.

clearly identify system components and flow of the product through a facility. Examples include kanban cards (visual signals indicated when and how much replenishment inventory is required based upon downstream pull demand), inventory/bar code labels, RFID tags (electronic tags to automatically identify and track inventory), and handheld computers. The benefits of visual inventory controls include shorter lead times, reduced inventory levels, improved on-time delivery, and faster troubleshooting.

Visual metrics/displays – To display and communicate kaizen schedules, supply chain, and operational metrics with the idea of letting employees know of key initiatives, track performance against goals, and recognize efforts and achievements. Examples can include visual dashboards, scoreboards, slogan banners, and kaizen improvement displays with benefits such as better alignment with corporate goals, improved accountability, real-time performance tracking, and increased employee involvement.

Visual safety – Visual signals to ensure that hazards are clearly identified and that employees know how to work safely. Examples can include equipment hazard labels, chemical labels, warning signs, and accident prevention tags, with benefits such as lower workers' compensation costs, improved employee morale, enhanced regulatory compliance, and reduced downtime.

Layout

Process flow and layout are central to the concept of lean (Figure 4.7). Flow patterns arrange process steps in a natural flow order, link process steps to minimize cycle time and travel distance, eliminate areas of congestion, and simulate a continuous flow process by putting internal customers and suppliers next to each other.

Facility layout is as important as the technology and materials it contains and has a major impact on business performance. The layout should be reviewed and improved continuously so that waste associated with poor layout be eliminated or reduced.

There are many reasons why the existing production facility layout isn't optimal. For example, an existing facility may limit the choice of a good layout without major reconstruction, and existing layout may not have taken into consideration future expansion or changes to the product mix.

Benefits of an improved layout include higher utilization of space, equipment, and people, improved flow of information, materials, or people, improved employee morale, and improved customer/client interface and flexibility.

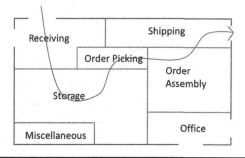

Figure 4.7   Flow example in a distribution center.

5S-Workplace Organization

One of the most popular lean tools is known as "5S" or workplace organization. 5S uses many of the previously mentioned tools such as standardized work, visual workplace, and layout to provide a safe, uncluttered, efficient environment to work. It is also a great place to start your lean journey for your company.

5S incorporates the use of standards and discipline and is not just about general housekeeping, but also safety, organization, and creating a lean culture.

The 5S's are:

1. Sort: Sort out and separate what is needed from that which is not needed in an area. The motto is "when in doubt, toss it out".
2. Set in order (or straighten): Arrange items that are needed so that they are ready and accessible and clearly identify locations for all items so that anyone can find them and return them once a task is completed.
3. Shine: Clean the workplace as well as equipment on a regular basis to maintain standards and identify defects.
4. Standardize: This involves maintaining the first three of the 5S's using standard procedures. This might involve going through an area on a regular basis to remove unneeded material and equipment (sort), checking at the end of a shift that materials are in their proper place as well as checking inventory levels if applicable and having a 10 minute cleanup at the end of shift using a checklist to identify what needs to be done and by whom.
5. Sustain: Perhaps the hardest "S" of all and it requires sticking to the rules to maintain the standards and to continue to improve every day. This involves everything from measurement, audits, rewards, training, and other support and really is part of the cultural change that may be required to be successful.

5S provides a solid base for a lean program. It is generic enough that it is applicable and successful in all industries, all areas of a company, and with all levels of employees as it allows teams to organize their workplace in the safest and most efficient manner.

Advanced Tools

Next, we will cover some more advanced tools that are commonly used in lean programs. While they may require more training and management participation and guidance, they can prove to be very effective if applied correctly and recommendations followed.

Value Stream Mapping

Value stream mapping (VSM) is a lean technique that is used to analyze the flow of materials and information currently required to bring a product or service to a consumer. A VSM is typically one of the first steps your company should take in creating an overall lean initiative plan (along with 5S-workplace organization, which allows you to develop the lean culture on a broader basis). In some cases, it may be appropriate to proceed with a lean opportunity analysis (LOA) that identifies the best places to start.

Developing a visual map of the value stream allows everyone to fully understand and agree on how value is produced and where waste occurs.

It typically involves the following steps:

1. Identify the target product, product family, or service and determine the "takt" or demand time that is typical at the current time. It is calculated by dividing total work time available by units required (e.g., make one and pass one unit every 10 seconds). This determines the pace of the value stream and determines where bottlenecks which limit capacity and create waste may exist.
2. Draw a current state value stream map (Figure 4.8), which is the current steps, delays, and information flows required to deliver the target product or service. This may be a production flow (raw materials to consumer) or a design flow (concept to launch). There are "standard" symbols for representing supply chain entities.
3. Assess the current state value stream map in terms of creating flow by eliminating waste.
4. Draw a future state value stream map (Figure 4.9).
5. Implement the future state.

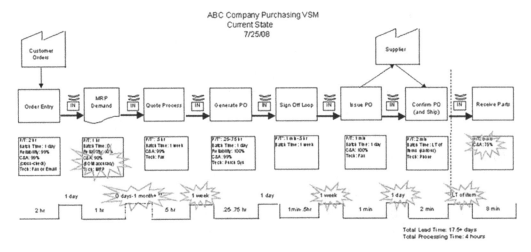

Figure 4.8   Current state value stream map example.

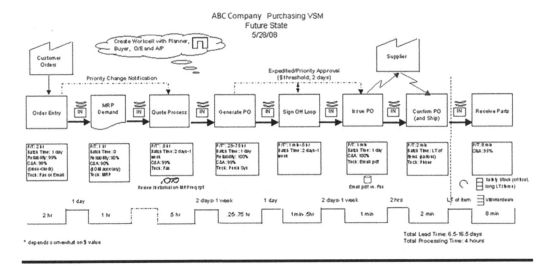

Figure 4.9   Future state value stream map example.

One of the major benefits of VSM is that the entire organization gains a common understanding of an entire value stream, not just their area, and learns to identify realizing where the wastes are throughout the organization and extended supply chain. The team then constructs a future state of a value stream with less waste and then develops an implementation plan to achieve that future state. The result of a successful VSM process is to have a tool to direct lean improvements.

Once areas of waste are identified, there are a variety of advanced lean tools and techniques described next which may be used in combination with some of the basic ones we have already covered.

Pull System with Kanban (JIT System)

Just-in-time or JIT refers to an inventory strategy companies use to increase efficiency and decrease waste by receiving materials or information only as they are needed in the process.

A kanban is a visual signal that is used to trigger an action (can be a card or even a line on a wall). Typically, the action is a request for material or information downstream in a value stream also referred to as a "pull" system.

In general, a downstream process may only withdraw items in the precise amounts as specified in the kanban and upstream processes may only send items downstream in the precise amounts and sequences also specified by the kanban. No items are made or moved without a kanban and typically a kanban card must always accompany each item. Of course, it goes without saying that defects and incorrect amounts should never be sent to the next downstream process and the number of kanbans should be monitored carefully to reveal changes to downstream demand as well as problems and opportunities for improvement (see Figure 4.10).

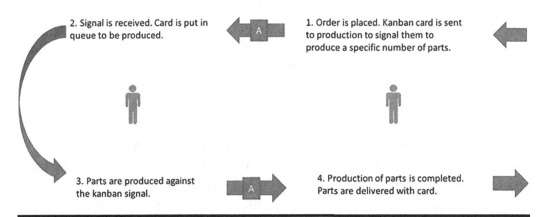

Figure 4.10   Example of kanban process with the card.

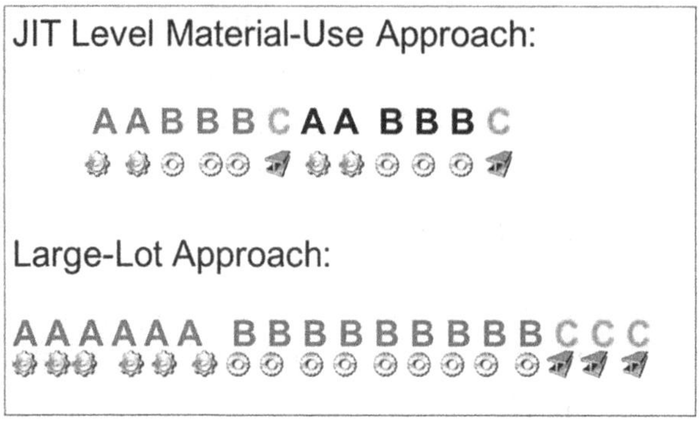

JIT Level Material-Use Approach:

A A B B B C A A B B B C

Large-Lot Approach:

A A A A A A   B B B B B B B B B C C C

Figure 4.11   Benefits of batch size reduction.

Batch Size Reduction and Quick Changeover

Batch or lot size reduction (ideally one piece, at least in some cases) is an important part of many lean strategies (Figure 4.11). Lot size directly affects inventory and scheduling. Other effects are less obvious but equally important such as throughput time and reduced effects when quality issues arise.

Small lots reduce variability in the system and smooth production. They enhance quality, simplify scheduling, reduce inventory, enable kanban, and encourage continuous improvement.

The effects of small lots differ somewhat between make-to-order (MTO) and make-to-stock (MTS) environments but are important in both production strategies.

In general, there is also a correlation between changeover time (i.e., the full time it takes to go from "last good piece to next good piece", not just equipment setup time) and batch size. That is, the quicker and easier a changeover is (in and of itself, a changeover is a waste as nothing is produced during that time), the smaller the batch size can be, helping you to move from a push to a pull environment.

This is true not only in manufacturing but also in the office, warehouse, and throughout the supply chain as setups for different activities exist for everyone. For example, batches of orders may sit in an inbox awaiting entry, while the employee does some other activities. To enter the orders themselves requires a "setup" including gathering other needed information and materials, accessing software screens, etc. Therefore, there is a tendency to batch orders, thus slowing up throughput time, which leads to orders taking longer to get to the shop floor or warehouse needed to ship and bill products.

Many lean tools such as layout, standardization, etc. can help to shorten changeover time. In many cases it is useful to have a kaizen event focused on the process where it is filmed and documented to come up with significant improvements.

Work Cells

A work cell refers to the arrangement of resources in a business environment that are organized to improve process flow and efficiency and eliminate waste. They are often found in manufacturing and office environments.

A work cell reorganizes people and machines into groups to focus on single products or product groups. As opposed to a long assembly line requiring a fair amount of labor, a work cell is typically "U" shaped with equipment that is suited to the family of products or services that flow through it. The labor tends to be cross-trained, empowered, and flexible to ensure the smooth flow of material and information (Figure 4.12).

Benefits include reduced raw material, work-in-process and finished goods inventories, better utilization of machinery and equipment, less floor space required, reduced direct labor cost, and a heightened sense of employee participation.

Total Productive Maintenance

Equipment-related waste can have a huge impact on throughput, efficiency, and quality. Yet it's surprising how many companies rely on what is known as "breakdown" (vs. preventative) maintenance.

Much more than just a preventative maintenance program, TPM focuses on equipment-related waste and involves a series of methods that ensure

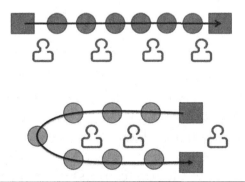

Figure 4.12   Assembly line versus work cell layout.

every piece of equipment in the production process is always able to perform its required tasks so that production is never interrupted. It is a comprehensive, team-based, continuous activity that enhances normal equipment-maintenance activities and involves every worker with the goal of keeping equipment producing only good products, as fast as needed with no unplanned downtime.

TPM includes designing machines that are reliable, easy to operate, and easy to maintain, emphasizing total cost of ownership when purchasing machines, so that service and maintenance are included in the cost, developing preventive maintenance plans that utilize the best practices of operators, maintenance departments, and depot service, and training workers to operate and maintain their own machines (also known as "autonomous maintenance").

Using TPM results in many positive outcomes, such as improved equipment performance and availability, increased first-time-through (FTT) quality levels, downtime due to emergencies, increased employee skill levels and knowledge, empowerment, job satisfaction, and safety.

TPM can be applied anywhere equipment is used, not just the shop floor, as distribution centers can't run without forklift trucks and carousel, trucks can't run without proper maintenance, and offices don't perform as well with copiers, printers, and computers that are frequently slow or out of service.

Problem Identification and Solving Tools

After identifying waste, but before coming up with solutions, it may be critical to find out the source of the waste or variability. This may involve the collection, compiling, and analysis of information to get to the root cause(s) of the problem.

Five Why's

The "5 Why's" is a simple but effective technique to get to the root cause of a problem. It is attributed to Sakichi Toyoda, one of the fathers of the Japanese industrial revolution, who had a "go and see" philosophy.

The way it works is when a problem occurs, you uncover its source by asking the people who are involved in the process "why" at least five times. This will usually lead you to the root cause(s) of the problem.

For example, you find that you shipped the wrong product to a customer.

1. *Why?* The wrong item was pulled from the inventory.
2. *Why?* The item pulled from the inventory was mislabeled.
3. *Why?* Our supplier mislabeled the item prior to shipping it to our warehouse.
4. *Why?* The individual applying labels to our product at the supplier placed the wrong label on the product.
5. *Why?* Labels for different orders are pre-printed, and it is easy to apply the wrong label.

So, in this example, the supplier is the cause of the issue. There may be a variety of things that can be done to eliminate the problem at both their end (e.g., print labels to order) and our end (e.g., random sampling upon receipt in our warehouse).

Seven Tools of Quality

The seven tools of quality are a set of graphical techniques that help in troubleshooting issues related to quality but can also be used in various forms of process improvement to get to the "root cause" of a problem, quality or otherwise. They are suitable for people with little formal training in statistics and because they can be used to solve most quality-related issues.

1. Cause-and-effect diagram (also called a fishbone chart) – Can identify possible causes for an effect or problem and sorts of ideas into useful categories.
2. Check sheet – A form for collecting and analyzing data that can be used for a wide variety of purposes.
3. Control charts – Graphs that are used to study how a process changes over time, within certain, stated parameters.
4. Histogram – A graph to show frequency distributions, or how often each different value in a set of data occurs.
5. Pareto chart (also known as the "80/20 rule") – Organizes and shows data on a bar graph from the greatest type and number of occurrences to least. The "Pareto" phenomenon states that it is typical that a relatively small number of causes generate most of the problems.

6. Scatter diagram: Graphs that pair numerical data, one variable on each axis, to look for a relationship (e.g., high absenteeism is related to low productivity).

7. Flow chart – Shows the steps in a process (i.e., actions which transform an input to an output for the next step). This helps in analyzing a process but should document the actual process used rather than what the process owner thinks it is or wants it to be. The differences between the actual and the intended process can provide many ideas for improvement.

Lean, Supply Chain, and Technology

It is debatable as to how much technology can help in lean manufacturing. Some "purists" think that it plays no role in it as it is traditionally known as a very visual tool. However, with the growing complexity of the **global** supply chain, many argue that technology is required to scale lean in this type of environment using some of the technologies mentioned in Chapter 3 such as control towers, AI, access to real-time data, the cloud, etc.

The reason for the lack of non-support by traditionalists is that, historically, ERP and MRP systems didn't do a great job supporting a lean philosophy as they were based more on a "push" philosophy, the opposite of lean.

Some reasons given for the need for technology with lean include:

- Using technology as a foundation to drive lean processes and information flow helps to institutionalize lean within the factory and supply chain, as over time, many lean initiatives, which rely on people and their knowledge of lean practices, tend to deteriorate (or at least go back to their "past" state).
- As product mix and production process complexity keep increasing, the "low tech" approach to lean can find it hard to keep up with things.
- Traditional use of kanban replenishment approaches discussed earlier must be resized ever more dynamically in complex environments.
- The increased use of outsourcing to make materials and components has made it harder to use kanban cards and visual processes to coordinate component replenishment from external sources. So more sophisticated supply network communication and collaboration capabilities are needed today.

- There is more of a need to have more "real time" data capture systems to have success with a lean philosophy as it is very dependent on timely and accurate information. Technologies such as EDI, bar code scanners, and RFID help to ensure greater accuracy and visibility in your internal and extended supply chain.

Organizations that apply proven technology to lean manufacturing and supply chain can significantly improve speed, efficiency, and profitability as lean-enabling technology has moved well beyond just electronic kanban and can include lean-based supplier replenishment extended into the multi-enterprise supply chain, integrating modeling and simulation and VSM to document the production process and value-added activities into more day-to-day applications.

Today, best-in-class companies use lean automation tools such as inventory levels planned based on the uncertainty of demand as well as order management integration with visibility into manufacturing constraints when order promising. Most are enabling lean manufacturing practices through demand planning and forecasting systems and segmenting their supply chain using systems for forward-looking inventory targets by customer, location, etc. for production and deployment planning and scheduling.

However, to leverage technology in a lean environment, it first needs to be a good match for your organization's needs, be reliable and tested, which is the general topic of our next chapter.

Chapter 5

The Software and Hardware Sourcing Process

Before delving into the various supply chain processes where both lean and technology can work together for a business, we need to discuss the identification of requirements and subsequent technology selection and implementation process. If this is not done in a thorough and thoughtful manner, it can lead to disaster, resulting in not only less than expected benefits but also additional costs and delays.

Technology Sourcing versus Procurement

Technology sourcing and procurement are often used interchangeably, but they are not really the same thing.

Technology sourcing is the process of identifying, evaluating, and selecting the best technology solutions for your organization's needs. It involves researching the market, comparing alternatives, negotiating contracts, and establishing partnerships with vendors or suppliers. So, it's more of a strategic first step.

Technology procurement, on the other hand, is the process of acquiring, installing, and maintaining the technology solutions that you have sourced. It involves ordering, receiving, testing, deploying, and supporting the technology assets and services that you have purchased or leased.

Together, these two processes can bring many benefits to your organization, such as reducing costs and risks, improving quality and performance,

DOI: 10.4324/9781003372639-6

enhancing innovation and competitiveness, and aligning technology with strategy. By finding the most cost-effective and reliable technology solutions that meet your budget and requirements, you can choose the best solutions for your specific needs and goals. Additionally, you can access the latest technology trends and opportunities in the market to support your organizational vision and mission.

When dealing with multiple technology options, vendors, contracts, and stakeholders, it is important to stay current with the technology market and customer expectations, both of which are constantly changing. Additionally, delivering technology solutions quickly and effectively without lowering quality or security is a key factor in evaluating technology solutions.

In order to effectively manage technology sourcing and procurement in a volatile market, you need to take on a strategic and agile approach. This should include clearly defining and prioritizing your technology needs and goals, conducting a thorough market analysis and benchmarking to find the best solutions, negotiating fair contracts that reflect your expectations, implementing a governance and management framework that promotes accountability, transparency, and collaboration, and monitoring and evaluating your solutions regularly to optimize performance.

When sourcing and procuring technology, it is important to involve key stakeholders from different functions and levels to ensure alignment and buy-in. Leveraging existing relationships and networks to find reliable vendors and partners is also beneficial. To maximize success, you should use a mix of different sourcing and procurement methods, such as competitive bidding or direct negotiation. Additionally, adopting a life cycle perspective that considers the total cost of ownership and the value proposition of your technology solutions over time is important. Finally, embracing a culture of learning and improvement that encourages feedback, experimentation, and innovation will help you achieve your technology goals.

The Procurement Process

In many ways, the software and hardware decision process has much in common with other sourcing decisions for goods and services. So, at this point, it is a good idea to go over a "generic" procurement cycle. These cycles may vary by the good or service being procured as well as the industry or company involved (Figure 5.1).

The steps in the procurement process are:

Figure 5.1 The procurement process.

Identify and Review Requirements

When discussing requirements, procurement activities are often split into two categories (direct and non-direct) depending on the consumption purposes of the acquired goods and services (Table 5.1).

The first category, direct, is production-related procurement and the second is indirect, which is non-production-related procurement.

Direct procurement is generally referred to in manufacturing settings only. It encompasses all items that are part of finished products, such as raw materials, components, and parts. Direct procurement, which is a major focus in supply chain management, directly affects the production process of manufacturing firms. It also occurs in retail where "direct spend" may refer to what is spent on the merchandise being resold.

In contrast, indirect procurement activities concern "operating resources" that a company purchases to enable its operations (i.e., maintenance, repair, and operations inventory as well as capital spent on plant, equipment, and technology). It comprises a wide variety of goods and services, from standardized low-value items like office supplies and machine lubricants to complex and costly products and services like heavy equipment, computer software and hardware, and consulting services.

Table 5.1 Direct versus indirect procurement

		Types		
		Direct procurement Raw material and production goods	Indirect procurement Maintenance, repair and operating supplies	Capital goods and services
Features	Quantity	Large	Low	Low
	Frequency	High	Relatively high	Low
	Value	Industry specific	Low	High
	Nature	Operational	Tactical	Strategic
	Examples	Resin in plastics industry	Lubricants, space parts	Resin and plastic product storage facilities

The source for requirements can come from material requirements planning (MRP) systems via planners and purchase requisitions from other users in the organization (a purchase or material requisition is a document generated by an organization to notify the purchasing department of items it needs to order, the quantity, and the time frame that will be given in the future).

During this step, purchasing will review paperwork for proper approvals, check material specifications, verify quantity, unit of measure, delivery date and place, and review all supplemental information.

Establish Specifications

To establish specifications, one must identify quantity, pricing, and functional requirements as described below.

- Quantity – In the case of small volume requirements, you need to find a standard item. If larger volume, then it must be designed for economies of scale to both reduce cost and satisfy functional needs.
- Price – This relates to the use of the item and the selling price of the finished product.
- Functional – There is a fundamental need to understand what the item is expected to do per the user(s). This includes performance and aesthetic expectations (e.g., hand can opener – how smoothly does it remove the top of cans as well as how ergonomically appealing is the design?).

In general, the description of the item may be by brand or specification. One might use a brand if the quantity is small, the item is patented, or is requested by a customer. It would be by specification if you're looking for very specific physical or chemical makeup, material, or performance specifications.

The source of the specifications themselves can be based upon buyer requirements or standards that may be set independently.

If the buyer sets the specifications, it can become a long and expensive process requiring a detailed description of parts, finishes, tolerances, and materials used resulting in the item being expensive to produce.

Standards, on the other hand, set by government and nongovernmental agencies, can be much more straightforward to use as they tend to be widely known and accepted, lower in price, and more adaptable to customer needs.

Identify and Select Suppliers

The next step in the procurement process is to identify and select suppliers. Typically, this involves coming up with a "long list" of suppliers who meet your requirements in general, then whittling the list down to final candidates before selecting the ultimate vendor.

Identification of potential suppliers can come from a variety of sources including the internet, catalogs, salespeople, trade magazines and directories.

Once you have identified potential vendors, a "request for information" or RFI is issued to them that states a bit about your company and its requirements as well as requested background on the vendor. It's usually not too difficult to refine the vendors that respond down to a smaller list of candidates (usually 5–10) and from there it's best to include a multi-functional team of employees to determine the finalist(s).

Once you have it down to a short list, a "request for quotation" (RFQ) or "request for proposal" (RFP) is issued. An RFQ is an invitation to selected suppliers to bid or quote on delivering specific products or services and will include the specifications of the items/services. The suppliers are requested to return their bids by a set date and time to be considered for selection. Discussions may be held on the bids, in many cases to clarify technical capabilities or to note errors in a proposal. The initial bid does not have to mean the end of the bidding as there may be more than one round.

Vendor Evaluation

I've found what is known as the "factor rating method" (see Table 5.2) to be useful in the task of vendor evaluation.

The factor rating method identifies criteria that need to be considered as part of what you will be buying and assigns weights as to the relative importance of each of these factors. You then score how well each supplier compares on each factor and give them a score which is weighted times the rating.

While this may not be the total decision-making factor, it can get you close enough to help you make a final decision. There are always "intangible" factors that can come into play such as personal opinions of executives, prior experience with a vendor, etc.

Table 5.2   Factor rating method for vendor evaluation

Criteria	Weights	Scores (1–5)	Weight × Score
Engineering and research capabilities	0.1	4.0	0.4
Production process capability (flexibility/ agile)	0.2	5.0	0.8
Delivery capability	0.1	3.5	0.2
Quality and performance	0.2	3.0	0.6
Location	0.1	1.0	0.1
Financial and managerial strength (stability and cost structure)	0.2	5.0	0.8
Information systems capability (e-procurement, ERP)	0.1	2.0	0.2
Reputation (sustainability/ethics)	0.1	5.0	0.5
Total	1.00		3.4

There are many factors besides price (and not always the lowest is selected) that are important when selecting a supplier such as:

Technical ability – As their product will become part of your product, can they help you to develop and make improvements to your product?

Manufacturing capability – Can they consistently meet your stated quality and specifications?

Reliability – Determine if they are reputable and financially stable.

After-sales service – Do they have a solid service organization that offers technical support?

Location – Are they close enough to support fast and consistent delivery and support service when needed?

Determine the Right Price

As was pointed out before, while price may not be the only determinant, it certainly contributes greatly to the bottom line as it can be upwards of 50% of the cost of goods sold.

There are three basic models that are used as a basis for pricing. They are:

Cost based – The supplier makes their financials available to the purchaser.

Market based – The price is based on published, auction, or indexed prices.

Competitive bidding – This is typically used for infrequent purchases but can make establishing a long-term relationship more difficult.

When preparing to negotiate a price, preparation is the key. On a personal level, if you are buying a house or car, the more research you do, the better idea you have of what is available and what is a "fair" price in the market area (at least to you). Thanks to the internet, there are many sources available to get a good idea as to what's available and a range of pricing based upon recent history. The same goes for business negotiations, where the buyer should have knowledge of the seller's costs to some extent.

Negotiation

For the most part, negotiations are based upon the type of product.

Commodities – The price is usually determined by the market.

Standard products – The price is set by catalog listings and there is usually little room for negotiation (other than volume).

Small value items – Companies should try to reduce ordering costs or increase volume where possible.

Made-to-order items – Prices are based upon quotations from a number of sources, and as a result, prices are negotiated where possible.

Where negotiations are possible, there are two general types of negotiation that can be used, distributive and integrative.

In distributive bargaining, the goals of one party are in fundamental, direct conflict with another party, resources are fixed and limited, and maximizing one's own share of resources is the goal for both parties. So, in this case, there is usually a "winner" and a "loser".

One needs to set a target point and a walkaway point to negotiate a final price that is satisfactory to the buyer. To determine these may take a good amount of research and judgment. The seller may have a listing or asking price and you will submit an initial offer or counter offer. This type of negotiating usually requires sufficient "clout" to justify lower pricing. Larger companies with multiple locations or business units may have sufficient volume to justify this.

When I was a member of General Electric's corporate sourcing, we were able to leverage over $1 billion/year spent annually on transportation corporation-wide by collecting freight volumes by mode for all of the 100+ GE units to negotiate significant savings. This was accomplished not only by collecting and analyzing the annual spend but also by reducing the number of carriers within each mode to a company-wide group of "core" carriers in order to maximize negotiation power.

Integrative negotiation, on the other hand, is more collaborative with a goal for a "win-win" conclusion by the creation of a free flow of information and an attempt to understand the other negotiator's real needs and objectives. This process emphasizes commonalties between the parties and minimizes the differences through a search for solutions that meet the goals and objectives of both sides.

Issue Purchase Orders

At this point, we move from procurement to more of the "day to day" supplier scheduling and follow-up which go more under the heading of purchasing activities. This involves execution of the master schedule and MRP to ensure good use of resources, minimize WIP, and provide the desired level of customer service. This usually falls under the auspices of what is known as a buyer/planner who works hand in hand with the master scheduler. Buyers/planners are responsible for the control of production activity and the flow of work through the plant and can also be responsible for purchasing, materials requirements planning, supplier relationship management, product life cycle and service design, and more. They also coordinate the flow of goods from suppliers.

The purchase order (PO) is used to buy materials between a buyer and seller. It specifically defines the price, specifications, and terms and conditions of the product or service and any additional obligations for either party. The PO must be delivered by fax, mail, personally, email, or other electronic means.

The types of purchase orders may include:

Discrete orders – Used for a single transaction with a supplier, with no assumption that further transactions will occur.

Pre-negotiated blanket – A PO made with a supplier containing multiple delivery dates over a period of time, usually with predetermined pricing which often has lower costs as a result of greater volumes (possibly through centralized purchasing and/or the consolidation of suppliers) on a longer term contract. It is typically used when there is an ongoing need for consumable goods.

Pre-negotiated, vendor managed inventory (VMI) – The supplier maintains an inventory of items at the customer's plant and the customer pays for the inventory when it is actually consumed. Usually for standard, small value items like maintenance, repair, and operating supplies (MRO) like fasteners and electrical parts.

Bid and auction ("e-procurement") – This involves the use of online catalogs, exchanges, and auctions to speed up purchasing, reduce costs, and integrate the supply chain. There are many e-commerce sites for industrial equipment and MRO inventory auctions and vary in format from catalog (e.g., www.grainger.com, www.chempoint.com) to auction (e.g., www.biditup.com). Websites can be for standard items or industry-specific.

Corporate purchase card (pCard) – This is a company charge card that allows goods and services to be procured without using a traditional purchasing process; sometimes referred to as procurement or "p" cards. There is always some kind of control for each pCard, such as a single purchase dollar limit, a monthly limit, and so on. A pCard holder's activity should be reviewed periodically independently.

To further enhance the speed and accuracy of transactions, many companies use what is known as "EDI" (electronic data interchange), which is the computer-to-computer exchange of business documents in a standard electronic format between business partners. In the past, EDI transactions either went directly from business to business (in the case of large companies) or through third parties known as value-added networks (VANs). Today, a large portion of EDI transactions now flow through the internet.

Sometimes included in the category of EDI is the use of electronic funds transfer (EFT) which is the electronic exchange, transfer of money from one account to another, within a single financial institution or across multiple institutions, through computer systems. This also includes e-commerce payment systems which facilitate the acceptance of electronic payment for online transactions which has become increasingly popular as a result of the widespread use of internet-based shopping and banking.

Follow up to Assure Correct Delivery

Enterprise Resource Planning (ERP) software modules such as MRP assume that scheduled dates will be received on time. However, a scheduled delivery date must be monitored and managed in order to identify and avoid possible missed dates in advance where possible. In some cases, delays may be inevitable, and as a result, recovery plans must be developed and managed.

It is also critical to have an understanding of the supplier's production process, capacity, and constraints in order to collaboratively resolve problems.

On occasion, expediting is necessary but should be on an exception basis. Supplier performance should be monitored on an ongoing basis. If a particular supplier is consistently being expedited, corrective action occurs.

In many organizations, purchasing may work hand in hand with either their traffic or transportation department or that of the vendors (depending on shipping terms).

Receive and Accept Goods

The key objective at receipt of goods is to ensure that proper physical condition, quantity, documentation, and quality parameters are met. To accomplish this requires a cross-functional activity among purchasing, receiving, quality control, and finance.

Receiving is technically a "non-value-added" activity from a customer perspective as it is designed to ensure that everything up to that point has been done properly. The goal is to ensure quality throughout and reduce or eliminate the need for inspection. In many cases, technology such as bar-code scanners and handheld computers can automate the process. Some of the inspection processes can also be reduced or eliminated by various inspection and certification processes being performed by the vendor.

Approve Invoice for Payment

The final step in the procurement process is approving an invoice for payment (see Figure 5.2) according to the terms and conditions of the PO. Typically, the data in the PO is matched with that found on the packing slip that was received and checked when the product arrived and the invoice.

Figure 5.2   Document flow.

Any discrepancies must be reconciled before payment is issued to the vendor. In some cases, small levels of discrepancies can be ignored (e.g., ±3% or ±$20).

Discounts for early payment should be taken whenever possible, although, in a sluggish economy, many customers try to extend payment as long as possible due to cash flow issues.

Software and Hardware Selection

It is always important to have a tailored methodology for the successful selection and implementation of technology which varies somewhat from the previously covered procurement process.

While no one method works best, it should include the following main phases:

Phase 1 – Planning and budgeting

The initial step in the technology selection process is your internal planning and budgeting. You need to set up your project team, get buy-in for the project, and put together a high-level budget.

Also having a project advisory or guidance team (or steering committee) to oversee the entire process beginning with the action plan or roadmap is a good idea. This team should include at least one key executive sponsor.

It's not a bad idea to consider using a consultant who has the expertise and knowledge about these steps and different systems and software and hardware products.

Phase 2 – Requirements analysis

Next, you need to put together your requirements document. Make sure it is focused on your requirements (key differentiating criteria) so that you can concentrate on your most important requirements and quickly, yet thoroughly, evaluate vendors.

During this phase, you should document processes to find potential areas for improvement using lean or other techniques. During the subsequent assessment stage, review every step. Examine all steps in each of the business process tasks and make sure each task adds value to the internal or external customer. This may eliminate steps and/or help improve your business workflow even before new software implementations or technology upgrade.

Prioritize business needs by determining which features you would like to have and features you absolutely need to have to determine a complete list of functional requirements.

Make sure to speak with end users to know more about what could improve their work processes and products and as a result, identify improvements to cost, time, and user satisfaction.

As there may be a long list of requirements, rank the priorities of these features in terms of what is really required (e.g., required, desirable, and nice to have).

Phase 3 – Vendor research

Now it is time to evaluate your vendor options. This phase focuses on how to start with a long list of vendors and efficiently evaluate them to get to a short list of approximately 3–4 vendors.

Typically, an RFI is issued first which is sent to a long list of qualified vendors (sometimes a request for proposal/quote or RFP/RFQ is issued if the list isn't too long; if it is, that can wait until a little later in the process).

This "winnowing" process can be accomplished by conducting additional research and learning more about the packaged combination of features and benefits available by visiting each service vendor's websites and links to their solutions.

Phase 4 – Demonstrations

When you have your short list, invite the vendors for demos. Make sure they follow a structured demo "script" so you can see how they will handle your key requirements and you can compare them in an equal manner.

Also, look for references that you can contact and possibly visit to "kick the tires" so to speak.

Phase 5 – Final decision

When you narrow the list to one or two vendors, it's time to do your due diligence and confirm your final decision.

Phase 6 – Contract negotiation

In many cases, software and hardware contracts are written by the vendor. Make sure you negotiate the contract to protect your interests and save you money.

Implementation Vendor/VAR Selection

A critical part of the selection process that most companies overlook is the selection of a qualified implementation partner or Value Added Reseller (VAR). In certain cases, you need to do this evaluation during the vendor research, and in other cases you will select the implementation partner after you select the software product. The selection of the implementation partner can make or break the success of your implementation.

Make or Buy

The first decision in this process, at least strategically, is the question of "make or buy" which is the choice between internal production and external sources.

A simple break-even analysis can be used to quickly determine the cost implications of a make or buy decision in the following example.

If a firm can purchase equipment for in-house use for $500,000 and produce requested parts for $20 each (*assume there is no excess capacity on their current equipment*) or they can have a supplier produce and ship the part for $30 each, what would be the correct decision … make (assume with new equipment) or buy (i.e., outsource production)?

To arrive at the correct decision, a simple break-even point could easily be calculated as follows:

$$\$500,000 + \$20Q = \$30Q$$
$$\$500,000 = \$30Q - \$20Q$$
$$\$500,000 = \$10Q$$
$$50,000 = Q$$

As the break-even point is 50,000 units, the answer is that it would be better for the firm to buy the part from a supplier if demand is less than 50,000 units, and purchase the necessary equipment to make the part if demand is greater than 50,000 units.

In terms of the technology decision, in the case of software, much has changed. 25+ years ago, there wasn't much packaged software available, so most companies coded and maintained their own applications and even outsourced computer hardware.

Since that time there has been a revolution of sorts starting with the invention of the PC and packaged software. As the year 2000 (i.e., Y2K) approached, the fear of old "home grown" software not accounting for the calendar change (and crashing) along with the plethora of ERP and other packaged software systems then available greatly reduced the need for in-house programming of entire systems as most organizations migrated toward these packaged systems which ran in a client-server (and later web-enabled and web-based) environment.

SCM System Costs and Options

The final cost of supply chain management software can be three to five times the cost of the software license as it also includes planning, implementation, training, customization, interfaces, hardware, and configuration of the software. SCM software vendors also typically charge a 15–20% annual fee for maintenance and technical support.

A newer alternative to installed software is what has become known alternatively as "SaaS" (software as a service), "on demand" or "cloud" supply chain software.

Cloud supply chain systems may reduce or eliminate up-front software acquisition costs by offering subscription fees for web-based applications, allowing you to "pay as you go" as fees are based on usage. In this model, there are typically no installation or maintenance costs for the customer.

The major concern of most potential users is security, which may or may not be as big a risk as imagined. Nevertheless, cloud software represents the single highest growth sector in the enterprise software market and some software vendors are expanding into the cloud by offering some of their SCM modules as SaaS (www.gartner.com, 2013).

According to a 2023 market research report, the global SaaS market size is projected to grow from $273.55 billion in 2023 to $908.21 billion by 2030, at a CAGR of 18.7% (Fortune Business Insights, 2023).

"Best-in-Class" versus Single Integrated Solution

For more specialized types of supply chain applications such as network optimization and forecasting, choosing a "best-in-class" solution may be the way to go as the number of supply chain vendors with a single integrated solution is limited to larger vendors such as SAP and Oracle. In many cases, companies may select one vendor for SCP and another for SCE.

When licensing "best-in-class" software, costs may be greater to implement, as they require additional interfaces when having multiple vendor relationships. An application known as an Enterprise Application Interface (EAI) system can reduce some of the integration costs.

The benefits of one integrated solution are many, including having a single point of contact, a common user interface, and a common IT architecture.

Consultants

There are three general types of supply chain consultants involved in the technology selection and implementation process. They are:

1. SCM experts or management consultants – SCM experts help with the planning and modeling.
2. Software vendor consultants – Consultants employed by the software vendor who are application software subject matter experts (SME) and help implement the software.
3. IT consultants – Information technology (IT) consultants who help with infrastructure, interfaces, and custom programming (www.erpsearch. com, 2014).

The number and mix of consultants in an SCM software implementation project will vary depending on the size and scope of the project.

Project Management

Many technology projects can be quite complex and involved. It is therefore important to follow good project management principles and techniques.

In general, project management is needed when there are the following characteristics:

- Single unit
- Many related activities
- Difficult production planning and inventory control
- General purpose equipment
- High labor skills

The use of good project management techniques can ensure the delivery of projects on time and within budget, achievement of project objectives, goal clarity and measurement, coordinated resources, and risk identification and management among other things.

So having a good project management methodology provides a reusable, structured roadmap to managing and executing projects with tools for capturing, analyzing, and improving project work efforts.

Heizer and Render (Pearson, 2013) identify three phases of project management:

1. Planning – goal setting, defining the project, team organization.
2. Scheduling – relate people, money, and supplies to specific activities and then relates the activities to each other.
3. Controlling – monitor resources, costs, quality, and budgets; revise plans and shift resources to meet time and cost demands.

All three phases are critical to the success of projects. This is especially important for technology projects as many studies have shown a high failure rate. For example, one survey found that 70% were satisfied or extremely satisfied with the quality of the project, 48% with the timeliness of the implementation, and 46% with the cost incurred (source: Information Week 2012 Enterprise Management Survey of 508 business technology professionals). Other surveys (and experience) that I've seen that are from the user side tend to be a fair amount lower in terms of satisfaction with the quality of the project and its results.

At this point, the reader should have a good fundamental understanding of the evolution of the supply chain and logistics function, lean concepts, the general types of software and other technologies that can enable it as well as the general sourcing process.

We will now look in more detail at specific software and technology and how they can enable a lean and smart supply chain using the "SCOR" model as described in the next chapter, starting with the "Plan" process.

SUPPLY CHAIN SOFTWARE SYSTEMS

Chapter 6

Supply Chain Software Systems: Plan

For ease of presentation and understanding, I have chosen to use the SCOR (supply chain operations reference) model to discuss the various supply chain software systems available today.

The SCOR model describes the business activities associated with satisfying a customer's demand, which include plan, source, make, deliver, return, and enable. There will be software system chapters on each SCOR category, except for "enable", as the technology applied within each area enables the supply chain to be efficient, agile, and responsive.

The SCOR model also segments the supply chain into logical business processes and categories. This standardized structure enables an analysis of all information, financial, and product flows within the extended value chain. Based on data analysis, companies can plan long-, medium-, and short-term increase the efficiency and effectiveness of their supply chain management and coordinate and compare the processes between suppliers, manufacturers, and customers.

Before we delve into the types of technology used for planning in the supply chain, it is important to note that some planning tools are more strategic in nature while others are more tactical and operational.

DOI: 10.4324/9781003372639-8

Planning Levels in the Supply Chain

Strategic Level

In general, a strategy is a road map for the entire supply chain process. Strategic supply chain decisions are usually the first step in developing a good process. The supply chain strategy should align with the organization's overall mission and strategy, especially in terms of cost, responsiveness, differentiation, and quality, for example.

Issues addressed at this level include:

- Choosing the site and purpose of business facilities.
- Creating a network of reliable suppliers, transporters, and logistics handlers.
- Long-term improvements and innovations to meet client demands.
- Inventory and product management throughout its life cycle.
- Information technology programs and systems to make the process more effective.

Tactical Level

Shorter-term decisions involving the supply chain occur at the tactical level where processes are defined. Tactical decisions play a big role in controlling costs and minimizing risks where the focus is on customer demands and achieving maximum customer value.

Contingency planning, which is a tool used to guard against issues related to unpredictable changes in distribution operations, can be used both strategically and tactically in an organization as their supply chain is greatly impacted by globalization and its inherent logistical complexity. This has resulted in having risks beyond just the demand and supply variability, limited capacity, and quality issues that domestic companies have traditionally faced, to now include other trends such as greater customer expectations, global competition, longer and more complex supply chains, increased product variety with shorter life cycles, security, political and currency risks.

As a result, it is becoming increasingly important for global supply chain managers to be aware of the relevant risk factors and develop suitable mitigation strategies.

Tactical concerns may include:

- Procurement contracts for required materials and services.
- Production schedules and guidelines to achieve quality, safety, and quantity standards.
- Transportation and warehousing solutions, including outsourcing and third-party logistics options.
- Inventory logistics, including storage and finished goods distribution.
- Achieving best practices in comparison to competitors.

The Operational Level

The operational level of supply chain management is where "the rubber meets the road" so to speak. This is where day-to-day processes, decision-making, and short-term scheduling take place. It is critical not to jump straight into operational management without focusing on the strategy and tactical levels. Effective operational-level processes are the result of strong strategic and tactical planning.

Operational-level management roles may include:

- Daily and weekly forecasting to satisfy demand.
- Production operations, including scheduling and detailed management of work-in-progress.
- Monitoring logistics activity for contract and order fulfillment.
- Settling damages or losses with suppliers, vendors, and clients.
- Managing incoming and outgoing materials and products and on-hand inventories (Po, 2012).

We will now discuss the technology used in more strategic decisions and then move to some applications used in tactical decisions. In some cases, such as forecasting, technology can be used to support all three levels of supply chain planning.

Supply Chain Network Optimization

Location is a strategic, long-term decision in nature that is not easily changed in the short term and applies to raw material sourcing, manufacturing, distribution, and retail.

Strategically, the major goal or priority of the location decision for a manufacturer is to minimize cost, while retailers look to maximize revenue where possible.

To remain competitive in today's global economy, the efficient movement of goods from raw material sites to processing facilities, manufacturers, distributors, retailers, and customers is critical.

Unlike transportation and inventory decisions, location decisions tend to be less flexible as many of the costs are fixed in the short term.

Picking the wrong supplier, manufacturing, or distribution location can have a long-term impact on the total cost of a product. This decision can be heavily influenced by transportation costs as they can average 3–5% of sales with warehousing costs being 1–2% on average, historically.

With that in mind then, the goal of supply chain network design is to determine the best location of facilities within the supply chain, while determining the capacity of these facilities, determining how to source demand through the network, and selecting modes of transportation in a manner that provides the required level of customer service at the lowest cost.

The Location Decision and Its Impact on Value

Like many aspects of the supply chain, there are many trade-offs. In terms of supply chain network design, there is the major trade-off of cost versus service (e.g., the level of investment spent on inventory, transportation, and distribution in relation to the service level offered to customers).

From the customer's perspective, service may be viewed in a variety of ways, including:

- Lead time – The amount of time for a customer to receive an order.
- Product variety – The number of different products offered by a distribution network.
- Product availability – The likelihood of a product being in stock when the customer places their order.
- Customer experience – This may have many dimensions, including how easy it is for customers to place and receive orders as well as how much the experience is customized.
- Time to market – The time it takes to develop new products and bring them to market.

- Order visibility – The ability of customers to track orders from time of placement to delivery.
- Returnability – How easy it is for a customer to return merchandise and the efficiency of the network to handle these returns.

In general, companies selling to customers who can handle a relatively long response time may require only a few locations, far from the customer. In these cases, companies may concentrate on increasing the capacity of each location.

On the other hand, companies that sell to customers who are looking for short response times and maybe even picking up products with their own vehicles need to locate facilities close to them. These companies typically have many facilities, each with a relatively low capacity.

So, the trade-off here is that faster response times required to meet customer demand increase the number of facilities required in the network, and, conversely, a decrease in the response time customer's desire increases the number of facilities required in the network (see Figure 6.1).

Changing the distribution network design affects other supply chain costs (see Figure 6.2) such as:

Inventories – The more locations, the harder to accurately forecast demand as there are smaller and smaller demand groupings, making the target smaller and harder to hit. As a result, safety stock requirements go up almost exponentially (i.e., the "square root" rule which states that average inventory increases proportionally to the square root of the number of locations in which inventory is held).

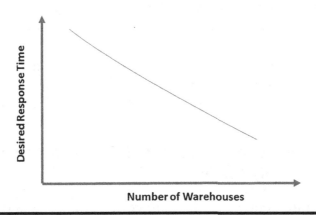

Figure 6.1   Relationship between the number of warehouses and response time.

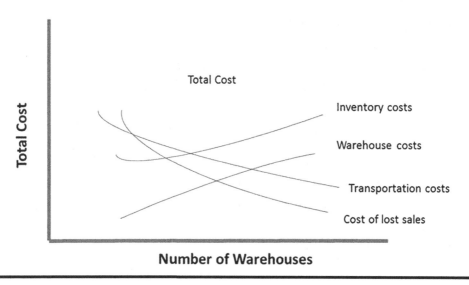

Figure 6.2 The number of warehouses and the impact on cost.

Transportation – Ideally, we want a "long in and short out" in field warehouses to gain economies in transportation on the inbound end (i.e.,
full truckloads versus less than truckload or "LTL"), but this of course
can reach a point of diminishing returns as it will increase inventory
and warehouse operating costs as demand is parsed too small.

Facilities and handling (i.e., warehouse operations) – There are certain
economies of scale that are gained by operating fewer warehouses
whether company owned or outsourced by consolidating volume. This
can result in lower unit handling and storage costs with fewer facilities
and must be analyzed thoroughly. On the other hand, the use of local
public DCs' may enable a company to have their products combined
with other company's products to gain some local transportation savings.

There is also the fact that as the number of distribution facilities increases,
the amount of information to manage increases. This can be somewhat
mitigated by having efficient and integrated information technology systems.

How and Why Network Optimization Technology Can Help to Enable a Lean Supply Chain

As customer requirements become more complex in today's demand-driven,
omni channel environment (resulting in more small shipments to the consumer), supply chain optimization studies are the foundation for some of

the most successful companies' logistics and fulfillment operations. As a result, supply chain networks need to be frequently re-evaluated, similar to the lean concept of continuous improvement, as organizations can strategically create value and enable profitable growth in new and existing markets by optimizing supply chain performance.

From a lean and agile supply chain perspective, an optimally designed supply chain can significantly improve margins, support expansion into new markets, enhance the customer experience, and reduce operating costs.

In many ways, the process of supply chain network optimization can help you achieve more value and less waste through lower inventories, maintaining the right stock levels, and choosing the right transportation modes and warehousing strategies throughout your network.

Without an optimized supply chain network, it becomes very difficult to execute a lean strategy. For example, if your business ships small sized orders and has grown in the southwest region of the US but your finished goods distribution centers are in the midwest and northeast, you know in general that it might make sense to open a new DC in the southwest. This type of analysis can determine not only the precise size, location, and market to serve but also the savings and improved service levels of various "what if" scenarios.

As supply chain network optimization studies can be fairly technical requiring specialized software and often needing consulting advice with a price tag of as much as $100,000, many small to medium sized enterprises (SMEs) tend to not do this type of study at all, put it off, or just use a rough "guesstimate", resulting in significant money being left on the table as well as leaving a variety of wastes in their internal and extended supply chains.

Network Optimization Technology

Network optimization software evaluates your total supply chain from manufacturing and suppliers through warehouses and distribution centers all the way to your distributors and end customers.

The typical tools used to perform supply chain network design are based upon quantitative modeling and optimization which refers to the selection of the best element (regarding some criteria) from some set of available alternatives.

The use of models enables you to evaluate complex relationships and trade-offs of the overall system by connecting large numbers of variables in a framework that makes it easier to define relationships. Quantitative tools to perform this type of analysis also make the translation of an operational strategy into a financial business case much more straightforward.

Types of models used in network design include spreadsheets, regression and statistical analysis, simulation, linear programming, mixed integer linear programming, and expert programs/heuristics.

In general, the trade-offs between these different approaches involve speed versus complexity and the need to achieve "good enough" versus optimal solutions.

Typical commercial network optimization solutions look to utilize long-term demand forecasts, supply chain facilities and capacities, lead times, and fixed and variable costs to identify the most cost-effective supply chain network.

The deliverables usually include where to locate facilities, what modes of transportation to use, and long-term sourcing decisions. As the name implies, network optimization tools seek to optimize performance across an entire supply chain network.

This breed of tool can be used either as an integrated part of a suite of advanced planning and scheduling (APS) tools or as a stand-alone application to only analyze supply chain design decisions. In many cases, as this type of analysis is performed relatively infrequently (maybe every 1–3 years), and requires some specific expertise, some companies choose to bring in consultants who may have their own software.

Integrated approaches can offer a distinct advantage in that the network design system may use the same or similar modeling criteria like the modeling used for day-to-day supply chain planning activities. As a result, integrated models will often be better maintained. However, this approach, as it involves the integration between the various systems, may take longer to obtain results than would be achieved using dedicated models based on more manually massaged data.

As network optimization tools model the entire supply chain, they require a lot of information including forecasts, product and facility information, manufacturing, storage and distribution rates, capacities, a variety of costs, as well as objectives such as inventory turns, services levels, etc.

Other planning tools, which we will discuss later in this book, typically model a supply chain at the SKU/location level, but this is not always the case for network optimization models. Many models such as this used to evaluate strategic decisions utilize somewhat aggregated data. Aggregated data is used because it reduces the challenges of adding new plants, distribution centers, or demand for "what-if" scenarios; and because aggregating data reduces model size and run times allowing what-if scenarios to be more easily solved and evaluated (www.spinnakermgmt.com, 2023).

Technology Options

There are a variety of network optimization solutions available today. They range from stand-alone systems to modules of larger supply chain systems and can be installed or on-demand "cloud software" systems.

JDA (since renamed as "Blue Yonder"), JD Edwards (Oracle), SAP, and Logility all have network optimization modules that are integrated with their other supply chain planning and execution modules.

Other systems like IBM® ILOG®, LogicNet Plus® XE and Logistix Solutions, for example, offer a stand-alone system (on-demand in the case of Logistix Solutions) for lower upfront costs, but as they aren't integrated with other supply chain planning and execution modules, they are perhaps a bit more data intensive.

Supply Chain Network Optimization Technology Case Studies

What follows are some actual examples of companies that have used supply chain network optimization technology to reduce waste and improve efficiency in their extended supply chain.

Case #1: North American Distribution Network Optimization

Challenge

In a not uncommon scenario, a leading industrial manufacturer had a complex manufacturing network and a large number of distribution centers across North America but didn't have an effective method to evaluate the options available and make good, strategic business decisions regarding the correct number and location of facilities. They have a small number of known competitors and wanted to model their supply chain and perform scenario analyses to evaluate how customers' sourcing and buying behavior might change in different industry-wide supply and demand situations.

Approach

Spinnaker (www.spinnakermgmt.com), a supply chain consulting organization, was hired by this client to help design and implement a network design analysis tool that could be used to model and analyze different what-if scenarios using Oracle's strategic network optimization (SNO) supply chain modeling software. This solution utilized data from the client's production systems as well as information for what-if scenarios that could be created and maintained outside of the production systems.

The network design model provided a tool to be used to evaluate changes in the client's supply chain and market environment including the addition or removal of warehouses/production facilities and changes in: (1) manufacturing capacities at existing facilities, (2) demand by product line and/or geography, (3) cost, and (4) current and potential competition sites and capacity.

Results

Supply chain network analysis used to take this company weeks to complete manually or it didn't occur at all because of the effort required. After the project, the client was able to evaluate over 50 what-if scenarios resulting in significant supply chain design changes including the opening and closing of facilities. The modeling effort has led to supply chain cost reductions generating more than 20 times the return on investment while providing an increase in customer service (www.spinnakermgmt.com, 2015).

Case #2: Global Network Design

Challenge

A client of Establish Inc. (www.establishinc.com), a supply chain management consulting firm that was a global manufacturer of semiconductor products, was utilizing two main global distribution warehouses in the Asia-Pacific region. They had some space constraints at their facilities as well as some business model and operational changes that were affecting the logistics flow.

Approach

The first step in evaluating the network was to determine if the current network was optimal with the changes that had taken place and, if not, recommend what should the optimal network look like.

Establish utilized its significant global modeling expertise as well as CAST software (a global supply chain modeling software from Barloworld Optimus) to design the optimal network.

The client had over 10,000 different products, delivery requirements of 48 to 72 hours, and diverse customers throughout North America, Europe, Asia, and the Middle East. So, the model needed to be both flexible and precise to identify the optimal network configuration.

The Establish team gathered data from multiple sources on different continents to document current supply chain flows and costs.

A baseline model was developed for an accurate representation of the current supply chain network. The baseline was used as the basis for comparison of all the various model runs.

Results

There were many runs of the model, which included changes in physical locations and number of locations, transportation modes, delivery requirements, potential customer changes, and product characteristic variations.

In the end, an alternative configuration was found that was more cost-effective with similar delivery service levels which was a combination of existing locations with the movement and consolidation of other locations to produce an optimal configuration.

Once implemented, the client would have a 20% savings in total supply chain costs with the new configuration (www.establishinc.com, 2023).

Even with an optimized supply chain network, the absence of a good demand forecasting process enabled by technology can result in waste throughout the supply chain.

Demand Forecasting Systems

Up until 25 years ago or so, forecasting was kind of the "outcast" that no one wanted to take ownership of. A lot of that, I believe, had to do with the fact that as it is basically a prediction of the future, there was (and still is to some extent) an air of mystery surrounding it. In many cases, this led to separate and somewhat disconnected processes and systems for forecasting.

Marketing and sales would forecast dollars by product and brand at least at an aggregate for budgeting and planning purposes, but these numbers tended to only be updated quarterly at most, thus becoming "stale", and were not truly statistically based (and in the case of sales, highly opinion based and potentially skewed toward bonus goals).

Manufacturing and supply chains needed to run the "day to day" business and therefore needed shorter term, accurate (i.e., at least partially statistically based) current, SKU based (i.e., an individual item at a stock keeping location) forecasts to drive inventory deployment, production planning and scheduling, procurement of materials, staffing and equipment requirements. So, in many cases, they developed their own set of forecasts.

In many cases, this led to a "two" number system causing financial, inventory, and customer service issues.

In the late 1980s, with the help of forecasting software systems such as American Software (which later became Logility), companies were able to tie it all together with "one number" systems which allowed for a kind of "pyramid" approach to forecasting. Statistical SKU forecasts (with qualitative adjustments) could be aggregated to higher levels such as brand or family, discussed among departments, and possibly adjusted at that level and the adjustments prorated back to the SKU level (and in a variety of units of measure), thus resulting in a consensus one number system.

Starting in the late 1980s, organizations began to create entire forecasting functions and departments with trained, experienced forecasters (aka "demand analysts", "demand planners", etc.) who were able to blend "art and science" (i.e., qualitative and quantitative forecasting methods) to develop more accurate, consensus forecasts. Often, this function can be found under the supply chain and/or operations organization, although in some cases, it can still be found under the sales organization.

From that time forward, companies have realized the importance of forecasting to all levels of business planning as when one thinks about it, most aspects of business strategy, planning, and operation are based upon some kind of forecast.

A Lean Approach to Forecasting

Forecasting, perhaps more than other processes, if it is not lean and efficient, can drive waste throughout an organization in the short, medium, and long term.

For example:

- Strategically – Its accuracy (or inaccuracy) can wreak havoc on a supply chain network in terms of locations, functions, layouts, inventory and operating costs, and ultimately customer service levels.
- Tactically – It can affect budgeting and production and deployment planning.
- Operationally – It affects purchasing, job scheduling, workforce levels, job assignments, and production levels.

Ultimately, forecast inaccuracy (at any level) can either lead to (1) waste to the customer in terms of short, late, or no delivery (and hence lost sales), (2) larger amounts of safety stock (and costs) to compensate for forecast inaccuracy, and (3) potentially any of the other eight wastes, in addition to excess inventory, as described in Chapter 4 of this book.

The first step in lean forecasting is to have a forecasting process in place. Assuming that is the case, you need to look for opportunities to improve the process. It should focus on minimizing the use of company resources to maximize customer value by creating meaningful, accurate forecasts as efficiently as possible.

Typical Forecasting Process

Typical steps found in a "best practice" forecasting process include:

1. Determine the use of the forecast – Forecasts can be used as a "driver" for many business decisions including budgeting, capital investments and improvements, production and inventory deployment, etc. Knowing this up front helps determine not only data and software requirements but also "best practice" processes.
2. Select the items to be forecasted – Many items rely on accurate forecasts, especially those most important to the success of an organization. Those items should get the bulk of the resources to have as accurate forecasts as possible. Other, slower moving items with lower profit margins may be best managed with simpler methods of forecasting or even rely on min/max inventory policies alone.
3. Determine the time horizon of the forecast – This will depend on the intended purpose of the forecasts. If they are to be used more for long-term capacity and new product planning decisions, then they may

need to go out several years and be in annual planning periods or "time buckets". If used to drive short- to medium-term processes such as master production scheduling and short-term planning, then an emphasis is placed on the short term and the data will typically be in smaller planning periods such as months, weeks, or even days.

4. Select the forecasting model(s) – Some items, such as slow moving, low margin items can utilize simplistic forecasting methods such as a moving average. A faster moving item with seasonality might require a range of more sophisticated statistical methods such as regression. Whatever combinations of statistical methods are used, they might be adjusted based upon qualitative methods, the forecaster's expertise or intuition, and information from elsewhere such as sales or the customer.

5. Gather the data needed to make the forecast – The system must be capable of gathering recent demand history in an efficient manner as many companies have many thousands of SKUs to forecast. This is usually done via integration with other modules or systems which are the source of this transactional data.

6. Make or generate the forecast – The forecasts need to be re-generated with more current information using the various models and methods discussed in step 4.

7. Validate and implement results – Forecast accuracy targets should be set based on some realistic and meaningful basis. This can include having tighter targets for "A" items (i.e., the "critical few" items that generate most of a typical business' sales and profits) and lower accuracy targets for the many "C" items (i.e., the majority of items, which individually don't generate much in the way of revenue or profits) or other criteria such as high shortage or holding costs, anticipated engineering changes, and delivery or quality problems. Once targets are set, it is important to not only measure forecast accuracy but also determine the cause(s) of higher than anticipated errors.

Lean Forecasting Process

Kahn and Mello (*Journal of Business Forecasting*, 2004–05) arrived at five steps to lean forecasting:

1. Specify the value that channel partners get from forecasting. Primarily this involves getting the product delivered to them at the right time, quantity, place, and price as well as helping to reduce their supply chain costs through reduced inventory.

2. Identify the value stream and focus on eliminating waste such as excess data collection and reporting, long queue times for information, over-analysis of data, too many or the wrong people involved in the forecasting process, and high system costs.
3. Create flow especially by reducing the time between receiving information and making decisions by focusing on reducing the time between creating a baseline forecast, adjusting, and final approval.
4. Facilitate pull by creating a procedure to initiate when a forecast should be made. Pull can also refer to which items will be forecasted, and which will be managed more through inventory control policies such as relying more on reorder points with safety stock or kanbans.
5. Strive for perfection to create the most meaningful forecasts from the customer's perspective.

They also pointed out a framework of focal elements to assist in lean forecasting initiatives. The elements are to:

1. Clarify the forecasting objective and the value that customers obtain from the process.
2. Measure the value the customer receives from a leaner forecasting process.
3. Identify the flow behind the delivery of value to the customer.
4. Determine the pull of the elements for efficiency.
5. Establish a continuous improvement process that serves customers best.

So, what if you don't have a good forecasting process in place? According to an SAS white paper titled "The Lean Approach to Business Forecasting" (SAS, 2012), the lean approach to forecasting is motivated by the fact that many existing forecasting process activities are not adding value. The failure can be due to failed systems, flawed forecasting models, or inadequate organization processes often due to internal politics and management opinions.

A lean approach consists of gathering data, conducting analysis to add value, communicating the results to management, and streamlining and improving the overall forecasting process.

As the objective is to eliminate non-value-added processes or waste, you need to identify where you are spending resources in the existing process. Figure 6.3 is a typical, generic forecasting process found in goods or service industries.

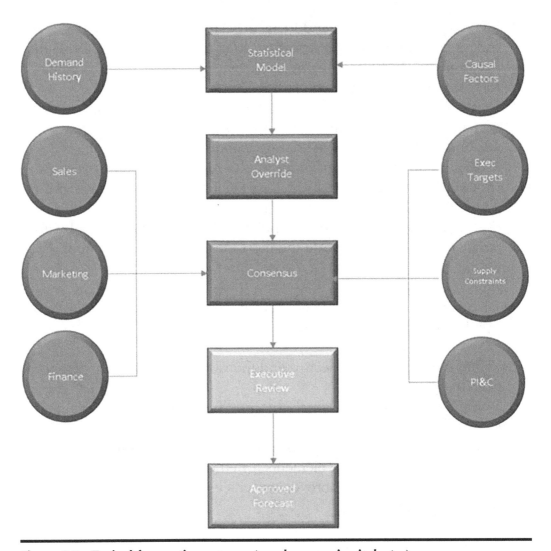

Figure 6.3 Typical forecasting process (goods or service industry).

Demand history and other causal variables are fed into statistical models to create an initial statistical forecast.

A forecast analyst may then enter a manual override based on knowledge of the market and products or information from sources such as sales and customers. Then the forecast, aggregated by family or class of products or services, is discussed as part of a consensus, collaborative, or sales and operations planning (S&OP) process.

As part of the consensus process, members of various functions such as marketing, sales, finance and accounting, supply chain and logistics, etc. give their input to the forecasts. This is not limited to the internal supply chain. Many companies have programs with larger customers such as collaborative planning, forecasting, and replenishment (CPFR), part of which includes collaboration on forecasts with major customers and will be covered in more detail in Chapter 13.

A last step in the process, after supply constraints are considered, is executive approval of the forecast and subsequent supply requirements.

The SAS white paper suggests starting with a "naive" forecast, which takes little effort and basically assumes that actual demand for an item the previous month will be the forecast for the upcoming period. The thinking is that the naive forecast shouldn't be nearly as good as your existing elaborate process. If it is, then something is extremely wrong with your current process.

Whatever software you are using (discussed later in this chapter), you should gather data on all steps (from Figure 6.1) and participants in your forecasting process. It is human nature to assume that by applying more sophisticated forecasting methods, developing a more elaborate process, and including more management participation in our forecasting process, we will get more accuracy, but this may not be the case, and to determine that we require supporting data and analysis.

SAS suggests using a forecast value-added metric to measure the change in a forecasting performance metric (such as forecast accuracy, positive or negative bias, or mean absolute percentage error or MAPE) that can be attributed to a particular step or participant in the forecasting process.

The forecast value-added metric allows you to see if each additive change has improved accuracy through added effort (i.e., demand history → statistical model → statistical forecast → management override) by comparing the results of each process activity to the results that would have been achieved without doing the activity.

Forecast accuracy can't be unrealistic as perfection is seldom achieved as unpredictable outside factors may impact the forecast. Other realities of forecasting include product family and aggregated forecasts are more accurate than individual product forecasts and the further out the time horizon is, the harder to forecast than it is to forecast tomorrow's demand. It's more about minimizing variance by setting meaningful targets and putting the appropriate time and number of resources into the development of the forecasts.

As touched on earlier, one common way to do this is using the Pareto principle or 80/20 rule which states that a small number of items generate the majority of your revenue or profits. These fast-moving products are considered "A" items and, therefore, considerable effort should be placed on determining their forecasts, with tighter (i.e., smaller) variance targets. The other items ("B" and especially "C" items of which there are typically many, which usually generate a much smaller amount of revenue or profits) generally have less accurate forecasts and as they don't contribute that much to the bottom line, they deserve less attention in the forecasting process.

Targets may also be tied to where an item is in its product life cycle (i.e., introduction, growth, maturity, or decline). Typically, new or declining items are more volatile (and rely more on "qualitative" approaches to forecasting) versus growth or mature items which tend to rely more on statistics for forecasting demand.

Smart Forecasting Technology Options and Requirements

Like most technology in the supply chain, there are a range of options when it comes to forecasting demand. They can range from simple spreadsheets, statistical forecasting tools more for analytical use, "point solutions" which allow for the efficient processing of large numbers of items and can be integrated with other more comprehensive (ERP) applications, to being one of many integrated modules in a packaged ERP solution.

There are also installed client/server and desktop solutions as well as software as a service (SaaS), "on demand" modules found on the web, also known as "cloud software".

From a lean perspective, this type of software attempts to minimize waste by tracking trends that will affect future demand and accomplishes the task by improving the forecasting process to eliminate errors or biases in the data and also by reducing data latency, which makes real-time (or at least closer to real time) demand planning possible.

Demand planning tools help an organization to reach two core objectives: (1) improved demand forecast accuracy and (2) greater control over demand "shaping" (i.e., influencing demand to match planned supply).

Demand forecasting systems attempt to accomplish the following:

- Historical analysis – Cross-functional or multidimensional statistical and judgment-based forecasting processes that analyze the historical demand for an individual product at various levels of detail (often factoring in broader macro- and micro-economic trends) to deliver an accurate forecast to supply chain executives.

- Data separation – The software gathers a wide range of data to improve past and future demand analysis. Often the data is filtered and separated by product, customer, seasonal, and market information.
- Demand shaping – The software factors in data that is related to promotions, advertising, planned introductions of new products, and upcoming competitor activity. It then accumulates and displays detailed plans for future marketing campaigns as well as the projected effects on demand and revenue that may occur.
- "What-if" analysis – The software can perform a series of scenarios and simulations based on "what-if" factors. The results of these what-if simulations can suggest potential deviations from planned demand which can then be communicated to other areas of the supply chain to adjust shipments or production.
- Supply chain communication – Demand planning systems are typically integrated with other elements of the supply chain management system to drive and change replenishment scheduling as part of the supply or capacity planning process, preventing excess inventory and reducing inventory carrying costs while at the same time helping to meet targeted customer service levels.

When deciding upon specific forecasting software, you not only need to consider your functional requirements but also be able to assess the potential system functionality and its value in the planning process. It also requires an understanding of the efficiency, accuracy, and relevance of the data that is provided, since that data is key to the effectiveness of the system.

As per the forecasting steps previously mentioned, when selecting demand planning software, you should consider:

- What specific, detailed data does it collect and interpret?
- How often is the data collected (and how often does the system need to be updated)?
- Will the system be used by itself as more of an analytical tool, integrated with supply chain planning or a comprehensive SCM system? You must also determine if it is compatible with legacy systems.

(Harris, 2015)

Artificial Intelligence (AI) and Forecasting

AI planning and forecasting is a field of AI used to make scientific predictions about the future without requiring oversight. A truly "smart" way to do things.

AI planning tools use time series data to estimate future developments for many industries, including sales, healthcare, financial services, and manufacturing. Planning and scheduling problems are much more easily solved with AI forecasting.

Artificial Intelligence versus Augmented Intelligence

As stated earlier, AI combines computer science and datasets to solve problems without human interaction. Machine learning (ML) and deep learning are both subfields of AI.

"Augmented" intelligence, also known as intelligence amplification, cognitive augmentation, and machine augmented intelligence, is limited to computers and software that augment the abilities of a human mind and cannot operate independently.

AI helps machines to think and act like humans, whereas augmented intelligence uses those same machines to assist humans with specific tasks.

Why Is AI Planning Important for Your Business?

AI planning and forecasting uses algorithms to make predictions and forecast trends without human judgment, leading to far less error, and can often outperform data scientists and experts. There have been studies comparing AI predictions with expert predictions from humans and they usually show AI performing better. Algorithms and AI will likely not replace human intelligence entirely in the future, but their ability to analyze data will always help data scientists and forecasters.

It's difficult for a human to analyze data as precisely and efficiently as AI. The main reason for this is that while businesses are aware of a variety of specific data (such as the number of products that can be manufactured in a day), there are also immense amounts of data collected daily and much of that data is unstructured.

Examples of AI Usage

The entire global manufacturing supply chain depends on AI planning and forecasting to balance supplies and sales in a way that maximizes profits.

Without AI for planning and forecasting, it would be increasingly difficult for modern large manufacturing companies, each having numerous suppliers, to even exist, let alone lead their industry.

High-tech industries depend on AI planning and forecasting because human intuition is not well-suited for forecasting novel things, but reliable planning is still critical to success.

Healthcare is starting to adopt AI planning and forecasting to overcome biases of doctors, researchers, and support staff to better understand illnesses and adapt treatments using data-driven approaches, saving lives and improving quality of life.

In the case of a global retail management system, forecasting when it is necessary to switch inventory from summer to fall is critical, and both hemispheres would also need to be considered separately, or winter coats would be shipped to Australia as temperatures begin to rise, for example (domo.com, 2023).

An example of an affordable tool for SMEs (small to medium sized enterprises) that includes some aspects of AI (or at least augmented intelligence) is Forecisely™ (www.forecisely.com; in all candor, the author is an investor in this business).

Lean and Smart Forecasting Technology Case Studies

What follows are some actual examples of companies that have used demand forecasting technology to reduce waste and improve the efficiency of their forecasting process.

Case #1 – Luxury Automaker Improves Forecasting Capabilities with AI

Challenge

A high-end auto manufacturer needed more accurate sales forecasting for its first electric model. The company wanted to go from "gut feeling" and manual regression analysis to full ML supported by centralized data.

Approach

Using both Snowflake's (software) powerful data platform and a custom ML framework, phData (consultant) introduced a faster, more accurate, and user-friendly sales forecasting approach. The team also set the client up with the ML models they'll need for better business intelligence in the future.

Results

The auto manufacturer:

- Built a forecasting platform to address complex data science use cases.
- Solved the short-term problem of forecasting the new electric model of vehicle without extensive historical data, while building a system that will improve over time and can address multiple types of forecasting problems within the business.
- Utilized data pipelines built on Snowflake to ensure that the system always uses the latest data for forecasting; by writing the data back to Snowflake, the customer maintains their single source of truth and is able to use their current BI dashboard natively to view the model output.

The outcomes included:

- A sales forecast model that can forecast results 6 months in advance with significantly higher accuracy than current approaches.
- In 87% of cases, the deviation between the forecast and the observed data was fewer than 10 cars over a 6-month period.
- The forecasting results are up to 50% more accurate than traditional forecasting models (phData, 2024).

Case #2 – Butterball

Challenge

Butterball produces a billion pounds of turkey products every year at five facilities in North Carolina, Arkansas, and Missouri and ships these products to the 98% of American grocers that carry part of the Butterball line, as well as retailers in more than 30 other countries.

As Butterball's products are highly seasonal, heavily promoted, and date-sensitive, they faced several significant supply chain challenges. To deliver a high level of customer satisfaction, maintain freshness, and minimize obsolete inventory, they needed to have highly accurate forecasts.

As a result, they turned to JDA ("Blue Yonder") Software (www.jda.com) for help to improve and manage its complex short- and long-term forecasting process.

Approach

Butterball's approach had been focused more on the short term with heavy use of manual data manipulation, which tended to cause wasted time for the planners. JDA demand software allowed them to focus more on exception monitoring, longer-range planning, and demand shaping.

It has also allowed them to focus more on product perishability and meeting retailers' different service-level expectations and product freshness requirements. Planners now can modify Butterball's forward plans to minimize excess product and maximize customer satisfaction. Planners now can separate normal demand from promotional demand streams.

Results

Benefits to Butterball include a 28% reduction in obsolescent inventory, a 2% improvement in the short-term forecast, and a 50% reduction in long-term forecast bias.

Butterball has leveraged this technology to create a VMI (vendor managed inventory) replenishment model with a key customer (this type of technology will be covered in Chapter 13). The increased level of retailer collaboration is providing the building blocks to further expand Butterball's demand network (www.jda.com, 2023).

Case #3 – Kimberly-Clark

Challenge

Kimberly-Clark makes personal care products including Kleenex facial tissues, Huggies diapers, and Scott's paper towels with worldwide sales of $20 billion in 2011.

In 2006, company executives decided to change Kimberly-Clark's supply chain strategy from focusing primarily on supporting manufacturing to meeting the specific needs of its retail and grocery customers.

To do so, Kimberly-Clark realized it would need to include point-of-sale (POS) information about actual consumer purchases to improve the resupply process with retailers.

In 2009, the company used some minimal downstream retail data in its demand-planning software, but for the most part relied on historical shipment data for its replenishment forecasts, knowing that forecasts based on historical sales are subject to errors, due to the bullwhip effect resulting in excess safety stock and unsold inventory.

Approach

They conducted a pilot program with the software vendor Terra Technology which incorporated POS data into its North American operation. The pilot was successful, and in 2010 they licensed and implemented Terra Technology's multi-enterprise demand-sensing solution.

Kimberly-Clark has three retail customers which generate one third of their consumer products business in North America and provide POS data, which is fed daily into the software, recalibrating the shipment forecast for each of those retailers. The software evaluates any new data inputs from the retailers along with open orders and the legacy demand-planning forecast to generate a new shipment forecast for the next four weeks. Kimberly-Clark also uses that forecast to guide internal deployment decisions and tactical planning.

The software processes data from the retailers, such as POS information, inventory in the distribution channel, shipments from warehouses, and the retailer's own forecast, and reconciles that data to create a daily operational forecast. It also identifies patterns in the historical data to determine how much influence each input has on the forecast. One example might be that POS is found to be the best predictor of a shipment forecast on a three-week horizon, but actual orders and legacy demand forecasts could be the best predictor for the current week.

Results

By incorporating demand signals from key retail customers into their shipment forecasting process, Kimberly-Clark has realized substantial improvements such as being able to develop a more granular metric for forecast errors. Ultimately, they found a reduction in forecast errors of as much as 35% for a one-week planning horizon and 20% for a two-week horizon.

Furthermore, forecast accuracy improvements, which resulted in reductions in safety stock, have helped Kimberly-Clark reduce its overall inventory reducing finished-goods inventory by 19% over the previous year and a half (Cooke, 2013).

While an improved forecasting process by available technology is critical to all businesses, the typical next step for goods and (some) service organizations is to answer the question of "how much" and "when" to produce or purchase additional inventory, which we will delve into next.

Master Production Scheduling

A master production schedule (MPS) takes a business plan and other inputs from financial plans, customer demand, engineering, and supplier performance to create a comprehensive product manufacturing schedule for independent demand inventory (i.e., end items or finished goods) SKU's. The MPS covers what is to be assembled or made, at what time, with what materials, and the cash required during each week of a relatively short-range planning horizon. MPS is a key driver of material requirements planning (MRP) which determines raw material and component requirements, known as "dependent demand" inventory covered in Chapter 7, as well as a short-term manufacturing schedule (Chapter 8).

The MPS must be copacetic with the aggregate production plan which attempts to create a supply plan that satisfies demand at the lowest cost; and as the process moves from planning to execution, each step must be tested for feasibility in terms of manpower, machine, and material constraints.

Rough-cut capacity planning (RCCP) involves a quick check on a few key resources to implement the MPS, to ensure that it is feasible from the capacity point of view. The MPS and RCCP are developed interactively. This determines the impact of the MPS on the key or aggregate resources such as man or machine hours. Rough-cut capacity plans can be "finite" or constrained because they must operate within certain constraints or can be "infinite" or unconstrained leaving adjustment decisions to the expertise and knowledge of the planners themselves.

Inputs for a master product schedule may include SKU forecasted demand, production costs, inventory, customer needs, lot size, production lead time, and capacity. Inputs may be automatically generated by an ERP system.

A typical output for a finalized MPS is a production plan, in a format often referred to as a "PSI" (production, sales, and inventory) report (see Figure 6.4) and may include quantities to be produced, staffing levels, quantity available to promise, and projected available balance. It is typically generated at the item level for a particular sourcing facility (internal or outsourced) or market zone and shown in weekly or monthly time planning buckets.

ABC Company
PSI Report
February 23, 2011

Plant/Market Zone : EAST														
Item : 016														
Description : WINDOW CLEANER 100Z														
Safety Time : 9														
Safety Stock : 1611														
Period	Past Due	23Feb11	28Feb11	07Mar11	14Mar11	21Mar11	28Mar11	04Apr11	11Apr11	18Apr11	25Apr11	02May11	09May11	Total
Periods of Supply	6.2	1.03	1.53	2.05	2.0	1.95	1.67	2.0	2.1	2.07	2.53	2.06	2.02	
Beginning Inventory	620	520	1037	1677	1638	1599	1260	986	1033	1020	1247	1534	1508	16479
Forecast	0	503	823	819	819	819	754	493	493	493	493	746	746	8001
Customer Orders	100	300	1200	0	0	0	0	0	0	0	0	0	0	1600
Dependent Demand	0	0	0	0	0	0	0	0	0	0	0	0	0	0
Scheduled Receipts	0	1700	200	0	0	0	0	0	0	0	0	0	0	1900
Planned Orders	0	120	840	780	780	480	480	540	480	720	780	720	780	7500

Plant/Market Zone : ALL														
Item : 016														
Description : WINDOW CLEANER 100Z														
Safety Time : 9														
Safety Stock : 1611														
Period	Past Due	23Feb11	28Feb11	07Mar11	14Mar11	21Mar11	28Mar11	04Apr11	11Apr11	18Apr11	25Apr11	02May11	09May11	Total
Beginning Inventory	620	520	1037	1677	1638	1599	1260	986	1033	1020	1247	1534	1508	16479
Forecast	0	503	823	819	819	819	754	493	493	493	493	746	746	8001
Customer Orders	100	300	1200	0	0	0	0	0	0	0	0	0	0	1600
Dependent Demand	0	0	0	0	0	0	0	0	0	0	0	0	0	0
Scheduled Receipts	0	1700	200	0	0	0	0	0	0	0	0	0	0	1900
Planned Orders	0	120	840	780	780	480	480	540	480	720	780	720	780	7500

Figure 6.4 Production, sales, and inventory ("PSI") report example.

The technology used to generate a MPS can range from complex spreadsheets to modules within ERP or supply chain planning systems. Integrated solutions offer the benefit of being connected to the aggregate, MRP, and short-term scheduling systems, creating more efficient and effective results.

Lean Scheduling

Scheduling is very important to manufacturing, as it focuses on the allocation of scarce resources to tasks over time. Scheduling problems can be very complicated to solve, and as a result, it's not always possible to find the best possible solution in a reasonable time frame.

Heuristic methods, a rule or a method that comes from experience (i.e., kind of a "shortcut"), have been developed to find near-optimal solutions in comparatively short periods of time. However, heuristics often applied in practice are dispatching rules that have minimal computational complexity and are simple to implement.

It is difficult to execute a schedule precisely, but the main objective of it is to be able to accommodate and anticipate uncertainties before they occur or have a plan to counteract them.

Production planning in a lean environment requires smoothing out the peaks and valleys in the production schedule, resulting in a level schedule. To deliver this kind of lean schedule, an organization must be able to make quick changeovers from one product to another and be able to produce in small lot sizes. This must be done in a demand "pull" type of system as opposed to the traditional "push" or large lot production.

In a lean operation, products are often produced to a buffer called a finished goods "supermarket", rather than directly to customer orders as that might not be feasible due to the relatively small quantities on each order.

The concept of "takt time" is critical to shifting to level scheduling. Takt time can be thought of as the "heartbeat" of the plan and is the rate at which a finished product (usually a family of products) needs to be completed in order to meet customer demand.

Once the takt time is known, the process bottleneck, a resource that requires the longest time in operations of the supply chain for certain demand and therefore limits capacity or throughput, can be determined. This "pacemaker" then drives the pull process both upstream and downstream.

Various lean methods can be used to relieve bottlenecks when they stop the process from meeting the required takt time.

> *For example, leveling of production by both volume and product mix. Products are not manufacturer in accordance with the sequence of customer orders; rather Heijunka, [a Japanese word that means "leveling"], calculates the total volume of orders in a period and levels them out so the same amount and mix are manufactured each shift/ day. Small-scale Lean organizations use spreadsheets to schedule their production to create Heijunka. However, IT systems are a crucial addition for most organizations and yield significant benefits.*
>
> *With the addition of the internet, this has exploded its potential. The spreadsheet approach can be helpful in a pilot context or small-scale entities, but it is questionable whether spreadsheets are a scalable technology in larger organizations, as it's known that they encounter issues with data reliability when used in isolation. Hence, there is a requirement to enable the scheduling method to integrate with an organization's Enterprise Resources Planning (ERP) or Supply Chain Management (SCM) systems.*
>
> *(Salman et al., 2010)*

Furthermore, executing a lean JIT type of schedule requires partnerships with suppliers, where future production schedules that drive purchasing requirements for parts and supplies are shared through visual or electronic kanbans (a system to control the supply chain from a production viewpoint). In many cases, suppliers replenish automatically through what is known as a "vendor managed inventory" system.

MPS/Production Planning Technology Options and Requirements

It is still somewhat common in many organizations for a production plan to be generated using a spreadsheet. Unlike other supply chain applications such as forecasting and MRP software, there isn't really much in the way of "stand alone" MPS software (usually including some kind of RCCP capability). However, it can usually be found as a module in many ERP systems as it needs to be tightly integrated with the information contained in these types of systems such as forecasting, inventory, purchasing, and manufacturing scheduling as well as aggregate planning and manufacturing short-term scheduling systems and/or modules.

Examples include the JDA Master Planning module (www.jda.com) and Logility Voyager Manufacturing Planning (www.logility.com).

Using technology such as this for production planning can help to create reliable, feasible master plans that can drive manufacturing and cost efficiencies while improving inventory management, usually featuring time-phased views of each product and manufacturing resource load. They do this by generating constraint-based schedules and capacity plans that maximize throughput (a major benefit or at least the goal of most lean processes).

Lean and ERP for Production Planning: A Fine Balancing Act

A corporate-wide ERP system can be a real challenge when it comes to working with lean initiatives on the plant floor as there can be some major conflicts, one of those being the conflict between materials planning and production scheduling.

ERP tends to use a top-down "push" approach, depending heavily on sales forecasts for materials planning, while lean is based upon a customer demand "pull" based production schedule keeping minimum inventory with a kanban system that replenishes materials and parts only when needed.

For example, TRW's European Foundation Brakes Division, manufacturer of brake calipers, drums, boosters, antilock braking systems, and electronic stability-control systems, as well as various suspension components, with eight plants in five countries has successfully used a strategy of keeping ERP mostly outside of lean-driven plants.

Internally, the plants in TRW's European Brake Division are focused on their lean initiative. However, when dealing with customers and suppliers, ERP provides them with transactional information.

On a weekly basis, a logistics planner in each plant, with the help of an automated calculation, takes customer-order data from the ERP and levels demand, producing a similar number of parts for every product every day for the upcoming weeks.

ERP provides the customer order information, but each plant builds its own level calculation of demand from that data. As they are building parts at the same pace that customers need those parts, sequencing of orders is generally not a problem.

Finally, ERP is used again at the end of the production process, when brake parts are finished and ready to be shipped to customers (Bartholomew, 2012).

Lean and Smart Production Planning Technology Case Studies

What follows are some actual examples of companies that have used technology to reduce waste and improve efficiency in their production planning process.

Case #1 – Energy Bar Company

The Challenge

A fledgling energy bar company wanted to create a flexible production plan driven by various demand projections over a 12-month period. They wanted to use a low-cost strategy to schedule hiring of additional workforce, ongoing raw material purchases, capital equipment purchases, and production facility decisions for current and forecasted demand. They initially did calculations in a spreadsheet, manually adjusting production and purchasing variables. They quickly realized that changes in demand caused issues in other areas not easily accounted for in the spreadsheet, causing this form of production planning to be a trial-and-error exercise.

Approach

ORM Technologies (www.orm-tech.com), having an optimization and operations research engineering software system, utilized their Production Planning software module with the energy bar client to include all known production, cost, and staffing constraints to produce a 12-month plan based on current and forecasted product demand.

This technology allowed their energy bar client to:

- Create quickly production plans that maximize profit with dozens of different demand profiles.
- Select the optimal timing to hire additional workforce, purchase raw materials, and make facility decisions to meet current and forecasted demand.
- Perform "what-if" analysis with current and forecasted product demand as well as facility, staff, production, raw material, and packaging costs and capacities.

Results

The system output provided the company with the information needed to make staffing and facility decisions as well as capital equipment and reoccurring raw material purchases, also allowing the company to save much needed capital by delaying a move to a new facility by several months and optimize the staffing plan. The client can now run a "what-if" analysis whenever they want to determine the production, cost, inventory, and staffing effects of changes in demand to plan rather than operate in a reactive mode (www.orm-tech.com, 2023).

Case #2 – Global Raw Materials Supplier

Challenge

A global manufacturer was running a production and materials planning process that must be highly integrated with demand (customer orders) to minimize waste on the manufacturing floor while allocating demand across all global plants to optimize output. They used a "production planning" data mart to provide synchronization and a consolidated production view across each of the manufacturing facilities.

This data mart urgently needed to be updated, both in terms of the technology and the logic driving the process.

Approach

Corporate technologies (CTI), a systems integrator and solutions provider (www.cptech.com), was brought in to reverse engineer the business logic and implement a new "production planning" data mart to reduce the cost of ownership while improving the maintainability of the system.

The strategic plan for all business units was to use an integrated SAP architecture, applying SAP business objects data services as data integration technology across the manufacturing systems.

This involved the analysis of hundreds of different data flows from thousands of different data sources. Business rule logic was re-engineered in SAP business objects data services and tested for business integrity.

Results

Ultimately the updated technology and logic significantly reduced IT maintenance costs and improved data inputs to the manufacturing planning process (www.cptech.com, 2023).

Case #3 – Techlogix Helps Nestlé Innovate in Milk Production Planning

Challenge

Nestlé Pakistan operates the largest milk collection operation in Pakistan working with approximately 190,000 farmers in the provinces of Punjab and Sindh. They produce a variety of dairy products including milk, powdered milk, cream, tea whiteners, and yogurt.

Even though demand for milk products is fairly constant year-round, not surprisingly, milk production varies very significantly from season to season. As the content of milk (fat, etc.) from farmers varies, Nestlé has the added problem of managing its production capacity in the most efficient way with both supply constraints and demand variations.

Although Nestlé had invested in an ERP system, they were unable to automate the complex milk production planning process and the manual planning that was being used had its own set of limitations.

To manage content variation, Nestlé prepares a production plan every month using several estimates and assumptions. Their typical production plan is generated in a spreadsheet by a production planner, following a set of objectives with many rules and constraints. Objectives of their usual production plan include:

- Minimizing milk waste.
- Reaching planned production quantities for each SKU.

- Producing material ahead for future months when fresh milk supply may be inadequate.
- Efficient utilization of imported material.
- Creating requests in advance of anticipated material shortage.
- Utilizing available plant capacity for bulk production and line capacity for packaging.

Rules and constraints used in planning include:

- Maintaining production ratios between products have to be maintained when increasing or decreasing production.
- Following plant and packaging line capacities and maintenance schedules.
- Tracking raw material availability and stock expiration dates.
- Selecting the most appropriate bill of material (BOM; from a large of number of potential recipes) which depends on raw material and fresh milk availability.

Their current SAP ERP system did not fully capture the complexity of the milk production planning problem and thus the reliance on manual planning, which has multiple flaws:

Suboptimal plans – The production planning process produced suboptimal plans, largely because of trying to solve a complicated multi-constraint optimization problem primarily using instinct, approximations, and heuristics from experience. This could be seen in line capacity remaining idle, the use of less desirable BOMs, etc.

Time-consuming and repetitive – The entire planning process, which included the generation of multiple plans, took a considerable amount of time. This process had to be repeated each month and took a significant portion of the month to complete.

Error prone – The production planner had to consider a wide range of conditions, rules, and constraints when creating the monthly production plan. As a result, human errors were common.

Expert dependent – The production plan at Nestlé is dependent on a very small number of experts and training new resources is difficult and takes considerable time.

As a result, Nestlé decided to develop an automated solution in order to simulate multiple what-if scenarios using rules and constraints to prepare a final production plan that met all set parameters.

Approach

Techlogix (www.techlogix.com), an IT services, consulting, and business solutions company, was engaged to create a customized planning system. They proposed a multi-phased approach starting with a feasibility study and part high-level solution design, followed by a detailed design, build, and delivery of the solution with a final phase of maintenance and ongoing support.

Techlogix designed and delivered a web application to be used as a simulation engine to produce a production plan along with a variety of reports. The reports helped the planner look at different aspects of the production plan.

The production planning algorithm has two distinct aspects: planning and scheduling. The planning algorithm uses fresh milk quantity, raw material stock quantity, and other inputs to determine the optimal production of bulk material.

This quantity is the input to the scheduling algorithm which attempts to schedule production on plants within specified capacities. If required production capacity is not available, the planning algorithm adjusts production and attempts a reschedule to find the best fit.

Reports are generated that allow a production planner to view productions in terms of bulk produced, SKUs produced, plant and line capacities used, etc.

The goal during testing was to manage multiple production lines based on the system output. Five months of parallel runs were conducted where the system output was compared with the manual plan as well as checked against all constraints.

Toward the end of testing, the system was able to consistently generate plans that met all criteria and significantly improved upon the manual plan.

Results

The automation of the production planning process now only takes a few hours versus days of effort previously, with more time now for maneuverability. The new production planning output is more precise and accurate than before, which helps to reduce costs and eliminate waste (www. techlogix.com, 2023).

Case #4 – Durabuilt Windows and Doors Balances Lean and ERP for Production Scheduling

Challenge

Durabuilt is a manufacturer of windows and doors and operates a 180,000-square-foot plant with 450 employees. They have been using Cantor, an ERP system, since 2008 and have had the challenge of integrating lean practices at their plant for the past three years with Cantor ERP, which was a real balancing act as they needed both to survive and prosper.

Approach

In the past, Durabuilt's workflow on the production floor ran through ERP and they would produce 50 or 100 boxes before going to the next order. As a result, large quantities of boxes waited for hours to be used. Before ERP they sent paper documents to purchasing to order materials and then to receiving to wait for the materials to come in.

Results

Durabuilt's IT staff had to adapt the ERP system to support the lean management principles used at the facility.

As part of the lean initiative, the plant had modified their assembly line to single piece flow and needed to configure the ERP to support that process. Now, instead of having batches of parts sitting around in boxes waiting for hours to be used, the parts are brought to the line as needed.

Management strongly believes that if they didn't have an ERP system, their lean initiatives wouldn't work.

For example, they no longer have a transfer of paperwork for purchasing as orders for materials go straight to their suppliers.

It's now a faster process, and they are not missing anything due to human error, with material lead time built right into the system providing an accurate delivery date to the customer up front.

In the new process, orders are entered into the ERP system by sales-people which then go to the scheduling department. Schedulers then create and adjust the production schedule in ERP, fine-tune it daily, factoring in variables such as the capacity of individual manufacturing lines versus complexity and time sensitivity of customer orders. Schedulers then put consideration into the transport schedule for Durabuilt's fleet of trucks that deliver windows and doors to customers (Bartholomew, 2012).

Some companies start with MPS/production planning and then aggregate those plans for collaboration purposes; others start at the aggregate and then disaggregate for production planning. In either case, they are directly linked and must be in sync. Next, we will discuss aggregate or S&OP, its impact on a lean supply chain, and how technology can greatly assist in this process.

Sales and Operations Planning

Sales and Operations Planning Defined

In its simplest terms, S&OP is a process for a business to ensure that supply can match demand, at least on the aggregate (the reason it is also often referred to as "aggregate planning"; thus, the reason for putting it later here in Chapter 6).

It is a process where executive-level management regularly meets and reviews projections for demand, supply, and the resulting financial impact (typically integrated with the results of more detailed work described earlier developing forecasts and in some cases production plans). S&OP is a decision-making process that makes certain that tactical plans in every business area coincide with the company's business plan. The net result of the S&OP process is that a single operating or aggregate plan is created that allocates company resources.

An even broader definition of S&OP has emerged in recent years, offering an even greater impact from a lean perspective on a supply chain, integrated (or advanced) S&OP (also referred to as "integrated business planning" or IBP) which represents the transition of S&OP from its production planning origins into the fully integrated business management and integrated strategy and financial planning process it is today. There is now more effort put into not only looking at your business's internal supply chain but also the extended supply chain, both downstream toward customers and upstream toward suppliers. This effort has been enhanced by many of the collaborative programs and technology-enabling tools used in demand and supply chain planning such as VMI and collaborative, planning, forecasting, and replenishment (CPFR).

S&OP increases teamwork between departments and helps to align your operational plan with your strategic plan. It is a process where various targets are set (i.e., forecast accuracy, inventory turns, etc.), and progress against the strategic and operational plans are reviewed in a series of meetings.

The objective of S&OP is to have a consensus on a single operating plan that meets forecasted demand while minimizing cost over the planning period. It should allocate people, capacity, materials, and time at the least possible cost while ensuring the highest customer service possible.

The executive S&OP process itself (Figure 6.5) actually "sits on top of" the number crunching and analysis being done at a lower level of the organization (e.g., item forecast generation, production planning, etc.) and involves a series of meetings prior to a final S&OP executive-level meeting which are used to create, validate, and adjust detailed demand and supply plans.

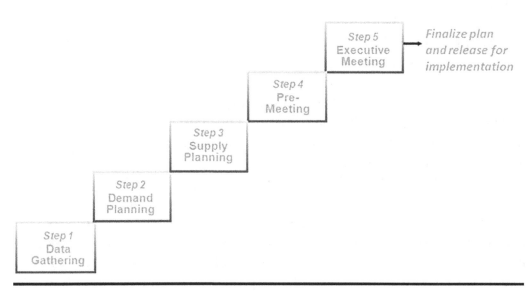

Figure 6.5 Steps in the S&OP process.

First Quarter			Second Quarter			Third Quarter		
January	February	March	April	May	June	July	August	September
50,000	30,000	55,000	60,000	80,000	150,000	150,000	125,000	80,000

Aggregate Plan

Months:	January					February		
Aggregate Plan Quantity:	50,000					30,000		
Weeks:	1	2	3	4	5	6	7	8
MPS quantity:								
26" Boys Blue	10,000		10,000		5,000		5,000	
12" Boys Red		12,500		12,500	8,500		8,500	
12" Boys Yellow		5,000					3,000	

Master Production Schedule (MPS)

Figure 6.6   Aggregate plan versus master production schedule.

The S&OP meetings are:

Demand planning cross-functional meeting (step 2) – Generated
forecasts are reviewed with a team that may include representatives
from the supply chain, operations, sales, marketing, and finance.
Forecasts have already been generated statistically and aggregated in
a format that everyone can understand and confirm (e.g., sales might
want to see forecasts and history by customer in sales dollars).

Supply planning cross-functional meeting (step 3) – After confirmed
forecasts have been "netted" against current on-hand inventory levels and
scheduled production work orders/purchase orders, future production/
purchasing plans are reviewed. Again, this data will usually be reviewed
in the "aggregate" by product family in units, for example (see Figure 6.6).

Pre-S&OP meeting (step 4) – Data from the first demand and supply
meetings are reviewed by department heads to ensure that consensus
has been reached.

The discussions from this series of monthly management meetings high-
light issues and look at possible resolutions before the outcome of the
discussions is presented to the senior management team as a series
of issues to be resolved. These issues form the basis of the **executive
S&OP meeting** (step 5).

S&OP and Lean

Lean teams plan and execute on a shop-floor level, but S&OP can be a
great tool to make the connection between lean kaizen event goals and
objectives and corporate ones. As we know, inventory is one of the eight

wastes and covers variability in a process. Using S&OP, inventory and other supply chain operating costs can be directly planned and controlled. In general, there are two general ways to reduce inventory: (1) more accurate forecasts and (2) shorter cycle times. The S&OP process attempts to improve and control both.

From a lean perspective, a robust S&OP process acts as both a planning and control method at an executive management level as various metrics indicating the level of waste such as forecast accuracy, inventory turns and on-time and complete shipments to name a few, are benchmarked externally to set objectives (as well as matching the company's strategic plan) and then measured to know when things are in or out of control.

According to an Aberdeen Group study in 2010, there are four key performance criteria to distinguish best-in-class in terms of S&OP. They are:

1. Forecast accuracy.
2. Perfect orders delivered complete and on time.
3. Cash to cash cycle.
4. Gross profit margin.

All of these, especially the first three, are measurements of how lean a company is in that the lower the score, the more "variability" your system has, which leads to many of the wastes we have discussed (Viswanthan, 2010).

Working Together

Dougherty and Gray, in their 2006 book *Sales and Operations Planning – Best Practices*, point out that in a study of 13 best practice companies, lean and S&OP help each other and according to one of their best practice clients, "continuous improvement is embedded in the S&OP process, and continuous improvement cannot be maximized without S&OP".

Furthermore, they point

> If you create a manufacturing environment where material flows with minimum waste (lean), but you can't predict capacity and material availability problems in enough time to avoid them (S&OP), you will inevitably revert to firefighting, finger-pointing and poor results. Similarly, if you do an excellent job of future planning but have poor flows, you can almost count on higher in-

ventory levels, longer lead times, and lower profitability … Traditionally lean manufacturing has been stronger on workplace management, S&OP on decision-making for the future. The tools and methods of lean manufacturing have tended to look most closely at the plant, and its immediate customers and suppliers, mostly over a short horizon. This leads to improvements like: "shorter, quicker, fewer, lower cost, more flexible, and better aligned". S&OP provides distance vision – providing the ability to predict capacity and material availability problems before they become crises, to identify market issues while they are still opportunities, and to prioritize improvements in a way that will create the most favorable results.

Tomorrow's supply chain will be driven, among other things, by effective S&OP which allows for effective supply chain planning, balances new and current products and services, employs timely, effective replenishment, enables timely success/failure measurement, and, with the help of technology, can generate data/analysis/correction.

When S&OP is implemented in a company that is focused on a team-based continuous improvement process, from top to bottom, success can be ensured.

S&OP/Aggregate Planning Technology

While many modules of ERP systems now offer a variety of "dashboards" with the ability to drill down into details demand and supply information, it is still not uncommon for Excel templates such as the one shown in Figure 6.7 from Weeks Software Solutions, LLC (www.ezmrp.com) to be used that integrate with tools ranging from other production planning spreadsheets to modules in ERP systems.

At the other end of the spectrum, there are much more complex offerings from companies such as SAP (www.sap.com), which is powered by their HANA in-memory data platform that is deployable as an on-premise installation, or in the cloud. It is best suited for performing real-time analytics (discussed in Chapter 15) and developing and deploying real-time applications. Using "in memory" applications such as HANA with S&OP offers a unified model of demand, supply chain, and financial data, at any level of granularity and dimension in real-time.

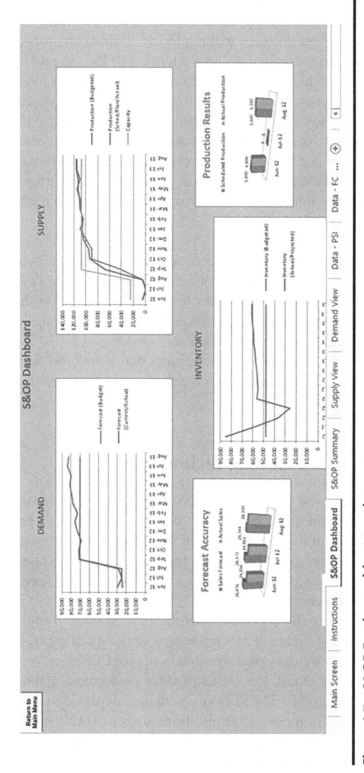

Figure 6.7 S&OP Excel spreadsheet template.

The linkages from the dashboard are driven by demand and supply planning activities that have been aggregated into product classes or families.

So, it's no surprise that they are typically integrated, on the aggregate with forecasting applications on the demand side.

On the supply side, they can be fed data from MPS or in many cases from (un)constrained or "rough cut" production (or capacity) planning (RCCP) modules in ERP or supply chain planning systems such as found in Logility (www.logility.com) and JDA/Blue Yonder (www.jda.com) software. These types of systems or modules allow for the optimization of manpower, material, and machine constraints of facilities or even production lines to minimize resource constraints sometimes reducing manufacturing planning time by as much as 75%.

Let's take a scenario where the aggregate monthly production requirements (using established crewing, equipment run rates, minimum lot sizes, changeover times, etc.) for a class of products that all run on the same filling and packaging line are beyond the stated monthly capacity for five of the planning months. In the case of unconstrained capacity planning software, the planner would use their own knowledge, judgment, and other information to handle the situation. In the case of constrained capacity planning software, the software itself, using rules (priorities, sequencing, etc.) established by the planner, will automatically create an optimal solution to the scenario.

There are a range of options to be considered. They include demand options such as cutting, delaying, and backordering customer orders and supply options such as running overtime and hiring temporary workers (short term), adding shifts and using contract packagers (medium term), and adding new production lines and even facilities (long term).

How AI Can Save Your S&OP Planning Process

S&OP has been around since the 1990s for businesses across nearly every industry. However, this important supply chain process is now under added pressure from departmental silos, complex trading partner networks, and geopolitical and environmental tumult. At the same time, planners skilled to handle these challenges are in relatively short supply.

Yet there is also a rich history of applying technologies to continuously resolve challenges and optimize S&OP outcomes. Currently, integrating

Generative AI with ML algorithms is part of that legacy which delivers a modern, more inclusive, and intuitive S&OP process.

Furthermore, advanced AI technologies, such as ChatGPT (*which is a "chatbot" which allows you to have human-like conversations to complete various tasks and enables users to refine and steer a conversation toward a desired length, format, style, level of detail, and language*) can translate complex information into informed decisions that can increase profit and growth. AI technologies can also connect and align cross-functional teams such as sales, marketing, finance, and supply chains to allow businesses to stay ahead of supply chain disruption.

One main area where AI is particularly transformative for the supply chain is demand forecasting where it goes beyond traditional backward-looking methods and helps forecast demand and inventory at the speed of a rapidly changing market.

Using AI-enabled S&OP planning solutions such as Logility's DemandAI+, companies can take advantage of peaks and valleys in their demand trends to make the right assumptions and best decisions and deliver optimal outcomes with speed and agility.

When leveraging these AI-powered capabilities, users can meet tough forecasting challenges and achieve supply chain performance improvements, such as:

- Faster weekly planning cycles
- Fewer forecast errors
- Lower inventory costs

Users can also leverage the incredible speed of today's AI algorithms. These types of solutions accelerate the information-gathering part of the S&OP planning process from weeks to a continuous stream of real-time information, from market shifts to business impacts, and everything in between.

For example, collaboration enabled by ChatGPT and Narrow AI (a type of AI that focuses on a specific task or a limited range of tasks) can be queried to get the right data or report. On top of that, scenarios can be created to see how the overall organization and different departments are impacted.

Using AI, companies can then predict and respond faster and more accurately to changes as they happen with algorithms that incorporate customer behavior data, market dynamics, and events into the forecasting and overall S&OP processes. In addition, they can improve the accuracy of their forecasting models by considering base demand, promotional lift, causal forecasts, and user insights into their overall analysis.

With the integration of ChatGPT and Narrow AI, supply chain planning is further enriched with more sophisticated insights and greater visibility (Logility, 2024).

S&OP/Aggregate Planning and Technology Case Studies

What follows are some actual examples of companies that have used technology to help reduce waste and improve the efficiency of their aggregate planning processes.

Case #1 – Infineon Technologies AG Takes Planning to the Next Level with JDA S&OP

The Challenge

Infineon Technologies AG provides semiconductor and system solutions, focusing on energy efficiency, mobility, and security. They have customers worldwide, including auto manufacturers, industrial electronics companies, chip card and security businesses, and information and communications technology companies. Their industry is known for having volatile demand, long product lead times, requiring significant capital investments, and increasing product and supply network complexity.

So, it is critical that they can identify and respond to demand changes while balancing global production capacity across its more than 20 facilities.

Approach

Infineon made the decision to re-engineer its planning processes and tools so they could respond quickly to market changes, across all planning levels and areas of the company. They determined that they needed new technology to accomplish this goal. It took two years and was jointly managed by their information technology and business departments.

At the time, they were using homegrown S&OP tools, which didn't work because of limitations in scalability and integration. So, they chose JDA Software for this project as they had worked together in the planning area in the past.

The JDA consultants tried to understand their processes first and then tried to match them with the appropriate JDA solutions. Through this partnership, JDA was able to develop an interactive RCCP functionality within JDA S&OP, enabling Infineon to synchronize demand, supply, capacity, and load planning into one multidimensional view.

Results

Sales forecasts, pricing, and production capacity are now reviewed and adjusted in real time in one simulation model which gives Infineon an overview of its operational and financial plans. They can then quickly react to changes in the market. They can also shape demand to meet production constraints or identify a need for additional capacity (e.g., at a subcontractor site).

As a result of implementing the S&OP solution, Infineon has:

- Reduced its planning effort by more than 30%.
- Cut the lead time for its rolling forecast from four weeks to two weeks.
- Decreased planning errors up to 90%.
- Reduced its "churn" (i.e., making minor adjustments to the plan) by a factor of 10.
- Forecast accuracy has also improved.

Most importantly, Infineon now has a new collaborative planning approach, enabling the business to be more agile and responsive so that demand, supply, capacity, and load are always synchronized and calculated together (www.jda.com, 2024).

Case #2 – Accelerated S&OP Collaboration at Lance

The Challenge

Lance produces and distributes snack foods including cookies, crackers, nuts, and potato chips, largely under the Lance, Cape Cod, and Tom's brand names.

Their products are distributed via direct-store delivery with over 1,400 sales routes, independent distributors, and direct shipments to retail customer locations.

Their challenge was to increase visibility, improve forecast accuracy, and increase shelf freshness for consumers.

Approach

To reach these goals, Lance implemented Logility Voyager S&OP software which transforms information from sales, production, finance, marketing, transportation, and procurement into one central database. It allows S&OP to work from a "one number" system, saving time and achieving better clarity. With this S&OP solution in place, it was determined that they could cut hours and days from their planning process, streamline the planning cycle, and complete analysis in a fraction of the time.

The goal was to allow Lance to have greater visibility into their business and be able to identify their most profitable customers and channels, optimize their product mix, improve procurement strategies, and maximize margins. Logility's S&OP best practices allow them to compare multiple "what-if" scenarios, evaluate critical decisions, and prepare contingency strategies to mitigate risk.

Results

After implementation, Lance improved forecast accuracy, reduced inventory days-on-hand, decreased finished goods storage, and improved S&OP collaboration.

Specifically, Lance:

- Improved forecast accuracy from 50% to 70%.
- Reduced inventory days-on-hand by 20%, from five days to four.
- Decreased finished goods storage by two warehouses.
- Accelerated S&OP collaboration.
- Improved acquisition integration effectiveness (www.logility.com, 2023).

Case #3 – Continental Mills Increases Productivity with S&OP Process

The Challenge

Continental Mills is a food manufacturer of products such as pancake mixes, bake mixes, drink mixes, and breading and batters in operation since 1932. They have three manufacturing facilities located throughout the US. Their current supply chain system and processes have been struggling to successfully cope with the increasing complexity of their business today, including many new SKUs and customers.

Their S&OP process was supported from the top down, with senior managers participating monthly. Up to that point, their supply chain team had calendar discipline, but with a very labor-intensive process.

The team had many challenges such as having many versions of spreadsheets emailed back and forth, some with corrupted data. They had no idea how much time and effort they put into chasing numbers and version control, only finding out after they didn't have to do it anymore.

They also have separate divisions that look outwardly in a different way with each division having forecasts at a different level of detail.

Approach

As a result, they looked for a new solution to manage that growth, selecting Logility's Voyager Solutions.

One benefit of the Logility solution is that it provides Continental Mills with a flexible solution that allows all four divisions to manage their business in their own way in different levels of detail, but still gives them a comprehensive corporate view through a single hierarchical structure.

Continental Mills has used the Voyager Demand Planning system to convert its businesses from its hard to maintain forecasting process using spreadsheets to a statistical forecast which reduced the time and effort previously dedicated to administration and "crunching" numbers.

They also can now do a much better job of driving the forecast and analyzing their options with a separate view for each one of the businesses. They have saved an estimated 40–50 hours of spreadsheet manipulation from the monthly S&OP process.

The S&OP software has allowed Continental Mills to streamline the production planning process and improve capacity planning for all its manufacturing facilities.

Results

Even with a record sales year, Continental Mills:

- Improved inventory turns by 20%.
- Increased resource efficiency in the forecasting process.

- Reduced forecast errors in one division by close to 50%.
- Achieved a record service level of 99.48%.
- Improved data accuracy and visibility throughout the business (www. logility.com, 2023).

Case #4 – Faribault Foods Plans with AI to Become More Agile

The Challenge

Faribault Foods is a leading manufacturer of branded, co-manufactured, and private label shelf-stable foods and beverages. In 2019, they set out to replace their on-premises demand planning and S&OP applications with a more modern cloud alternative.

The old system was also not very easy to use and required extensive training for new users. Faribault decided to search for a new cloud solution that would take advantage of the latest technologies to achieve better forecast accuracy while being easier to use and lower cost to operate.

Approach

Faribault evaluated three solutions: New Horizon (NH) software, a module from its ERP vendor, and a new cloud application from its legacy system vendor. After a careful evaluation, they decided to go with NH for the following reasons:

- Better forecast accuracy by using advanced technologies including AI, ML, and Facebook Prophet forecasting technology.
- Fastest implementation time and time to value.
- Modern and intuitive user experience.
- Lowest total cost of ownership (TCO).

They then started the NH S&OP implementation in January 2020 and went live that April.

Eighteen users from Faribault's supply chain and sales organizations use the system. Transaction data is imported from their SAP ERP system, and plans are exported to Faribault's SAP advanced planning and optimization (APO) application. Trade promotion plans are imported from Faribault's Vistex trade promotion management solution.

At the same time, the pandemic hit. So, to adjust to the demand shock, Faribault modified its business processes and took advantage of New Horizon's advanced capabilities:

- Faribault focused on fast movers and monitored them weekly while reviewing slow movers monthly. This was facilitated by NH's automated demand segmentation capability.
- NH's forecasting engine automatically compensated for the skewing of demand history caused by the pandemic so that future forecasts would be accurate.
- Faribault increased the frequency of its S&OP process from the traditional monthly cycle to weekly and even daily in some cases. This was facilitated by NH's ability to integrate up-to-date information from ERP systems in as little as a minute.
- Cross-functional teams consisting of sales, manufacturing, planning, and the executive team collectively resolved what products to produce and how to allocate limited inventory.

Results

Faribault's forecast accuracy understandably took a hit because of the pandemic, but it quickly recovered, and in fact they gained market share because they anticipated changes to demand better than the competition.

Faribault has achieved the following business benefits from their implementation:

- Low implementation costs and quick time to value resulting from the rapid deployment (one month for demand planning and one month for S&OP).
- Up to a 10% decrease in forecast error compared with the prior solution.
- Quick and agile response to the COVID-19 pandemic and other disruptions.
- Intuitive user experience resulting in greater adoption, higher planner productivity, and less need for training.
- Lower support costs and TCO.
- Increased service levels, sales, and market share resulting from more accurate forecasts and improved inventory availability (New Horizon, 2021).

Continuing to follow the SCOR model, we will next look at the "Source" component of the model from both a process and technology view, as it can have a huge impact on a company's cost and efficiency as purchasing and logistics costs can range from 50% to 70% of a company's sales dollar.

Chapter 7

Supply Chain Software Systems: Source

There are parts of the sourcing process that are strategic in nature and those that are more tactical to support planning and operational activities.

We will first briefly describe the topics and then look at technologies and cases for both.

Strategic Sourcing vs. Procurement

Strategic sourcing should not be confused with simply using centralized procurement to leverage volume buying. In fact, it is a systematic and fact-based approach for optimizing an organization's supply base and improving the overall value proposition and is the process of taking advantage of purchasing opportunities by continually reviewing current needs against purchasing opportunities.

Procurement, on the other hand, involves the process of selecting vendors, strategic vetting, establishing payment terms, the negotiation of contracts, and actual purchasing of goods and is concerned with acquiring the goods, services, and work vital to an organization.

In its broadest sense, strategic sourcing expands an organization's focus to the supply chain impacts of procurement and purchasing decisions, with goals to achieve large and sustainable cost reductions, long-term supply stability, and minimization of supply risk.

DOI: 10.4324/9781003372639-9

The approach, first established by General Motors in the 1980s and now a common business purchasing tool, is founded on a detailed understanding of both the spending profile of the organization and of the supplier market. This understanding is continually updated to deliver ongoing improvements to the organization's sourcing and procurement performance.

As we described in the previous chapter, once the S&OP process has been completed, the aggregate plan is "disaggregated" into a master production schedule (MPS) for a production facility, which shows net production requirements for the next 2–3 months, usually in weekly or monthly time periods by SKU for independent demand items (see Figure 7.1). This is known as "time phased planning".

However, in many cases, organizations have complex distribution networks. Consumer packaged goods companies, for example, may start at the MPS level (or even more detailed item-distribution center level) using a tool known as distribution requirements planning or "DRP" (to be covered in Chapter 9) and summarize upwards to the aggregate plan. In either case, this aggregate/disaggregate iteration may occur multiple times until it is finalized.

The net requirements above and beyond existing known ones which are referred to as "scheduled receipts" are called "planned orders" and "planned receipts"; the only difference is that planned orders are planned receipts that have been offset by the item's lead time.

It should be noted that the lead time for manufacturing, which is the time required to manufacture an item, is the estimated sum of order preparation time, queue time, setup time, run time, move time, inspection time, and put-away time. In the case of purchased items, the lead time is usually stated by the vendor and may or may not include inbound transit times.

First Quarter			Second Quarter			Third Quarter		
January	February	March	April	May	June	July	August	September
50,000	30,000	55,000	60,000	80,000	150,000	150,000	125,000	80,000

Aggregate Plan

Months:	January				February			
Aggregate Plan Quantity:	50,000				30,000			
Weeks:	1	2	3	4	5	6	7	8
MPS quantity:								
26" Boys Blue	10,000		10,000				5,000	
12" Boys Red		12,500		12,500	8,500		8,500	
12" Boys Yellow		5,000					3,000	

Master Production Schedule (MPS)

Figure 7.1 Aggregate plan versus master production schedule.

Material Requirements Planning

Once the MPS has been solidified, it can then be "exploded" through a bill of materials (BOM) file to determine raw material and component (i.e., dependent demand) requirements typically used to generate purchase orders or releases.

The most common tool for this is material requirements planning (MRP), which is a production planning, scheduling, and inventory control process (and system) used to manage manufacturing processes and generate direct goods requirements (i.e., raw materials and production goods).

We should also consider here requirements planning for indirect goods referred to as "maintenance, repair and operating" (MRO) goods which are typically run outside of an MRP process. MRO, for our purposes, includes machinery, tooling, and parts used to create a product as well as fluids, lubricants, office supplies, shop supplies, furniture, light fixtures, toolboxes, safety protection, and other consumables.

It should be noted that MRO items are often given a lower priority but without which businesses wouldn't be able to operate in an effective fashion. In fact, indirect procurement can range from 15% to 25% of a company's total revenue.

The information needed to run an MRP model includes the MPS, a BOM, inventory balances, lead times, lot sizes, and scheduled receipts (i.e., purchase orders and production work orders). These inputs need to be accurate and up-to-date. Otherwise, it's the old "garbage in garbage out" situation, resulting in poor execution and ultimately customer dissatisfaction.

MRP and Technology Case Studies

Case #1 – Gables Engineering Moves to a "Real" MRP System

The Challenge

Gables Engineering is an avionics manufacturer in business that builds custom cockpit controls including the design and building of the switches, housings, and LCD display modules for the airline and airframe industry.

Gables had a pseudo-MRP system based on reorder points which used current customer demand, as well as historical demand, to determine what they needed to buy. It was basically moving forward by looking backward (which assumes the past will repeat itself, which, as we know, isn't always the case). The company wanted a product using the Oracle® database that had a Windows® front end and that would seamlessly interface with other third-party systems.

Approach

Gables formed a team to look at its business processes to see if they needed a new enterprise application system. A request for quotation (RFQ) sent to several software vendors.

Gables selected IFS enterprise resources planning (ERP)/e-business that includes a true MRP module with a better understanding of actual demand. Previously at Gables, demand was determined by customer orders as well as by a factor for historical demand causing them to buy and build unnecessary parts, loading shops with unnecessary work and inflated purchased inventories.

Results

Once Gables implemented the new IFS system, it was able to calculate demand using actual customer orders and a forecast, enabling them to order and build parts by looking at forecasts, not at history. This reduced work in process and overall inventory by 50% and 30%, respectively. It used to take two days to get a spare part shipped out, from time of order to time of shipment, and now same-day shipping is possible.

The software also tracks the history of changes made to a product down to serial number including the parts removed from inventory to manufacture it are maintained for now. During a customer audit, Gables was able to show the traceability of a component using the audited part's subassembly, which they could never have done previously.

Gables has also reduced kitting time to less than one month before assembly, kitting almost 99% of the entire product right before assembling it. They also now have notebooks allowing stockroom personnel to review pick lists online and pick and update inventory instantly (www.top10erp. com, 2023).

Case #2 – A Picture Perfect MRP Implementation Helps Traffic Enforcement Camera Maker to Profitability

The Challenge

Transport Data Systems (TDS), a $2 million company founded in 1995 and located in San Diego, California, manufactures license plate recognition and capture systems (cameras) for toll roads, parking lot security, and traffic violation processing and enforcement.

TDS never knew how much stock they had of anything, which, with increasing demand for their products, drove the company to look for an MRP system.

At the time, workers would make a spreadsheet for each job that included every required part and its estimated cost. In some cases, they didn't have any idea if they had some inexpensive parts on hand until they got ready to build them and they weren't there.

Results

Once TDS had licensed E-Z-MRP, it freed up their VP of Operations' time from administrative tasks, allowing him to focus on product improvements, strategic projects, and other aspects of his work that only he could do.

It also allowed TDS to determine a selling price quickly, instead of recalculating from each new spreadsheet how much it would cost to build the product.

The MRP system is now consistently being used as a standard operating platform, no matter who used the MRP system to help achieve stability and accuracy in the process (www.e-z-mrp.com, 2023).

Case #3 – Raytheon Streamlines and Automates Its Material Requirement Planning Processes with Exostar's Supply Chain Platform

Challenge

Raytheon is a technology and innovation leader specializing in defense, homeland security, and other government markets throughout the world that provides electronics, mission systems integration, and other capabilities as well as a broad range of mission support services.

Raytheon divisions relied on a variety of MRP processes and "home grown" and packaged software systems for the delivery of products and services to customers, but as a result had the following issues:

Siloed processes and systems – Each of Raytheon's six business units had implemented its own MRP solutions.

Manually intensive interactions – As the MRP systems couldn't be accessed directly by suppliers, all scheduling communications required an excess of manual intervention, resulting in increased cost, time, and risk.

Approach

Raytheon decided to transition to a collaborative MRP (cMRP) supply chain platform (SCP) solution from Exostar that would deliver the following benefits:

- Automate processes as much as possible.
- Leverage existing infrastructure to minimize impact and cost.
- Enable increased collaboration between buyers and suppliers.
- Standardization and integration across all existing MRP systems.

Results

Raytheon's Integrated Defense Systems (IDS) group was the first business unit to transition to SCP and connect its existing MRP systems with SCP. They have been able to modify their existing MRP process to make it a leaner, more automated, standardized, and collaborative process that reduces manual processes, increases productivity, and increases integration with suppliers.

Overall, Raytheon anticipates that after full implementation at all business units, they will be able to have savings of up to $3 million per year by:

- Increasing reliability – On-time delivery of goods from suppliers will increase by 10% or more.
- Streamlining the process – The new system should reduce manual re-entry of information, printing/faxing, and phone/email communications.
- Optimizing resources – Move 12–15 employees per business unit from administrative to more high-value tasks.

- Reducing supply chain risk – Better performance visibility and exception management.
- Improving consistency – Implement the cMRP solution across all six Raytheon business units over time (www.exostar.com, 2023).

The Procurement Process

Today, technology is heavily used not only in the short- to medium-term purchasing process in a variety of sources such as an MPS, procurement plan, MRP, etc. but also for the broader, longer-term needs of an entire procurement/sourcing process (see Figure 7.2).

As described in Chapter 5, procurement (also known as sourcing and supply management), the focus of this chapter, is the process of managing a broad range of processes associated with a firm's need to acquire goods and services in a legal and ethical manner that are required to manufacture a product (direct items) or to operate the organization (indirect items), the foundation of which is provided by the purchasing function. Per Figure 7.2, the procurement process typically includes the functions of determining purchasing specifications, selecting the supplier, negotiating terms and conditions, and issuing and administrating purchase orders.

Preparing and managing purchasing documents involved in this process has always been a time-consuming process. Most firms have streamlined the document flow process using lean and other process improvement techniques to reduce the paperwork and handling required for each purchase.

Automation of Procurement Documents and Processes

The types of purchase orders generated as a result of this process may include:

Discrete orders – Used for a single transaction with a supplier, with no assumption that further transactions will occur.

Pre-negotiated blanket order – A purchase order made with a supplier containing multiple delivery dates over a period of time, usually with predetermined pricing which often has lower costs as a result of greater volumes (possibly through centralized purchasing and/or the consolidation of suppliers) on a longer-term contract. It is typically used when there is an ongoing need for consumable goods.

Figure 7.2 The procurement process.

Pre-negotiated, vendor managed inventory (VMI) – The supplier maintains an inventory of items at the customer's plant and the customer pays for the inventory when it is consumed. Usually for standard, small value items like maintenance, repair, and operating supplies (MRO) such as fasteners and electrical parts.

Bid and auction ("e-procurement") – This involves the use of online catalogs, exchanges, and auctions to speed up purchasing, reduce costs, and integrate the supply chain. There are many e-commerce sites for industrial equipment and MRO inventory auctions and vary in format from catalog (e.g., www.grainger.com, www.chempoint.com) to auction (e.g., www.biditup.com). Websites can be for standard items or industry-specific.

Corporate purchase card (pCard) – This is a company charge card that allows goods and services to be procured without using a traditional purchasing process; sometimes referred to as procurement or "p" cards. There is always some kind of control for each pCard, such as a single purchase dollar limit, a monthly limit, and so on. A pCard holder's activity should be reviewed periodically independently.

To further enhance the speed and accuracy of transactions, many companies use what is known as "EDI" (electronic data interchange), which is the computer-to-computer exchange of business documents in a standard electronic format between business partners. In the past, EDI transactions went either directly from business to business (in the case of large companies) or through third parties known as value-added networks (VANs). Today, a large portion of EDI transactions now flow through the internet.

Sometimes included in the category of EDI is the use of electronic funds transfer (EFT) which is the electronic exchange, transfer of money from one account to another, within a single financial institution or across multiple institutions, through computer systems. This also includes e-commerce payment systems which facilitate the acceptance of electronic payment for online transactions which has become increasingly popular as a result of the widespread use of internet-based shopping and banking.

There are numerous other documents and/or information requirements which can be automated and integrated with an e-procurement process including:

- Identify and review requirements and establish specifications – Specification sheet, statement of work, product requirement, customer order/MRP requirement, and purchase requisition.

- Select suppliers (approved) – Purchasing card, e-catalog, EDI, stock check, and reorder point.
- Select suppliers (unapproved) – Request for quote/information (RFQ/RFI) and request for proposal (RFP).
- Issue purchase orders (PO) – Purchase order approval and release/acknowledgment and blanket order.
- Delivery and receipt – Bill of lading (B/L), packing slip, discrepancy report, kanban, receipt acknowledgment.
- Payment – Supplier invoice, match PO and invoice, pay invoice, and update supplier scoreboard.

So, it should come as no surprise that procurement is an area where technology has been heavily applied over the past 25 years. In fact, every one of the steps involved in the procurement process typically utilizes technology to one degree or another.

In its totality, the suite of tools used to achieve efficiency in purchasing transactions is broadly defined as "e-procurement". Companies are using e-procurement tools to manage the flow of documents by (1) automating the document generation process and (2) electronically transmitting purchase documents to suppliers.

Procurement Technology

There is a variety of technology available today to help an organization automate and improve their various procurement processes. For our purposes, we will define e-procurement as the business-to-business purchase and sale of supplies and services over the internet which can be integrated with internal computerized procurement processes and systems as identified in Figure 7.2.

In the area of procurement, which may sometimes include e-procurement functionality, there are two types of software vendors: (1) enterprise resource planning (ERP) providers offering both internal procurement (including individual MRP vendors; see example in Figure 7.3) and e-procurement as one or part of their modules and (2) services or vendors focused specifically of e-procurement.

Procurement software itself is a computer program or suite of products that helps to automate (and thereby improve) the processes of purchasing materials and inventory maintenance of goods. Following the typical

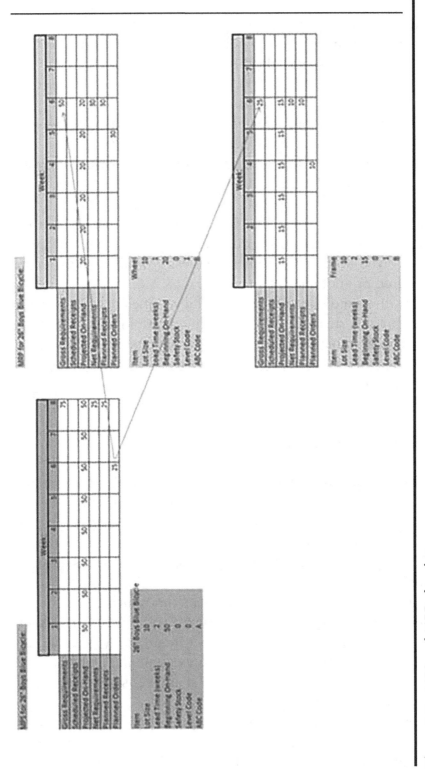

Figure 7.3 MPS and MRP planning.

procurement process, it can generate purchase orders, execute the ordering process online, match invoices to materials received, and pay bills electronically. Again, more often than not, systems today include e-procurement functionality as well as leveraging the benefits of the internet.

As a result, the benefits of using procurement software include ease of administration and potential cost savings as well as having a single interface for procurement to monitor their companies' spending.

Procurement software helps us to efficiently manage a variety of activities. Specifically, they include the ability to:

- Create a purchase order based on need.
- Verify a purchase order.
- Submit a pending purchase order for approval or rejection.
- Automate an electronic purchase order transmission.
- Purchase order confirmation or cancellations.
- Help to execute financial and inventory transactions when ordered materials arrive.
- Gather data and analyze it to improve profitability.
- Streamline and standardize administration. For example, procurement systems generally offer multi-currency support as well as tools that can automate purchases and purchasing approvals.

These systems can also connect users with large networks of qualified suppliers, which is a critical capability for supply chain professionals who are trying to identify the most reliable raw materials suppliers at the best price, wherever they might be sourced from.

As opposed to procurement modules internal to ERP systems such as SAP and Oracle, there are also "stand-alone" procurement solutions coming in a variety of forms. Dominick identified ten types of stand-alone procurement software systems:

1. Spend analysis – Allows you to find purchasing patterns within categories, by suppliers, etc. that might offer cost savings, performance improvements, and overall efficiencies. Most spend analysis vendors have been acquired by other types of procurement software vendors.
2. Supplier discovery – Allows you to search for suppliers that meet specific criteria, such as capabilities, location, supplier diversity, etc. Examples: ThomasNet, Ariba.

3. Supplier information management – Allows you to efficiently collect and maintain accurate supplier information including contact information and certification status directly from suppliers. Examples: HICX Solutions, Hiperos.

4. eSourcing – Allows you to get quotes and proposals electronically from suppliers quickly. This can be done privately or let suppliers see their rank among bidders to increase competitive pressure. Examples: WhyAbe, K2Sourcing, Trade Extensions.

5. Contract management – Enables you to prepare contracts using various templates. It can electronically route contracts for approval, track revisions, notify contract expirations, and store executed contracts. Examples: Selectica, Prodagio.

6. e-Procurement – Allows end users to search catalogs of pre-approved products and services from contracted suppliers, create requisitions, and have some requisitions turned into purchase orders (either manually by buyers or automatically). Example: ePlus, eBid.

7. e-Invoicing (also known as "ePayment") – Enables you to efficiently receive accurate supplier invoices electronically. May include "dynamic discounting", allowing suppliers to reduce the amount your organization owes in exchange for faster payment. Examples: Taulia, Tradeshift.

8. Supplier management – Enable you to track and/or rate supplier performance using manual or scorecard-style ratings. Also, integrate with other systems to gather actual performance. May include risk assessment capabilities. Examples: Aravo, BravoSolution.

9. Combination solutions – A type of e-procurement system allowing for direct payment to suppliers, commonly referred to as "procure-to-pay", or P2P. Ones that offer the option of soliciting quotes from suppliers are called "source-to-pay solutions". Examples: Coupa, Puridiom.

10. Complete suites – There are some software vendors that have many or even all of the solutions listed above. They are referred to as "suites". Examples: GEP, Zycus, SciQuest, and iValua (Dominick, 2015.

Lean and Procurement

Supply chain costs can range from 50% to 70% of a company's sales depending on the industry you're in, so it's not difficult to see why it's an area of interest in terms of looking for waste.

Lean sourcing or *procurement* is a different way of looking at and working with suppliers. There is a greater use of partnerships and alliances as well as a greater need for coordination and collaboration, often utilizing some of the technological tools mentioned previously for accuracy, timeliness, and efficiency.

Traditional supply chains are managed more on a cost basis, negotiating with many suppliers. While this may still be effective in some instances (e.g., commodities), lean procurement is all about long-term partnering with fewer, longer-term suppliers with less reliance on low-cost bidding. Motorola, for example, has eliminated traditional supplier bidding by adding emphasis on quality and reliability and in some cases may sign contracts that are in place throughout a product's life cycle (Heizer & Render, 2020). In this way, the relationship can be mutually beneficial. The value is created by economies of scale and long-term improvements (see Figure 7.4).

As a result of this type of relationship, where trust is very important, suppliers are more willing to get involved in just-in-time (JIT) partnerships and share in the design process and be willing to contribute technological expertise. For example, when Cessna Aircraft opened a new plant in Kansas, they set up consignment and VMI programs with some select suppliers. One supplier, Honeywell, was allowed to maintain avionic parts on-site. Other vendors who participated kept parts at a nearby warehouse to supply the production line daily. This was a "win-win" situation as Cessna was able to execute JIT inventory replenishment for parts and their suppliers gained better insight into Cessna's production requirements and

CHARACTERISTIC	TRADITIONAL SUPPLY CHAIN	LEAN SUPPLY CHAIN
Suppliers	Many	Few
Interactions	Confrontational	Collaborative
Relationship Focus	Transactional	Long Term
Primary Selection Criteria	Price	Performance
Length of Contract	Short Term	Long Term
Future Pricing	Increased	Decreased
Lead Times	Long	Short
Order Quantities	Large Lots	Small Lots
Quality	Extensive Inspection	Quality at the Source
Inventory (Supplier and Customer)	Large	Minimal
Information Flow	One Way	Two Way
Flexibility	Low	High
Product Development Role	Small	Large (Collaborative)
Trust	Limited	Extensive

Figure 7.4 Lean supply chain characteristics.

could offer suggestions for product improvements, thereby strengthening the relationship (Heizer & Render, 2020).

Some suppliers may be somewhat hesitant because of issues such as having too much reliance on one customer, shorter lead times, smaller order quantities, etc. As a true partnership, the customer must be willing to work with the supplier and share costs, training, and expertise so that they're not just "passing off their problems upstream". Of course, you need to always have a "backup" plan and only a single source (i.e., one supplier for an item) where there is very little risk involved (e.g., commodity type item, easily substituted part, etc.).

There are many lean opportunities in procurement including:

- JIT, such as in the Cessna example above. There may also be a potential application for VMI, where a supplier manages its customer's inventory of parts and supplies which will be covered in more detail in Chapter 13, "integration and collaboration".
- Batch size and lead time reduction – Producing smaller quantities of items more frequently, thus reducing inventory and cycle time.
- Blanket orders – Where a customer places a single purchase order with its supplier containing multiple delivery dates scheduled over a length of time, in many cases at predetermined prices.

As they say, "if you can't measure it, you can't improve it". This applies to all the applications mentioned in this book. By performing "lean assessments" and "supplier reviews", you can determine how "lean" your supplier is and what progress has been made toward that goal.

Besides process improvement itself in the procurement process, the benefits of electronically generating and transmitting purchasing-related documents include:

- A virtual elimination of paperwork and paperwork handling.
- A reduction in the time between need recognition and the release and receipt of an order.
- Improved communication both within the company and with suppliers
- A reduction in errors.
- Lower overhead costs in the purchasing area.
- Purchasing personnel spend less time on processing purchase orders and invoices and more time on strategic value-added purchasing activities.

Procurement and Technology Case Studies

Case #1 – Enabling Online Supplier Collaboration at Toshiba Semiconductor Company

Challenge

Toshiba Semiconductor Company wanted real-time information for its global operations to stay a global leader in the industry and the lack of this information would limit the company's success in the future.

At the time, purchasing employees bought products locally with no sharing of information among buyers, factories, or headquarters as these activities were being conducted separately primarily because no central database existed.

Approach

Toshiba selected JDA (now known as "Blue Yonder") software for spend optimization to help manage its supplier relationships using a web interface with their customers and suppliers. This would enable Toshiba to operate on a real-time basis using accurate information enabling them and their suppliers to collaborate on sourcing and procurement for supply management. In this way, they could integrate product development, sourcing, supply planning, and procurement across the entire supply chain.

Toshiba decided to implement JDA Negotiate and Strategic Sourcing for direct materials and information-gathering and decision-making processes.

This would enable them to send out RFQs to suppliers via the internet and help the company to create a supplier database shared by all their purchasing staff to assist in the selection of the best suppliers in future negotiations and to make balanced scorecards for each supplier.

Results

As a result of its successful implementation, JDA solutions enabled Toshiba to gain a competitive advantage by refining its supplier base and adding speed, efficiency, and reliability to purchasing.

They can now handle between 7,000 and 8,000 RFQs per site at six of their major factories in Japan.

Toshiba feels that they have achieved a competitive edge due to the increased level of speed and intelligent decision-making from using JDA software.

They firmly believe that it will help the company reduce its number of preferred suppliers using a balanced scorecard from information contained in the new database and that purchasing agents will become more strategic by enabling them to collaborate with product designers in the design stage, where 80% of a product's cost is determined (www.jda.com, 2023).

Case #2 – Clariant: Increasing Interenterprise Productivity and Extending Its SAP Software Investment Value

Challenge

Clariant, a global leader in specialty chemicals, markets innovative chemicals in a variety of business areas. They wanted to improve the accuracy of their catalogs for their global supply base and to develop more collaborative supplier relationships. Additionally, they wanted to improve invoice cycle times.

Approach

By deploying Ariba Procurement Content, PO Automation, and Invoice Automation solutions, they determined that they would be able to purchase all indirect goods and services through their existing SAP ERP software system.

Results

Clariant eventually deployed the Ariba Procurement Content solution to manage more than 300 catalogs, deployed the Ariba PO Automation solution in 21 countries, and rolled out the Ariba Invoice Automation solution in Germany and Switzerland.

This integrated smoothly with the existing SAP supplier relationship management application for order initiation.

It enabled a consumer-like shopping experience, covering all countries with one user-friendly solution. To accomplish this, they utilized Ariba services which incorporated catalogs and suppliers on the Ariba Network.

Clariant reached their goal of purchasing all their indirect goods and services through the integration of Ariba PO and invoice automation with their SAP ERP application, thereby increasing order accuracy, reducing non-catalog orders, and streamlining invoice processing in Germany and

Switzerland. It allowed procurement personnel to focus on higher-value activities and improved collaboration internally and with suppliers (www. sap.com, 2023).

Case #3 – New Purchase-To-Pay System Allows Smarter Processes at Atea

Challenge

Atea is a leading supplier of IT infrastructure in Europe that helps to enable their customers' IT purchases, delivery, and service processes to run smoothly by delivering the necessary hardware and solutions.

Other than their hardware purchases, which are most items purchased and are handled by central purchasing, Atea lets employees do their own purchasing for indirect items.

Currently, department heads must provide authorization twice: once to authorize a purchase, and later to authorize the invoice after delivery was made.

Approach

Atea looked for a combined technology solution that included purchasing, automated invoice processing, and travel and expense management. It had to support their decentralized (indirect item) purchasing strategy and integrate with their existing ERP and payroll systems, all the while being user-friendly.

They needed the solution to help optimize their purchasing, invoice, and expense handling processes as well as integrate their invoice processing and travel and expense management systems. A system that would enable department heads to deal with purchases just once.

Results

Atea licensed a purchasing system from Basware. Employees can now create a purchase requisition and get it approved electronically by their department head. When the invoice arrives, it's already been approved and can be sent for payment automatically, thereby reducing the work of two people by 50%.

They no longer must search for invoice documents, ownership of invoices or approvals, while at the same time ensuring the right purchases are made.

The purchasing system now integrates with invoice and travel and expense processing and with the entire payables side, enabling many approvals to be granted automatically.

The responsibility for invoice posting has now been delegated to individual departments with decentralized invoice posting.

There is no need to send invoices from one department to another anymore and departments have a better idea of what they are spending.

Atea also chose to shut down expensive manual advances and is switching as many staff as possible to personal liability credit cards (www.basware.com, 2023).

The type of procurement and purchasing systems described in this chapter are typically part of or integrated with ERP systems, technology drivers of the "make" topic of our next chapter.

Chapter 8

Supply Chain Software Systems: Make

Enterprise resource planning (ERP) systems have grown to incorporate a huge diversity of functionality, including topics covered in other parts of this book. In this chapter, we will discuss it more from a perspective of enabling production and related internal supply chain and logistics operations processes that support manufacturing processes.

The discussion of ERP systems in general will be followed by discussions of manufacturing planning and execution systems which may be internal modules in an ERP system or external integrated "best in class" applications.

ERP Systems Defined

ERP systems are a suite of integrated applications that an organization can use to collect, store, manage, and interpret data from many business activities. They can be locally based or cloud-based.

ERP systems initially focused on automating back-office transactional functions that did not directly affect customers and the public. They later became integrated with customer and supplier relationship management and e-business when the internet simplified communicating with external parties. Many of the systems then became web-enabled and then web-based.

While some may not consider ERP systems as supply chain management tools, a great deal of the functionality is supply chain and logistics related (see Figure 8.1), especially when you consider potential "add on" modules

DOI: 10.4324/9781003372639-10

such as forecasting, warehouse management systems, etc. ERP systems were originally an extension of an MRP system (a production planning, scheduling, and inventory control system used to manage manufacturing processes) and is used to integrate all internal processes as well as customers and suppliers. They allow for the automation and integration of many business processes including finance, accounting, human resources, sales and order entry, raw materials, inventory, purchasing, production scheduling, and shipping, resource and production planning, and customer relationship management. An ERP system shares common databases and business practices producing information in real time and coordinates business processes ranging from supplier evaluation to customer invoicing.

E-businesses must also keep track of and process a tremendous amount of information and as such have realized that much of the information they need to run an e-business such as stock levels at various warehouses, cost of parts, and projected shipping dates can already be found in their ERP system databases. As a result, a significant part of the online efforts of many e-businesses involve adding web access to an existing ERP system.

ERP systems have the potential to reduce transaction costs and increase the speed and accuracy of information but can also be expensive and time-consuming to install (one of the advantages of using cloud-based "on demand" vs. installed systems).

Figure 8.1   Typical modules in a basic enterprise resource planning (ERP) system.

ERP Systems and Lean Supply Chain

As the philosophy of lean, which in its simplest form is a team-based form of continuous improvement, has often been referred to as "a pen and pencil" type of tool, some supporters have talked about the elimination of the ERP systems entirely.

However, the reality is that a manufacturer's ERP system should be simplified as they can include a vast array of day-to-day functionality including general ledger, accounts payable, purchasing, receiving, and order management, to name a few areas. An ERP system is not only needed to manage existing business practices but also for tracking and analyzing current manufacturing processes to help find areas that need improvement.

Additionally, many of today's ERP systems have extended their applications to support basic lean principles of value definition and specification, value stream mapping, flow, and demand pull.

Furthermore, ERP and lean production offer many of the same benefits to an organization such as inventory and lead time reduction, quality improvement, and customer service improvement.

As manufacturing (and service industries to a degree) has moved from mass to lean production with the supply chain now heading in that direction as well, it can be said that we are now evolving into a phase of technology-enabled lean.

However, it must be understood that ERP systems support and enable lean but don't drive it. It's the lean culture, training, and tools that make it happen. ERP systems support and help to enable lean initiatives.

There are many things that can be re-configured or modified in an ERP system that can help enable lean manufacturing and the supply chain.

However, first, it is critical for an organization to resolve any conflicts between manufacturing efficiency and customer service/sales departments. Typical lean processes require a shift to smaller batch sizes, lead times, setup times, etc. which can conflict with the revenue goals of the sales department which would like to have excess inventory "just-in-case". These "leaner" production schedules should be tied to sales projections and actual customer demand, which can be configured in an ERP system. Then metrics and measures can be set in the ERP system for tracking and controlling purposes.

Regardless of your manufacturing operation, it is a good idea for an enterprise application to support multiple production strategies including make-to-order (MTO), make-to-stock (MTS), engineer-to-order (ETO), configure-to-order (CTO), and others. Even MTS manufacturers must consider the different levels of demand for various products and part numbers and should consider having a parallel MRP system that allows stable products to be run MTS and the many, volatile, small volume "C" items to be run in an MTO environment (and/or MTS with excess safety stock to compensate for poor or non-existent forecasts). This helps you to be efficient on products that make sense to manufacture in large quantities and responsive on products that are best handled as special orders.

An ERP system should at least have some tools that allow production to become pull-based, using processes such as a kanban (Japanese for "visual signal" which, based upon downstream demand, tells you what to produce and when to produce it). Having this functionality allows companies to pull products through a "leaner" supply chain while minimizing work-in-process (WIP), maximizing flexibility and responsiveness, and avoiding excess quantities of finished goods.

Enterprise applications should allow for operations at multiple sites as with any complex supply chain you really are operating in a multisite environment. The more integrated the operations between these different sites are, the more responsive you can be as the information flows seamlessly through your internal supply chain processes as well as customers and suppliers, whether these sites are under your direct control or not. This will allow your company to see multisite functionality as a tool for collaboration throughout the supply chain.

Master data management is critical for companies that have recently been through a merger or acquisition, especially where different parts of the company have multiple part numbers for the same item. It is hard to have enterprise-wide visibility and integration through the supply chain (critical to lean) when you have duplicate data and records for identical parts. Even if you are within a single global company, it is important to have multicurrency and multiple language support, as with any extension of the application to a customer or vendor overseas you may end up with duplicate data, hampering your lean supply chain improvements. In general, you need to have a common language for customer numbers, item codes, etc. to integrate the business and share plans and bring lean efficiencies to your supply chain (www.ifsworld.com, 2009).

ERP Technology

Enterprise system software is a multibillion-dollar industry that helps to support a variety of business functions and is the largest category of capital expenditure in United States businesses over the past decade or so. While early ERP systems focused on large enterprises, smaller enterprises increasingly use ERP systems to run their businesses in industries such as manufacturing, wholesalers/distributors, health care, government, retail stores, hotels, and financial services.

There are literally hundreds of ERP software vendors that range from the very large ones with expensive offerings (SAP and Oracle; up to millions of dollars) to mid-sized/priced and relatively small vendors costing as little as $100K and up. They can vary in terms of functionality and platforms (e.g., client-server and "cloud" based, on-demand "software as a service" or "SAAS") and serve general or only specific industries.

It is beyond the scope of this book and chapter to get too much into the detail of this technology beyond what we've already covered in terms of basic functionality and impact on the supply chain. However, the actual selection and implementation of these very critical systems can mean success or failure for an organization as speed and accuracy can offer a company a distinct competitive advantage in today's global economy.

Additionally, when poorly managed, the selection and implementation can be very costly and wasteful to a company as not only is the software license itself expensive but also the "total cost of ownership" can be 3–5 times the cost of the software license and include items such as training, consulting, technical and maintenance, hardware upgrades, and customization costs.

An article in CIO magazine offered "9 Tips for Selecting and Implementing an ERP System" (Schiff, 2014):

1. Get upper management support – Lack of upper management support and involvement can lead to resources at lower levels not being as dedicated and engaged in the implementation project.
2. Make a clear and extensive list of requirements before you start looking at vendors – Any good project must start by defining its scope. This includes identifying specific business processes and their functional and system requirements. It is critical that you work with end users, IT, and senior management from the start so you can find an industry-specific ERP system, with tools and features designed to solve your business requirements. This up-front effort will pay off in the long run.
3. Don't forget mobile users – Accessing ERP systems from desktops only is no longer an option, so look for an ERP solution that allows users to also connect securely via smartphones and tablets.

4. Carefully evaluate your options before selecting your ERP system – Make sure you have clear requirements and priorities as well as participation and input from key stakeholders during the evaluation stage to ensure better acceptance and user adoption.

   Reporting and metrics in the selected system are also important. So, make sure the existing reports in the system have available metrics you will need to drive your business, hiring, and resourcing.

   Integration is important as it must work with your existing legacy and/or critical office systems.

   If possible, try to find a vendor that specializes in your industry, or at the very least has referenceable clients in your industry.

5. Get references – So you can ask the customers what went right, what went wrong, and what they might have done differently.

   You can also network with industry associations that you might belong to and ask colleagues for ERP recommendations.

6. Think before you customize – Think about the amount of customization required for the ERP system as the more customization that is required, the higher the cost, not only initially, but when upgrading to new releases.

   Also, understand your tolerance for longer implementation cycles, as while turnkey solutions may have less flexibility, they will also likely have more stability and less initial and ongoing cost.

   Many companies' basic business processes are very similar such as paying invoices, collecting revenue, and procuring supplies (even though they may not think so!). So, there may be an opportunity to take advantage of standard "best practice" processes that have been tested by many other companies.

   If a business function believes they have a case for a customization, make them justify it as the cost of the customization is not only writing and testing the code but also providing long-term support of the custom code that may require special handling when you upgrade your software.

7. Factor in change management – Most ERP projects entail huge changes in organizations and impact the culture of your company. So, you need to develop control and communication plans and workshops to help with implementation and adoption of the systems.

8. Appoint an internal ERP product champion – Don't just use a vendor-appointed project manager. Make sure to have someone on your staff who is highly qualified as it's important to put your best people on the job as a lot is at risk.

9. Provide the necessary time and resources for training on the ERP system – You should identify department-specific needs up front and allow for sufficient time to develop and deliver training programs and, where possible, use employees within departments who can be given the opportunity for more in-depth instruction (i.e., "train the trainer") to become expert resources for their fellow employees. This can help to reduce the "us vs. them" dynamic which can often occur.

Supply Chain and ERP Systems Case Studies

Case #1 – Radio Flyer Teamed with Ultra Consultants on ERP Selection, Business Process Improvement, and Implementation Management

Challenge

Radio Flyer is one of North America's most recognizable wagon and toy manufacturers best known for its "Radio Flyer" red wagon.

Radio Flyer looked to standardize their global operations onto a single ERP platform. They had an AS-400-based ERP system which limited them as they wanted to improve visibility into the supply chain, optimize inventory, increase accuracy of sales forecasting, automate sales and financial operations, and improve reporting with real-time data analytics.

Approach

As is commonly the case, Radio Flyer didn't have in-house ERP expertise, so they brought in Ultra Consultants to help with the system selection and implementation process.

Ultra helped Radio Flyer identify gaps between the current state and the desired future state of operations and identify systems that would help to close those gaps. The maps helped to show them their pain points, bottlenecks, and waste in their processes and how to eliminate them.

During the software evaluation process, this helped them to be able to focus on key functionality and understand which ERP features and functions would be needed for business process improvement. It also helped to speed up the ERP selection process. Radio Flyer ultimately chose Oracle's JD Edwards EnterpriseOne system.

Results

With the help of an outside consultant, Radio Flyer was able to leverage their insight, knowledge, and methodologies to keep their internal team on course, reducing effort and helping them to efficiently reach their goals of the identification of process gaps, using ERP modules, features, and functions to improve their processes and ultimately pick and implement the best solution for their business in the shortest amount of time possible (Ultra Consultants, 2023).

Case #2 – Flexpipe Systems Inc.

Challenge

Flexpipe Systems Inc. manufactures and sells spoolable composite pipeline systems used for oil & gas gathering systems, water disposal, and other applications where a corrosion-resistant, high-pressure pipeline is required. Flexpipe Systems used a heavily customized (and non-upgradable) ERP system which was handcuffing them and had a lot of the standard functions which were beginning to be hampered because of the changes to the source code.

Approach

In 2008, Flexpipe Systems, which was anticipating significant future growth requirements, felt that additional functionality that could be incorporated into a new system such as the use of recipes that could give them extra flexibility and IFS Applications provided the right solution. The IFS ERP system would offer major and measurable efficiencies to the company's inventory management system, allowing the reduction of safety stocks and faster shipping of orders.

Results

At the time, it took Flexpipe approximately a day and a half to receive inventory from a shop order. Now with IFS, transactions are live within 20 minutes. They can finish a product, get it on a truck, and ship it out of their facility within 20 minutes of it being completed. In the past, this process could take a few days.

Flexpipe also experienced problems with their weekend production schedule. On Monday mornings they would spend considerable time closing shop orders that had been created during the weekend. Now, with their new ERP system, this process happens instantly and on the shop floor and delays caused by receiving three days of production into inventory on Monday morning have been eliminated.

Previously, they had to maintain four days of safety stock of their semi-finished inventory parts because they had a weekend of shop orders that had not been closed out. After the implementation of IFS, they were able to significantly speed up the shop order closing process, resulting in a 60% reduction in safety stock.

Furthermore, lot tracking for the company's pipe fitting products is critical. With their old ERP system and initially with IFS, Flexpipe Systems was performing extensive non-value-added work by recording inventory and shop floor transactions manually and then entering them into IFS Applications. Shipping or receipt details, including the part number and serial tracking numbers, would then be entered into IFS by someone when there was time.

After implementation of the new system, they were able to leverage IFS Applications' service-oriented architecture, using web services to drive data directly through IFS Applications' business logic. Handheld devices now read barcodes to capture serial, lot, and batch data and automatically enter it in IFS Applications. Barcode integration has delivered lean improvements and allowed Flexpipe Systems to reduce the risk of a recall (Top 10 ERP, 2023).

Case #3 – Automotive Supplier Nissen Chemitec America Accelerates Lean Operations with IQMS ERP

Challenge

Nissen Chemitec America (NCA), a leading automotive supplier operating in an industry where many suppliers compete for relatively few customers, understands the importance of lean manufacturing.

They had an ERP system that conformed to automotive customers' very strict requirements. However, it hindered NCA's ability to advance lean manufacturing principles. It was designed for suppliers of the Big Three automakers, so it didn't meet many of their needs. It was cumbersome, required heavy data entry, and blocked their efforts to be lean as it required a lot of maintenance.

As a result, NCA began looking for a more tailored ERP solution, one that was built specifically for contract manufacturers serving the automotive industry. They were looking for a fully automated system that met automotive compliance requirements like electronic data interchange (EDI), labeling, and quality functions, but was also robust and scalable. It also had to comply with customers' quality standards and business transaction requirements.

Approach

Ultimately NCA selected EnterpriseIQ from IQMS which has specific functionality designed for the auto supply industry, featuring a combination of manufacturing-specific functionality and automotive industry compliance standards.

Their previous ERP system slowed lean progress in a number of ways. For example, it was built upon multiple databases that required repetitive data entry across various modules and functions and was not automated and had limited barcode scanning capabilities. They had to do production scheduling manually using spreadsheets and production data had to be keyed in separately for reporting. One of the most significant areas of concern for NCA was that while the system supported EDI, the actual transactions were sent via modem, which delayed the company's ability to find and correct problems before and after they occurred. This slower than desired method also cost them between $3,200 and $3,600 monthly to transmit data and support customer requirements. On top of that, the company was experiencing between 30 and 40 EDI-related shipping errors per month.

Results

After implementation, NCA reduced its monthly EDI cost by 90% to only $300 and eliminated most shipping errors. In fact, from the moment they turned the IQMS system on, they started shipping error-free.

Incoming EDI files were now automatically translated into the ERP system, instantly updating all related records, and outgoing files were automatically transferred back to customers and suppliers. Now there's never a need for manual data entry, so they benefit from accurate, automatic, and timely communication across their entire supply chain.

NCA relies on EDI data to set daily schedules, forecast demand, and communicate with customers and suppliers, so this new automated processing of EDI data has resulted in new levels of accuracy because the company also uses RealTime Production Monitoring by IQMS. It supports powerful, graphical, scheduling screens and reports that can be used by anyone from anywhere to assess job status, track downtime, view quality data, and more.

Previously, they had created an infinite schedule based only on demand. Now, RealTime uses a graphical, finite schedule to assess not only machine capacity but labor capacity as well.

They also utilize the Quality Management suite of products to control pre-production items including statistical process control (SPC) and data is now communicated more quickly, error-free, and available for review at any time.

As all modules are built on one database, the functionalities NCA relies on, such as the EDI translator, finite scheduling, purchasing, RealTime production monitoring, and quality management, work together within the system to ensure tighter control and better visibility over the company's procedures and processes, both internally and externally, resulting in a leaner supply chain.

Additionally, they have reduced maintenance costs alone by over 70% and achieved lean objectives such as reduced cycle time, automated work-flow, and the elimination of redundant processes. As a result of less delivery errors, better quality, and streamlined communications, they have secured additional business from its largest customer (IQMS, 2015).

Next, we will look at "short term scheduling" software which can help enable a lean and agile process on the shop floor.

Short-Term Scheduling

The actual short-term, detailed scheduling of the production of goods and services, often executed and managed by an manufacturing execution system (MES; discussed later in this chapter), can be very complex leading to wasted capacity, "firefighting", and poor customer satisfaction.

If a business wants to use tools such as JIT, visual workplace, and quick changeover on the shop floor with the aid of an MES, to take full advantage of this, one should use sophisticated planning technology as it can get complex. While one could argue (and rightfully so) that short-term schedul-ing involves planning, it is also directly tied to day-to-day manufacturing and thus the reason to include it under the "make" chapter of this book.

As scheduling deals with the timing of operations, the main objective is to allocate and prioritize demand (generated by either forecasts or customer orders) for available facilities in the most effective and efficient manner. The methods can range from "back of the envelope" and spreadsheets to optimization using tools such as linear programming.

Effective and efficient scheduling can give an organization a competitive advantage through the faster movement of goods through a facility with better use of assets and lower costs, additional capacity resulting from faster throughput, and improved customer service through faster and more dependable delivery to the customer.

However, this is not an easy task as in manufacturing, as there exists the major, and sometimes conflicting, goals of short-term scheduling to minimize processing time, maximize utilization of assets, minimize WIP inventory, and ultimately minimize customer waiting time.

Service systems differ from manufacturing in that there is seldom inventory (at least in the case of a pure service business such as insurance), and scheduling is more about matching staff to variable demand. Complicating things further in service is the fact that sometimes legal or contractual issues may constrain flexible scheduling (e.g., inflexible union rules).

A manufacturing schedule decides which "job" (a customer order or forecasted demand in the case of MTS processes) can have resources allocated to it and for how long. The short-term scheduler determines the sequence that jobs run with the highest-priority jobs first. This may involve making on-the-spot decisions where a process may need to be interrupted and changed or swapped out for another job. The short-term scheduler must then redo the schedule without sacrificing much if any capacity or output.

As a result, the job of short-term scheduling involves detailed knowledge of the organizations' priority rules, equipment setup and run times, job routing, scrap rates, scheduled downtimes, etc. A real blend of "art and science".

Since scheduling is dynamic and rules need to be revised to adjust to changes and do not necessarily look upstream or downstream or beyond due dates, it may be necessary to use sophisticated software. To manage this, a breed of software known as "finite capacity scheduling" (FCS; discussed later in this chapter) can overcome the disadvantages of rule-based systems by providing an interactive, computer-based graphical system. It often includes rules and expert systems or simulation to allow real-time response to system changes and allows the balancing of delivery needs and efficiency.

Short-Term Scheduling Process

At this point, it is important to note the difference between medium-term planning models described in Chapters 6 and 7 and detailed, and short-term scheduling models discussed here.

A medium-term planning model is designed to allocate the production of the different products to the various facilities in each time planning period while considering inventory holding and setup costs, transportation costs, and lateness. Aggregate planning looks at different product families, but usually doesn't differentiate between different products within a family. It may determine the lot size for a product family at a facility. MPS, on the other hand, does schedule at the finished good SKU level, but is usually in weekly planning buckets.

On the other hand, a short-term detailed scheduling model is usually confined to a single facility and takes more detailed information into account than a planning model. They are typically planned in daily (and possibly in shifts) or even hourly planning buckets and can include both interrelated independent and dependent (e.g., components or modules) scheduled production. There are usually several jobs, and each one has its own parameters. The jobs must be scheduled so that one or more objectives are minimized (e.g., lateness, average completion time, etc.).

Medium-term planning and short-term scheduling models also should tie to long-term strategic models, facility location models, demand management models, and forecasting models. If there is a disconnect, service and profitability will be less than optimal.

Continuous versus Discrete Industry Scheduling

Short-term scheduling in continuous manufacturing industries such as chemical and food and beverage versus discrete manufacturing industries such as automotive and consumer electronics differ significantly.

Continuous manufacturing industries (Figure 8.2) typically have main processing operations with very high changeover and fixed costs. Scheduling tools in this area can be quite sophisticated and include cyclical scheduling procedures and mixed integer programming approaches.

Continuous industries also may have finishing operations which convert the output from the main production facilities. It may involve cutting of the material, bending, folding, and possibly painting or printing and is usually a

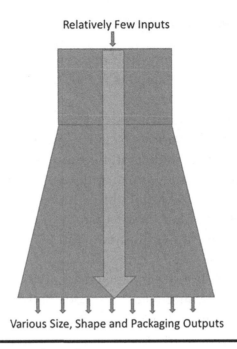

Relatively Few Inputs

Various Size, Shape and Packaging Outputs

Figure 8.2 Continuous manufacturing.

mix of MTO and MTS production strategies. Sequencing of customer orders may be important (MTO) as well as forecasts and inventory targets (MTS).

Discrete manufacturing (Figure 8.3) may involve three operations: converting such as cutting and shaping of sheet metal, main production, and assembly operations.

The end product of a converting process is usually not a finished good and usually feeds a downstream operation. Main production operations require multiple different operations using different machine tools. The product and its parts may have to follow a certain route through the facility going through various work centers. Each order has its own route through the system, quantity and processing times, and shipping date.

Assembly operations may be organized into work cells or assembly lines and usually require material handling systems but not typically machine tools.

There are some basic differences between the parameters and operating characteristics of discrete versus continuous facilities:

1. The planning horizon in continuous manufacturing facilities tends to be longer than the planning horizon in discrete manufacturing facilities.

Raw Material and Module inputs

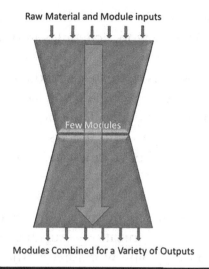

Few Modules

Modules Combined for a Variety of Outputs

Figure 8.3 Discrete manufacturing.

2. In discrete manufacturing facilities, plans and schedules may have to be changed or adjusted more often, and as a result, planning and scheduling tends to be more reactive.
3. In discrete manufacturing, there may be a significant amount of mass customization and product differentiation. In continuous manufacturing, mass customization does not play a very important role. The number of SKUs in discrete manufacturing tends to be significantly larger than the number of SKUs in continuous manufacturing.

As a result, the planning and scheduling issues in discrete versus continuous processes can be very different (Kreipl & Pinedo, 2004).

Scheduling in Service Industries

In the service industry, the primary issue is employee scheduling at a reasonable cost to meet demand varying with the time of day and with the day of the week.

In general, there are three kinds of staffing problems:

- Shift scheduling – Finding the optimal crew size and assigning each member of the crew to various shifts during the day.

- Days-on scheduling – Need to define the working and non-working days of employees in their work schedules in order to satisfy their days-off requirement.
- Tour scheduling – Contains both shift scheduling and days-on scheduling and it plans working days of each employee in a planned period which is covered by the schedule. The objective of tour scheduling is to find the least costly way to staff the system at the targeted levels by determining the ideal number of employees to be assigned to each feasible work schedule.

Some application areas of staff scheduling are hospitals (especially in nurse scheduling), mail processing organizations, trucking systems, airlines, call centers, catering, and housekeeping workforce in the hospitality industry.
  Solution techniques include:

- Manual "back of the envelope" techniques which, while not optimal, use common sense and experience.
- Cyclical scheduling – Where the objective is to meet staffing requirements with the minimum number of workers. Schedules need to be smooth, and personnel kept happy. Many techniques exist from simple algorithms to complex linear programming for optimal solutions.

Lean, Agile Short-Term Scheduling with the Aid of Technology

Planning and scheduling in a global supply chain requires the coordination of operations in all stages of the chain, so models and solution techniques described above must be integrated within a single framework. Separate models that represent successive stages in the supply chain must exchange information and interact with one another in various ways. For example, a continuous model for one stage may have to interface with a discrete model for the next stage.
  Planning and scheduling procedures in a supply chain are typically used in various phases. It is common to have a first phase with a multi-stage medium-term planning process (using aggregate data), and a following phase that performs short-term detailed scheduling at each one of those stages separately. Typically, once a planning procedure has been applied,

each facility can apply its own scheduling procedures. However, scheduling procedures are usually applied more frequently than planning procedures (Kreipl & Pinedo, 2004).

Advanced Planning and Scheduling Systems (APS)

Historically, manufacturers have relied heavily on the planning functionality in their ERP legacy systems. These systems are based upon early 1980s concepts such as infinite capacity, time buckets, and backward scheduling. The software that drives MRP applications was primarily designed to address the needs of MTS manufacturers and entailed the use of excess buffers of inventory and time at all levels of the manufacturing process.

On the other hand, lean systems are manually intensive, and over time, they tend to become disconnected from a company's legacy planning systems. It is also harder to implement in companies that have many SKUs, limited capacity, and unpredictable demand, at least one reason for the high failure rate of lean initiatives in the United States.

A bridge to this disconnect are what is known as "advanced planning and scheduling" (APS) systems, which can accurately manage time, react to changes at the operation level, and still create a schedule that quickly and accurately synchronizes multiple constraints.

An APS system is a manufacturing management process by which raw materials and production capacity are optimally allocated to meet demand. APS is especially well-suited to environments where simpler planning methods cannot adequately address complex trade-offs between competing priorities. Production scheduling is very difficult due to the interaction of limited capacity and the number of items/products to be manufactured.

Finite Capacity Scheduling Systems

A specific tool of APS used to deal with this complexity from a short-term scheduling perspective is known as "finite capacity scheduling" systems (Figure 8.4). FCS is an approach to understanding how much work can be produced in a certain time planning period, with limitations on different resources taken into consideration. The goal is to make sure that work proceeds at an even and efficient pace throughout the plant. Software applications for determining the best way to schedule work are called "decision support tools". Finite scheduling tools are different from infinite capacity scheduling tools. Infinite scheduling tools, which are simpler, don't account for limitations on the system that occur in real time.

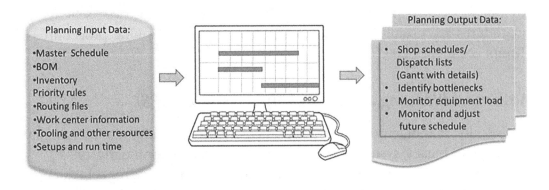

Figure 8.4   Finite capacity scheduling system inputs and outputs.

Different types of FCS tools are:

Electronic scheduling board (ESB) – Provide a graphical view of all jobs currently in production. If the digital board receives data from the factory floor, it can calculate performance times automatically, even if the administrator makes changes, and issue a warning if there's a bottleneck.

Order-based scheduling (OBS) – The scheduler (person or software application) prioritizes which work will be completed first by selecting only the orders that meet the plant's pre-set work in progress (WIP) criteria.

Constraint-based schedulers (CBS) – Bottlenecks in the production line determine the schedule for the rest of the components in the system.

Discrete event simulation (DES) – Model random events and predict the domino effect one event would have on the rest of the system.

Genetic algorithms – Like the scientific theory of natural selection where new schedules (children) are developed by using characteristics, such as sequences of work, from previous (parent) schedules.

Advanced Planning and Scheduling Systems Technology

Many of the larger ERP software vendors offer APS modules. There are also "best of breed" solutions offered by vendors such as Asprova and Preactor.

Detailed scheduling software is an important tool for many companies where it can have a major impact on the productivity of a process.

The difference between planning software and scheduling software is that planning systems are "bucketed" (monthly, weekly, daily) and don't preserve operation sequences within the time bucket. Scheduling systems are "bucket less" and preserve sequencing and can generate dispatch lists or shop schedules. The assignment of an operation to a resource is a critical component of an FCS system to achieve operational efficiency and optimized performance. Detailed scheduling uses a shorter time horizon and a much more detailed process route than a planning system.

The input to an FCS system is manufacturing work orders which have a process route associated with each order that defines the operation steps to make the product. The user then can load the orders onto individual resources using scheduling rules and interact with the schedule using the Gantt charts and plots that are generated. A typical output would be a dispatch list for each resource.

Supply Chain and Short-Term Scheduling Systems Case Studies

Case #1 – Auto Parts Manufacturer Chooses Asprova for Its Good User Interface Reduces Labor of Adjusting the Schedule

Challenge

An auto parts manufacturer had been using a custom-made scheduler before switching to Asprova, an APS system. Over time, as the number of products increased, they exceeded the capability of their existing scheduling system, causing issues such as:

- The inadequate data processing capability of the existing custom-made scheduler forced them to limit the number of products and divide orders into several scheduling runs.
- Numerous typing errors when manually scheduling products left items out of their schedule.
- An inability to restrict colors at each facility led to manual schedule modifications by an experienced schedule manager.

Approach

After learning more about Asprova's functions by using a trial version of the software and attending a training seminar, they decided to introduce

Asprova. They especially liked the ease of understanding and modifying the schedule in Gantt chart form and the ability to restrict colors in each facility.

They decided that the initial implementation work, including worker education, creation of the master data based on schedule managers' knowledge, and development of peripheral functions, were to be done mainly by the company itself, with the support of a consultant. Development of peripheral functions was done in parallel with the test run but designing and altering the functions to meet the demands from the production site was not an easy task.

Results

Since the installation of Asprova, the auto part manufacturer is now able to schedule all the products simultaneously and can create a complete schedule in the same amount of time it took to create one of the partial schedules before.

The time required to make a working schedule is significantly reduced as Asprova automatically creates a schedule that considers the color restriction of each facility, so they don't need to do nearly as much adjusting work.

They have also been able to standardize most of the scheduling work by codifying schedule managers' knowledge in the form of master data that was set into Asprova at the initial installation. Furthermore, it has become much easier to explain the procedure for scheduling to new employees because of how simple it is to verify and modify the schedule using Asprova's Gantt chart (www.asprova.com, 2023).

Case #2 – Mueller Stoves Reduces Assembly Line Stops after Preactor Deployment

Challenge

Mueller Stoves, started in 2001, produces a variety of stoves, domestic ovens, and cooktop stoves. They had been using the concept of mini factories pulled by kanban from the assembly line.

Despite all the efforts of their lean manufacturing team, the kanban was not bringing the expected results, mainly since the assembly lines were extremely dynamic because of the high variability of items per day on each assembly line and the high volatility of quantities and reschedules caused by unforeseen events.

While each mini factory was producing its own scheduling, other information was not considered, such as the availability of material (supplied by other areas or outsourced). As a result, the assembly lines often did not produce as planned because the mini factories could not respond in time to changes. They tried to supply the components for the items scheduled on the assembly lines through daily inventory lists and urgent production requests of missing parts, but often had to stop the lines due to lack of parts.

Additionally, they had:

- Difficulties balancing loads across several resources.
- Difficulties properly evaluating production bottlenecks.
- No visibility of the consequences of unforeseen events.
- No possibility of coordinating a preventive maintenance plan without sacrificing productivity.
- Lack of capacity analysis to give adequate responses to the demand.

Approach

As a result of these limitations, both the planning and production departments independently began to look for other solutions.

Both departments independently found Preactor and APS3 (Siemens partner for Simatic IT Preactor products) and realized that a scheduling tool based on finite capacity, which considered materials and resources, represented a possible solution to the challenges they faced.

The first step for the project was to generate finite scheduling only on the stamping area to load level the assembly lines, to prevent the internal parts supply shortage that was causing lines to stop.

Results

The results were impressive and highlighted that there was also an opportunity to schedule the painting area with the same principle adopted for stamping.

The most immediate results included:

- Improved visibility reducing production uncertainty through a scheduling horizon of 5 days and a firm schedule of 1 day.
- Increased reliability of the supplier to the JIT process due to their perception of the improving factory scheduling process.

- Reduction of stamping stocks from 3 days to 1.5 days of parts needed for future assemblies.
- Significant reduction of semi-finished stocks.
- Unplanned stoppages on the assembly lines went from 13 to 6 hours, a 22% reduction in WIP and a 98% improvement in overall inventory turns (www.preactor.com, 2023).

Finally, we will look at a breed of software known as "manufacturing execution systems" (MES) to see how technology can also help support a lean conversion process on the shop floor.

Manufacturing Executions Systems

A MES is a control system for managing and monitoring WIP on a factory floor and tracks manufacturing information, typically in real time, receiving data from robots, machine monitors, and employees (see Figure 8.5). In the past, MES operated as self-contained systems, but today are commonly being integrated with ERP software suites. The goal of a MES is to improve productivity and reduce cycle-time, the total time to produce an order. When MES

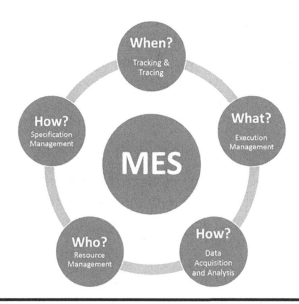

Figure 8.5 A manufacturing execution system (MES) should answer these five questions.

with ERP software is integrated, factory managers can be proactive about ensuring the delivery of quality products in a timely, cost-effective manner.

MES can operate across multiple function areas such as stages of the product life cycle, resource scheduling, order execution and dispatch, production analysis and downtime management for overall equipment effectiveness ("OEE"; a measurement of equipment-related waste), quality, or materials tracking and tracing. They also capture and record data, processes, and results of the manufacturing process, especially important in regulated industries such as food and beverage or pharmaceutical, where documentation of processes, events, and actions may be a requirement.

MES Role in Today's Competitive Environment

MES software can help a company to keep pace with an increasingly complex and fast-moving global environment, and better align your complex manufacturing operations to market needs. An MES uses three key functionalities to accomplish this:

1. Operations management – An MES can help you better coordinate the totality of production operations for both MTS and MTO manufacturing. This includes synchronizing production activities, improving work-instruction delivery to plant personnel in complex flexible-manufacturing operations, and better managing the flow of materials from warehouses and suppliers.
2. Integration gateway – An MES also enables integration between plant-floor and business networks. This is the key to bridging historically separate information technology (IT) and operations technology (OT) systems to create what's known as the connected enterprise, which is a unified network architecture that connects the people, processes, and technologies across your entire organization.
3. Information management – Automating data collection in an MES can replace costly, time-consuming, and potentially mistake-prone manual data collection. Data can be displayed in dashboards and as KPIs for better decision-making and consistent performance measurement. Production data can also be used for regulatory compliance and warranties, while genealogy and traceability can help limit the scope of recalls and shorten containment response times.

Manufacturing Execution Systems Implementation

Production environments face constant pressure to produce better and faster to remain competitive. It is a continuous struggle to eliminate unnecessary production costs; improve manufacturing, process, and business performance; increase throughput; reduce cycle times; maintain quality; etc. In support of those goals, an adequate level of automation is strived for. Efficient manufacturing operations can be provided by a MES. Nowadays, efficient manufacturing operations without software support have become unthinkable in many cases, due to legal provisions (e.g., tracking and tracing in the food and pharmaceutical industry), high product mix, etc. Company strategies and business requirements need to be continuously adjusted to follow the latest customer requests and industry trends. Production environments are dynamic, with constantly changing products and manufacturing processes.

Most software implementations are done in phases. The incremental MES implementation can start with functionalities such as data collection, order tracking, material tracking, KPI reporting, etc. As each implementation is somewhat unique, a thorough analysis is needed. At the start, user specification requirements are set up along with an "as is" model of the current process. While modeling the "as is" processes, everyone is forced to question the current way of working. Problems are uncovered and inefficiencies revealed, resulting in a "to be" model. This helps to define the conditions for initial MES selection.

Goodness of fit and flexibility of software can be conflicting goals. Packaged systems may have "best practices" but may not be best suited for your organization. It is important to balance natural tendencies toward over-complication, over-automation, and rigidity to get the full benefits of MES systems. As processes will change over time, it is important that the MES system is flexible as well.

Over time, there are three general types of changes to be aware of when implementing MES systems: updates, operational changes, and model changes.

- Updates – Small incremental (automated) software improvements to fix errors and bugs or to boost performance.
- Operational changes – Changes introduced within the boundaries of a company's existing manufacturing operations management (i.e., a new product introduction, installation of new equipment, a revised product flow, etc.).
- Model changes – More radical (and more expensive) changes requiring a change of the system itself.

Ultimately the MES technology must be able to support change to a process, as well as control the achieved improvements (Cottyn et al., 2011).

As previously mentioned, MES are often used in conjunction with ERP systems to streamline and enable actual manufacturing processes. MES is useful for delivering standard work instructions, labor charging, and recording quality checks.

MES and Visual Management Systems

Visual management can help to regulate inventory levels and production activities.

Specifically, the use of visual signals traditionally found on the shop floor provides information such as:

- Production line or work cell instructions that answer the question of who, what, where, when, and how for production.
- Provide accountability and ownership to labor and support staff.
- Process indicator to maintain safety, quality, on-time delivery, inventory, and cost.
- Display abnormal conditions (right part-wrong place, wrong part-right place, missing part, etc.).
- Show production status (e.g., ahead, behind, on schedule).

A visual management system can also, through an MES, enable upstream suppliers and downstream customers when linked in the ERP system to provide better supply chain visibility. Furthermore, awareness generated through a visual management system helps to enable improvement of related enterprise metrics.

For example, visual work instructions help companies achieve standard work by presenting the employees with the information they need to know when they need to know it.

Some visual work instruction software only presents the information to the employees in a visual format but does not capture production information or give you live visibility of your production floor. Where possible, it is important that the MES provide this information in a way that is easy to understand and allows the employees to interact with the instructions in a way that captures all the necessary production information.

Another example of visual tools in MES would be the use of product flow boards which can be done manually, by operators moving magnets on a whiteboard, or using entry and exit barcode scans to keep an electronic product status board current.

Supply Chain and Manufacturing Execution Systems Case Studies

Case #1 – Full Sail Brewing Taps Manufacturing Intelligence to Enhance Brewing Process

Challenge

Full Sail Brewing Company, a top 25 Oregon-based brewery, produces three core varieties of craft beer, along with several seasonal and specialty brews.

They realized that not only would future production demands strain their manual mash filtration system, but also that efforts to increase efficiency, cut costs, and further improve quality were limited under the existing system.

The mash filtration system at Full Sail required continuous manual data-testing and reporting.

In addition, the spent grain, a by-product the company sold as livestock feed, contained 82% moisture content, so liquid was going out the door with the by-product, and transporting the heavy waste was expensive. Basically, Full Sail was losing money on the transaction, paying farmers to take the spent grain off their hands.

Approach

The goal was to upgrade the process to improve product quality and increase filtration efficiency, capacity, and throughput. They also wanted to minimize operator dependency through automation.

So, they decided to upgrade its traditional, manual lautering process (where mash is separated into the clear liquid wort and the residual grain) to a fully automated, networked mash filtration system.

The new mash filtration system Full Sail implemented leverages the PlantPAx™ Process Automation System from Rockwell Automation which incorporated role-appropriate, real-time key performance indicators (i.e., manufacturing intelligence) that Full Sail can use to improve operations.

Results

Real-time data is now retrievable over variable time spans, helping to achieve optimum functionality of the system and catching discrepancies or problems that may have occurred during a batch.

With the new PlantPAx system, brewing capacity has increased by 25%, plus the time of each brew cycle has been cut by almost half. The visibility operators now have in their brew process allows them to optimize ongoing brews in real time.

The new MES will also:

- Cut raw material costs by 5% annually.
- Remove significantly more moisture from the spent barley grain and the by-product is now sold at a profit.
- Decrease water use by one million gallons annually helping to supplement its sustainability goals (Allen-Bradley, 2011).

Case #2 – Merck Pharmaceutical Asian Factory Implements MES

Challenge

A new Singapore-based pharmaceuticals factory that is owned and operated by Merck Sharp & Dohme (MSD) wanted to minimize risk by getting the plant operational, then implement MES before the plant reached full capacity.

Approach

They considered three different MES packages. Ci Precision's DMS suite of products was found to be the most easily configurable, and they felt that it had the greatest scope for future expansion.

Ci-DMS would be used to control all dispensing and material addition in the factory, both automated and manual, and be seamlessly integrated with the existing ERP system and automation hardware.

The system would have two supervisory stations – one on the shop floor and one for system administration. There would also be two manual dispensing stations with a Ci-DMS Silo Dispensing module to control dosing from three "big bag" silos into an intermediate bulk container (IBC).

The plan was to use barcode readers and a specially configured interface to communicate directly with the plant's ERP system and the AZO automated bulk dispensing system.

Results

The use of remote support saved around $60,000 by reducing the need for site visits. Manual dispensing and automated dispensing have both been reduced from two-person operations to one-person operations. This resulted in an annual saving of $150,000. Furthermore, the software has eliminated over 50,000 manual transactions that were previously entered into the ERP system.

The entire dispensing operation is now paperless, resulting in a reduction in overhead costs. The dispensing cycle time has been reduced as there is no longer any need for manual checks to be made and for paperwork to be completed. Quality assurance has been improved significantly using barcode scanners to reduce the chance of operator error (www.ciprecision. com, 2023).

Case #3 – EZ-MES Production Tracking System at a High Power Laser Company

Challenge

A manufacturer of high-powered lasers offers a variety of specialized laser products that use similar production flows. During the production process, individual product data is recorded and items are serialized requiring a complete history tracking, including sub-parts.

To do this, they used a combination of spreadsheets and a paper-based traveler system. The process was manual and required someone to physically search for all the parts.

As demand increased for its products, it became very important to be able to access accurate, real-time production status information. This would tell them where the lasers were in the production process, the inventory status of raw materials, WIP and finished goods, who performed a specific operation and when was it done, and recent throughput measurements.

The system had to be able to give real-time information about the location of all parts and products on the production floor, create travelers with barcodes that could be printed and show a list of barcoded attached parts, have complete traceability of parts including when parts are assembled into other parts and have no significant negative impact on the current IT structure.

Approach

After comparing several systems, they chose to implement the EZ-MES system. An account was set up online and EazyWorks implemented a first production flow in EZ-MES. There was no training needed and most support during the implementation was supplied with the built-in chat feature of the EZ-MES system. No hardware was required, and no software had to be installed.

Results

Once up and running, 50% of all the paperwork work was replaced with EZ-MES.

It has helped to enable growth as they would not have been able to handle the increased volume and increased product mix without EZ-MES.

The system had a low implementation cost as the configuration of the system is entirely maintained by the client without any training. There was no hardware, software, or any additional load in the IT department.

They were able to reduce inventory by knowing exactly what was on the production floor in real-time and quickly tell them what raw materials to buy for each order and when to start a new batch for the same order.

Real-time information is very valuable to the laser manufacturer to make immediate decisions. In the past, they had to err on the side of caution, resulting in too much work in progress, or too many parts on order. Now they were able to reduce inventory and WIP, improving cycle times and increasing revenue.

They also were able to improve operational efficiency as the system improved visibility for management with current production status now being available in real time, quick, and efficient decision-making.

Additional realized benefits included:

- Improved data integrity, transparent handling of nonconformities, and less time spent manually entering data into the system.
- Decreased employee turnover by having a system that is easier to use.

- Improved customer retention by being able to respond to customer questions about specific products quickly.
- Being able to show potential customers that the system provides full traceability of all parts (www.eazyworks.com, 2023).

Even if a company has done a great job in planning, sourcing, and making a product (with the aid of enabling technology), they still must deliver the product or service in an accurate, timely, and efficient manner to the customer, the topic of our next chapter.

Chapter 9

Supply Chain Software Systems: Deliver

For the purposes of this chapter, we will include all aspects of the order cycle under the category of "deliver" software systems.

The order cycle is the time between when a customer places an order and when it is shipped, which includes the storage, processing of orders, and delivery of goods in the supply chain. There are a variety of software systems used during planning and execution just prior to and during the order cycle which we will now discuss.

Distribution Requirements Planning Systems

Distribution requirements planning (DRP) is a technique that helps businesses determine the quantities, location, and timing of goods needed to meet anticipated demand. It helps in the efficient delivery of goods to distribution facilities by determining item quantities, location, and timing required to meet forecasted demand. The goal is to maximize product availability and reduce the costs of ordering, transporting, and holding products (see Figure 9.1).

DRP generates time-phased requirements for single and multi-facility distribution organizations (i.e., where a central facility supplies regional facilities which then supply other facilities in a "tree-like" structure). This process calculates inventory requirements over time and automatically generates gross and net requirements, which can be turned into inventory transfers, production work orders, and purchase orders.

DOI: 10.4324/9781003372639-11

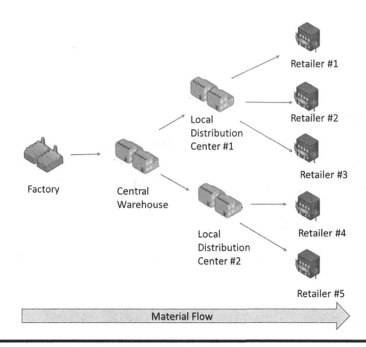

Figure 9.1 Distribution network.

The mechanics of DRP, which will be discussed later, are like MRP (material requirements planning) in that it develops replenishment plans by evaluating information such as order size, desired safety times/service levels, on-hand inventory, scheduled receipts, and both forecasted and actual demands. However, in the case of DRP, replenishment requirements are for independent demand inventory (i.e., finished goods) versus dependent demand for MRP.

DRP compares future forecasted and actual demand versus available inventory (plus scheduled receipts such as purchase orders or transfers) to predict future shortages and schedules planned replenishment orders (factoring in lead times) based upon user set criteria including safety stock or safety time targets.

DRP is "hierarchical" as the net requirements can be summarized up the supply chain to the plant level to create the item master production schedule (MPS) which can then be "exploded" with a bill of materials or "BOM" to generate requirements for raw materials and components (Figure 9.2).

DRP is ideal for organizations that want to transition from a "push" to a "demand pull" process, resulting in a more efficient, lean supply chain, but only if they have the philosophy and processes in place to take advantage of a pull-type system like DRP.

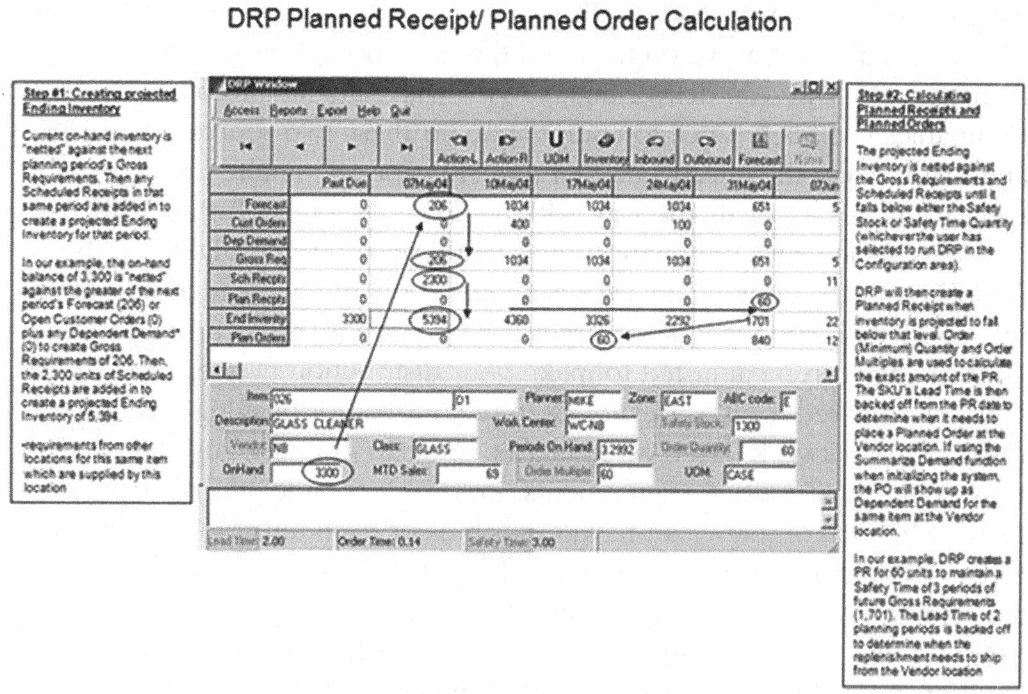

DRP Planned Receipt/ Planned Order Calculation

Figure 9.2   Sample DRP screen and description. (*PSI Planner* for Windows™, Copyright 1998–2024; printed with permission from Weeks Software Solutions, LLC.)

DRP Technology for Efficiency and Effectiveness in a Lean Supply Chain

Distribution inventory can either be "pushed" from the central supply down through the network or "pulled" up through the network by orders from the consumer. Pull provides the best availability for the customer (local management has control of what's available), but it is difficult to manage distribution inventory in a pull system environment because every order is a surprise to the supplying location as demand flows up the network. Pull is characterized by the so-called bullwhip effect: a small change in demand at the consumer end can generate large swings in demand higher up in the network and in the factory.

Push can generate the best inventory and transportation performance, resulting in the lowest cost. Shipments and stock levels can be centrally and globally planned. Central planning is furthest removed from actual demand, however, so service level is likely to suffer.

DRP can theoretically deliver the efficiencies of push with the service levels of pull. The hedging in that statement reflects the dependence on the forecast and stable processes. With an accurate forecast and performance as planned (shipments arrive on time and there are no unexpected losses, damage, etc.), DRP can deliver high service with minimal inventory. Companies use safety stock to compensate for these two sources of variability and that reduces the effectiveness of the DRP strategy – more inventory and more shortages – exactly the way MRP works in the plant (Turbide, 2023).

So, in some ways, the methods and assumptions used in DRP are the opposite of lean thinking, as DRP is all about planning ahead and optimizing, and lean responds to the market faster and more efficiently. However, DRP settings can be adjusted to make your distribution network as lean as you are prepared for it to be. For example, instead of pushing inventory through the network based on forecasts, one can only use customer orders to generate deployment requirements. In today's volatile, global environment, where a company can have thousands or even tens of thousands of SKUs (an item at a stock keeping location) at many distribution points that are remote from manufacturing facilities, this is probably not the best way to go (unless you have a local manufacturing facility that is extremely flexible and agile and ships to local customers only).

Instead, it may be best to utilize a "consumption" methodology (i.e., how customer orders consume the item forecast at each distribution center) along with using scientific safety time (periods of supply inventory targets based upon variability of lead time and demand) instead of fixed safety stock targets with reorder points in order to catch the "peaks and valleys" of predicted demand while still considering established replenishment lead times, lot sizes, and demand and lead time variability. This can be considered a "happy medium" between pure push and pure pull when using DRP.

DRP systems are also useful as a collaboration tool with customers to improve forecast accuracy, minimize retail stockouts, and improve inventory turns and productivity (more on that in Chapter 13).

DRP Software Mechanics

Like many APS systems, DRP traditionally was an "add-on" type system, as many of its inputs (inventory balances, existing purchase and production work orders, forecasts, etc.) and outputs (deployment/transfer requirements, new purchase and work orders, etc.) come from ERP or accounting systems.

Today, many ERP vendors have added DRP as a module as the demand for it has significantly increased.

As was mentioned, DRP software is a continuation of the MRP logic used for the outbound movement of finished goods from facilities. The deployment requirements, after being summarized by item, are used to generate the item MPS which then drives the MRP system through the bill of material file to create raw material and component requirements (Figure 9.3).

The software itself is similar from vendor to vendor, using the previously mentioned logic. However, it can vary in terms of user interface and ability to collaborate and share internally and externally. Additionally, like most software today, it can be installed at a company on their IT infrastructure (and possibly be web enabled or web based as well) and in some cases be offered as "SaaS" (software as a service or on demand) cloud software.

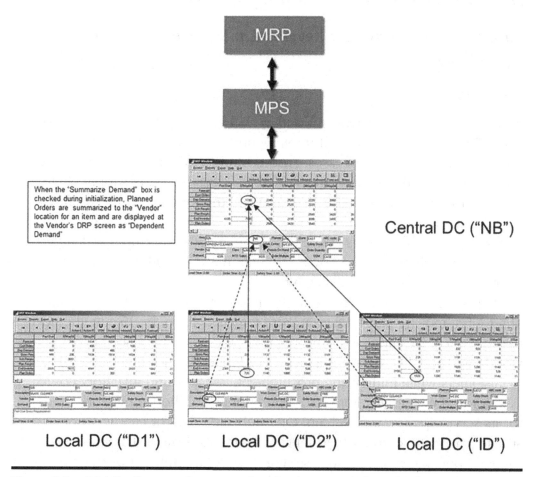

Figure 9.3   Distribution requirements planning in a network. (*PSI Planner* for Windows™, Copyright 1998–2024; printed with permission from Weeks Software Solutions, LLC.)

MRP and DRP were pioneering technologies for the computerization of supply chain planning. In the late 1980s to mid-1990s, the APS software vendors marketed aggressively against the ERP vendors. The ERP vendors, for their part, tried to downplay the importance of "best in breed" external solutions. That is until they began acquiring APS applications including DRP themselves (some ERP vendors developed the capabilities on their own rather than through acquisition). Eventually, many mid to large companies implemented MRP and DRP. In the case of DRP, it had become more prevalent in make-to-stock (MTS) companies with extended distribution networks such as is found in the consumer products industry.

DRP Replenishment Technology Cases

Case #1 – Auto Logistics: Revving Up Service Parts Logistics Operations

Challenge

In 2011, to improve efficiency and its global service parts logistics management, Ford was in the midst of implementing a 10-year plan to revamp its service parts network, processes, and technologies. They had undergone huge changes in these three areas to create a service parts supply chain that is lean, fast, efficient, cost-effective, and laid the foundation for the firm's global supply chain vision.

Ford's U.S. service parts operation alone includes around 250,000 part numbers (which equates to about 1.5 million SKUs) with approximately 1,500 suppliers and 4,000 dealerships.

High service levels are crucial in the auto parts business. When dealers order a fast-moving part by 4 p.m., Ford targets delivery by 10 a.m. the next day for 98% of its shipments. For bulk parts, they promise a second-day service. In addition, like most companies, Ford must balance high service levels to customers while minimizing procurement, logistics, and inventory costs.

Prior to the changes, Ford had a traditional warehouse network model for its service parts supply chain. One hub served eight facing depots spread across the country that delivered parts to dealers. The hub sent parts to the depots based on a "pull" strategy where the hub depot shipped a part when a specific facility was at risk of dropping below safety stock levels.

Approach

Ford now operates 26 smaller warehouses located throughout the USA, closer to its customers. They segregate different part types by volume, size, and frequency of use in different facilities.

As a result of this change, they switched to a push deployment strategy for most of its volume as they felt that they would have too many warehouse transfers with a pull strategy. They were able to do this as Ford shrunk its order sizes, shipping smaller quantities more frequently using lean techniques. As a result, the warehouse now generally receives only the parts and quantities it needs, rather than getting excess parts that get put into reserve.

One critical element of its service parts supply chain change is the selection and implementation of SAP's Service Parts Management (SPM) solution.

When implementing in the USA, they first conducted a mini pilot to test the infrastructure and make sure SAP's system could talk to Ford's remaining legacy systems, then began launching SPP in 2010.

Results

Ford found a variety of benefits in different functional areas such as:

Inventory planning – They now can optimize combined safety stock and economic order quantity values which helps Ford better determine the optimum order quantity for each part in inventory. This ends up driving safety stock down on low-volume parts when we buy in large lot sizes.

Distribution resource planning (DRP) – The SAP DRP system features with future-dated orders and supplier shutdown logic, among other functionalities, plus it will give them multiple short-date expediting options as their current system has only one process for expediting parts. SAP will allow it to differentiate between suppliers' preferences on how, when, and how much inventory to expedite.

Parts deployment – SAP's automatic rounding algorithm will enable Ford to better marry actual demand with packaging hierarchy logic.

Operation benefits to date (reflects the full implementation of SPP in Europe only):

- 20% improvement in forecast accuracy.
- 15% reduction in service parts inventories.

- 10% reduction in obsolescence.
- 10% improvement in referral cost.
- 0.5% increase in local fill rates (Partridge, 2011).

Case #2 – Everlast Builds a Championship Company with New Product Lines

Challenge

Everlast, founded in 1910, is an American brand active in the design, manufacturing, licensing and marketing of boxing, mixed martial arts and fitness-related sporting goods equipment, clothing, footwear, and accessories.

Recently, in addition to working with retailers who are outside the usual sporting goods arena, Everlast is expanding its marketing to specific groups in the athletics sectors such as the Latino and women's markets.

Everlast does the bulk of its sales through the major sporting goods stores and through broad-based consumer outlets like Walmart, Sears, Target, and Kmart.

The growing number of sales outlets is mirrored on the supply side as Everlast expands the number of overseas manufacturers it relies on.

Everlast's expansion into new areas has resulted in 2,000 SKUs, up from 500 just five years ago. As a result, the company realized it needed better ways to handle forecasting and resupply.

Approach

Demand Solutions Requirements Planning (DSRP; now owned by Logility) was initially recommended to Everlast by their new SVP of manufacturing. The increased complexity really made their work a lot more intricate, so DSRP is what they were counting on to help them go forward.

They found the application to be very user-friendly. Demand Solutions had already written an interface to MAS200, the host system that Everlast uses, so the company could get a quick start.

Results

Since implementation, Everlast has benefited in terms of speed and accuracy.

In the past, it took 24–48 hours, even a week, to roll up all the projections from sales reps. Now the company gets to a starting point in half an hour.

It gives them more data, more quickly in a very presentable format than they have ever had access to before, as previously they used spreadsheets and "feel".

They strongly believe it will help them keep their fill rates at 99% or 100% (DS Magazine, 2007).

Case #3 – Canadian Tire Keeps Stores Rolling with Replenishment Program

Challenge

Canadian Tire, a tire and auto parts retail chain with over 600 tire and auto parts locations (also featuring sports and leisure and home products), realized its aging stores and out-of-date replenishment system were costing it business.

Canadian Tire operates two huge distribution centers in the Toronto suburb of Brampton with a combined 1.6 million square feet of space.

The stores are operated by independent dealers and who were not happy as stock replenishment to the stores was performing below industry standards.

Partially driving this was the fact that inbound service from their supplier base was in the low 70% area, at best, in terms of on-time delivery. The goal was to get inbound on-time service levels into the 90's.

Approach

Canadian Tire began to ask themselves why they didn't apply DRP to retail. As a result, they eventually selected Manugistics software (now owned by JDA), which had years of experience working with planning and scheduling issues in consumer-packaged goods and other industries. It would be the first use of core applications that were not written in-house at Canadian Tire.

The process started with a gap analysis which led them to change some processes so the software wouldn't have to be modified. The following quarter they went live with a pilot involving three buying teams.

They took their time rolling it out over a yearlong period to make sure they got it right.

Results

Previously, the company used in-house reorder point software to trigger replenishment requests.

The heart of the new system is a rolling 26-week replenishment plan for each of the retailer's approximately 60,000 SKUs. This plan is regenerated and sent out weekly to all suppliers.

The numbers are based on actual and projected orders from the stores. The stores receive a "deal book" months in advance of each weekly flyer detailing the items that are to be featured. These orders, and standard replenishment orders, are filed daily via EDI and pulled into the Manugistics system overnight. This visibility is crucial not only for promotions but also for seasonal items.

Once it was able to provide this longer view, Canadian Tire asked suppliers to reduce their purchase-order lead-time to 14 days or, in a very few cases, 21 days.

After one year of full operation, supplier lead times had dropped from a 46-day average to 15 days, and on-time service from suppliers was up 20%. As a result, on-time delivery to the stores had improved 1.9%. These improvements came during a period when shipment volume grew significantly (25% over 24 months). Inventory turns at the DCs also had increased by 1.7 times.

Next, they would start to turn their attention to other areas of execution where they could leverage the information provided by the Manugistics system. This effort had two major thrusts: to improve transportation efficiency, inbound and outbound, and to increase productivity at the distribution centers.

Also, at the time, the system, which was driven by batch data received via EDI, did not allow for true, real-time collaboration with suppliers. So, they planned to look at using the internet for real-time communication and collaboration with customers and suppliers (Murphy, 1999).

While distribution inventory replenishment systems like DRP tell you what you need, when and where you need it, transportation management systems (TMS) focus on getting the product to the destination as we will discuss in our next section.

Transportation Management Systems

TMS which are used to connect your supply chain must be managed and controlled properly with complete visibility and great communication between partners. Transportation and logistics (primarily warehouse operations) costs can account for as much as 7–14% of sales depending on the industry you are in. Transportation costs alone comprise much of this expense for most companies. Best-in-class companies have transportation and logistics-related costs in a range of 4–7% depending on the industry sector. So, it's not hard to see how both operationally and financially important transportation is to a successful business.

So not surprisingly, TMS have existed in one form or another to manage this process for quite a long while. Historically, they have been an "add-on" to an existing ERP or legacy (i.e., "home grown") order processing or warehouse management systems (WMS).

Like most software today, they can be installed as resident software or web-based and accessed on demand.

A TMS offers benefits to an organization such as automated auditing and billing, optimized operations, and improved visibility (see Figure 9.4).

They typically include functionality to plan, schedule, and control an organization's transportation system with functionality for:

Planning and decision-making – Helps to define the most efficient transport schemes according to parameters such as transportation cost, lead time, stops, etc. Also includes inbound and outbound transportation modes and transportation provider selection and vehicle load and route optimization.

Transportation execution – Allows for the execution of a transportation plan such as carrier rate acceptance, carrier dispatching, EDI, etc.

Transport follow-up – Tracking of physical or administrative transportation operations such as traceability of transport events, receipt, custom clearance, invoicing and booking documents and sending of transport alerts (delay, accident, etc.).

Measurement – Cost control and key performance indicator (KPI) reporting as it relates to transportation.

Ultimately, a supply chain system is made up of connecting links and nodes, where the transportation system provides the "links" and the facilities the "nodes". As the saying goes, "a chain is as strong as its weakest link", so the efficient, timely management of the links is especially critical in today's global supply chain.

Yard management systems (YMS), which may be a module of a TMS (or WMS) or a "stand alone" application, integrate warehouse operations with

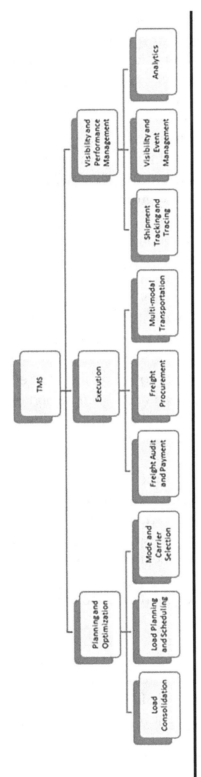

Figure 9.4 Transportation management system (TMS) components.

inbound and outbound transportation and maximize yard and warehouse efficiency by managing the flow of all inbound and outbound goods.

The YMS enables a business to plan, execute, track, and audit loads based on critical characteristics like shipment type, load configuration, labor requirements, and dock and warehouse capacity.

The YMS is used to arrange dock appointments for receiving orders and for arranging and scheduling outbound transportation equipment and helps to manage materials and transportation equipment in the warehouse or factory yard.

Transportation Management Systems for a Lean and Agile Supply Chain Network

As stated earlier, a TMS helps companies move freight from origin to destination efficiently, reliably, and cost effectively. Lean principles when used in conjunction with a TMS can deliver lower transportation costs, customer service improvement, reduced inventory levels, and progress toward business goals.

To help accomplish this task, we need to focus on total logistics costs and not just individual costs such as transportation, warehousing, inventory carrying costs, etc. Furthermore, it is a good idea to consider some guiding lean principles to apply to your transportation system (supported by functionality commonly found in a TMS) such as:

1. Develop and execute transportation strategy – Develop inventory strategies designed to support inventory strategy and customer expectations.
2. Eliminate transportation waste – Transportation more than necessary requirements is waste and should be eliminated. Focus on how transportation could be your strategic differentiator in the industry.
3. Measure transportation performance – Do not view transportation providers as transactional, but rather as strategic partners. Transportation service providers have distinct and measurable levels of performance capability. To build a lean supply chain, organizations need to build long-term relationships with quality carriers that are stable, dependable, and committed to servicing the organization.

4. Understand transportation cost structure – Transportation cost is made up of two distinct areas: unit costs and productivity costs. The significant opportunity for transportation cost reduction is in productivity costs. Focusing on unit costs, or carrier rates, will only result in creating instability in the transportation network. Rather, focus on productivity: trailer utilization, total miles run, equipment waiting time (which is pure waste), and adherence to core carrier routing guides…

5. Perform transportation daily event management – Cost savings result from disciplined, daily event management and hour-to-hour focus on waste identification and reduction… Create daily route designs, complete real-time track and trace, generate real-time metrics, and complete daily problem-solving. This investment and focus on process discipline is the lean way (Martichenko, 2023).

Types of Savings and Improvements Resulting in the Use of a TMS

TMS offer a strong ROI. The primary area where a TMS can save a company money is to lower its freight spend.

Types of saving can be put into three general categories:

1. Better data collection leading to improved decision-making in areas such as increased usage of core carriers and better procurement negotiations.
2. Process enforcement, by ensuring that the best carriers on a lane are selected for moves, for example.
3. Optimization of processes such as loading and routing of equipment.

Additionally, through lean thinking, there are other non-cost related advantages of using a TMS including:

• Improved understanding of the cost of serving customers.
• Reductions in the size of the transportation department.
• Lower carbon footprint (and lower fuel costs) through optimized routing of vehicles.

- Access to a greater number of carriers and increased ability to utilize capacity over the long term.
- A reduction in the number of warehouses required.
- Better tracking and compliance with transportation-related health, safety, and environmental regulation requirements.

These freight savings and other benefits also do not reduce service levels in any way, shape, or form and in fact will most likely significantly improve them (Banker, 2011).

Transportation Management Systems Technology

As a TMS is a component of an overall supply chain management system, it is typically part of, or integrated with, an enterprise resource planning system.

A TMS usually "sits" between an ERP or legacy order processing and warehouse software module and typically includes inbound (procurement) and outbound (shipping) orders which need to be considered by the TMS to offer routing suggestions. After review by the user, the routes are then analyzed by another TMS module to select the best mode and low-cost carrier. The system then electronically generates load tendering to set up the shipment with the selected carrier, and to later support track/trace, freight audit and payment. This information is then fed back to ERP systems as well as possibly to a WMS system.

The most common types of TMS installations are:

1. Traditional on-site installation and licensing (often offered as a separate module by many ERP vendors)
2. Remotely hosted licensing (i.e., SaaS/on-demand or cloud software)
3. On-site hosted licensing (a combination of the two above options)
4. Hosted – TMS free of licensing (same as #2, but free with no license requirements)

Many of the leading-edge TMS provide web and electronic interfaces to enable collaboration with transportation companies, trading partners, suppliers, and customers, in some cases in real time.

TMS Case Studies

Case #1 – Papa on the Platform – Hold the Anchovies: Papa John's Pizza Orders "Optimization Supreme" with Manhattan's Supply Chain Process Platform

Challenge

Although Louisville, Kentucky, based Papa John's Pizza is one the largest pizza companies in the world, with more than 3,000 restaurants, it still had supply chain inventory, visibility, and accuracy issues that were hurting its businesses. In fact, they were having to use outside storage for inventory that ended up being written off because its shelf life ran out before they could ship it to the restaurants.

At the same time, there were increases in commodity prices, fuel, and the minimum wage plus the usual limited-time consumer offers, which require immediate supply chain responses to temporary spikes in demand.

They needed a solution to align all the elements of their supply chain to reduce inventory levels and eliminate outside storage and inventory write-offs.

Approach

Papa John's selected Manhattan Associate's supply chain process platform which provided the perfect solution for optimizing all replenishment, inventory, and performance operations which included Manhattan's leading-edge WMS solution integrated with their TMS solution featuring transportation procurement, planning, and execution.

Papa John's did a phased implementation of the individual solutions starting with centralized purchasing/inbound inventory, addressed by Manhattan's replenishment and transportation procurement solutions, followed by warehouse management, with a final phase covering outbound delivery, with Manhattan's transportation planning and execution.

Results

The solution provided improved visibility along with reduced expenses, improved efficiency, and productivity in every part of the supply chain.

Papa John's now knows when a purchase order was created and can track a delivery all the way to their customers. They can now manage inventory levels accurately, efficiently, and more dynamically based on actual need, resulting in reduced overall inventory levels. They achieved a 10–15% reduction in freight spend after just six months of implementation.

Papa John's also had the following transportation-related benefits:

- 10% reduction in freight costs
- 66% reduction in outside storage costs
- 83% lower inventory write-offs
- 25% improvement in vehicle cube utilization
- 11% lower mileage
- 15% increase in stops/truck
- 16% increase in tractor fill (Manhattan Associates, Inc., 2013).

Case #2 – Leading Dairy Trims 18% from Transportation Costs Using Optimizer Software

Challenge

A leading dairy required inbound transportation planning for both its private fleet and for-hire carriers. They were using manual processes, moving data back and forth between an order management system (OMS) and a fleet telematics tool (a device which merges telecommunications and informatics used heavily in fleet tracking and management) from various providers.

This arrangement was especially cumbersome for a dairy due to the high perishability and fluctuating demand for milk production. On top of that, the grades, types, and qualities of milk, each with its own specific delivery requirements, added more complexity to the inbound transportation planning process. As a result, a high level of man-hours was used to attempt to manually optimize their inbound shipments. Despite the effort, the result was an under-utilization of equipment and drivers resulting in higher transportation costs.

Approach

After much searching, the dairy selected the "LoadFusion Transportation Optimizer" module of UltraShipTMS to control all inbound transportation planning for its private fleet of tanker vehicles.

It was configured to capture numerous inputs such as farm pick-up requests (histories, schedules, frequencies, etc.), the quantity of milk produced at each farm, etc. and was set up to capture real-time information from the client's fleet telematics system and their OMS. They were now able to see that during certain peak periods, equipment utilization and capacity were strained.

Transportation planners now had the ability to review farm schedules identifying potential modifications to farm pick-up request times and were also able to balance order demand with the specific types of supplies available at multiple farms, sourcing products from the location with the lowest transportation costs.

Results

Soon after going live, transportation planners were able to determine an optimal plan that used the fewest trucks, miles, and number of drivers to pick up the maximum volume of the product to meet their customer demands. Route optimization saved this client 10% on transportation and an additional 8% via improved demand planning for a total optimization savings of 18%.

Additionally, they were able to cut planning time by 90% through automation, reduce empty miles and increase compliance with business rules, Department of Transportation regulations, and better enforce union work rules (www.ultrashiptms.com, 2015).

Case #3 – Miller Brands UK Uses Transwide TMS to Manage Growing Transport Volumes

Challenge

Miller Brands UK is one of the world's leading beer producers. Miller Brand UK's rapid growth presented new challenges to their supply chain organization making it increasingly difficult to efficiently manage all their inbound transportation and placing greater workload on their already taxed transportation planning organization.

Approach

They looked for a TMS solution to increase efficiency, support growth, and improve customer service. Specifically, they were looking for a solution that could automate their labor-intensive transportation planning processes and provide more visibility so they could be more proactive.

Miller Brands UK selected and implemented Transwide TMS to automate previously manual processes. Phone, fax, and e-mail communication with carriers was replaced by a web platform for communication. Real-time transportation status updates, event notification functionality, and centralized transactional data provided increased visibility for their transportation planners and customer service teams.

Results

Processes are now centralized and standardized. There is an audit trail, detailing every communication and action associated with a transportation order. As a result, Miller Brands UK has seen a 50% reduction in internal processing time for their transport operations.

The planners and customer service agents now receive e-mail alerts when unforeseen things occur such as when there is an incident during the pick-up or delivery process.

Thanks to integration with SAP (their ERP system), any updates or changes to the transport are automatically updated in the respective systems.

The visibility to real-time information provided by Transwide TMS has allowed them to better manage direct deliveries to customers and to improve on-time delivery metrics, increase service levels, and respond more quickly and accurately to customer inquiries.

In the end, Miller Brands UK was able to realize savings of $220,000 per year and a return-on-investment ("ROI") within 2 months.

In the future, Miller Brands UK is planning on using the TMS to drive their continuous improvement process. They have already reduced carrier wait times and demurrage charges but are looking to make additional adjustments in their appointment scheduling process. They are also looking to reduce unloading "turn times" from 3 hours to down to 45 minutes (www.transwide.com, 2023).

Distribution Facilities Operations Technology

Now that we have discussed TMS, which cover the "links" in a supply chain, it is logical to follow with a discussion of technology used in the "nodes" of a supply chain (i.e., warehouses and distribution centers).

Order fulfillment is the process from point of sales order to delivery of a product to the customer and, in general, refers to the way firms respond to customer orders. In many instances, it is used to describe the act of distribution or the logistics function only.

For our purposes, in this chapter, we will use this term to include warehouse, order, and customer relationship management (CRM) and the systems used to manage these processes. The actual physical delivery of goods to the customer was covered in the previous section on transportation systems. All these processes and accompanying systems, whether referred to by these names or not, are typically linked together to help fulfill customer demand.

Warehouse Management Systems

Warehouse management systems (WMS) are software applications used to manage the receipt, movement, and storage of materials within the "four walls" of a facility and process the related transactions necessary for receiving, put-away, picking, packing, and shipping. Early WMS only provided simple storage location functionality. Today's "best-in-class" systems such as those offered by Manhattan Associates and High Jump Software (now known as Korber software) go beyond basic picking, packing, and shipping and use advanced algorithms to mathematically organize and optimize warehouse operations and may include tracking and routing technologies such as radio frequency identification (RFID) and voice recognition.

While many ERP vendors include WMS modules, more typically, companies license WMS from vendors that specialize in that type of system and then integrate them with their ERP or accounting systems. They can be run as installed systems or cloud-based, on-demand "software as a service" (SaaS) systems.

As mentioned above, many sophisticated WMS can use automatic identification and data capture technology, such as barcode scanners, mobile computers, and potentially RFID, to efficiently manage and monitor the flow of products as speed and accuracy are paramount in a warehouse. Once data has been collected, data is synchronized either via batch or real-time wireless transmission to a central database which provides a variety of reports about the status of material in the warehouse.

In warehouses where there are multiple picking locations requiring fast and accurate picking, a "pick-to-light" or light-directed system can be used to enhance the capabilities of the employees. A pick-to-light system has lights above the racks or bins the employee will be picking from. The operator then scans a barcode that is on a tote or picking container representing the customer's order. Based on the order, the system will require the operator to pick an item from a specific bin. A light above the bin will illuminate showing the quantity to pick. The operator then selects the item or items for the order. The operator then presses the lighted indicator to confirm the pick. If no further lights are illuminated, the order is complete.

Voice directed picking systems are gaining popularity. In this type of picking system, workers wear a headset connected to a small wearable computer, which tells the worker where to go and what to do using verbal commands. The operators then confirm their tasks by saying predefined commands and reading confirmation codes printed on locations or products throughout the warehouse. These systems are used instead of paper or mobile computer systems requiring workers to read instructions and scan barcodes or enter information manually to confirm their tasks, thus freeing the operator's hands and eyes.

Order Management Systems (OMS)

An "order management system" (OMS) is a computer software system used in many industries for order entry and processing. In most cases, it is part of a larger ERP, WMS, or accounting system (see Figure 9.5).

OMS applications manage processes including order entry, customer credit validation, pricing, promotions, inventory allocation, invoice generation, sales commissions, and sales history.

A distributed order management (DOM) system is different from OMS in that it manages the assignment of orders across a network of multiple production, distribution, and/or retail locations to ensure that logistics costs and/or customer service levels are optimized.

An OMS is usually deployed as part of an enterprise application such as an ERP system as its sales engine is integrated with the organization's inventory, procurement, and financial systems.

Customer Relationship Management Systems

The term "customer relationship management" (CRM) refers to processes, strategies, and technologies that companies use to manage and analyze customer interactions and data throughout the customer lifecycle. Its goal is

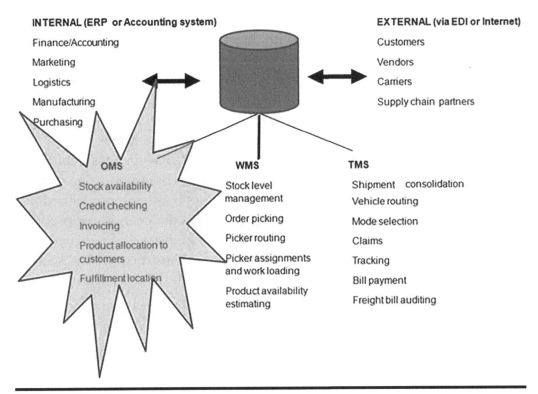

Figure 9.5 Order management system (OMS) and other supply chain execution systems.

to improve business relationships with customers while assisting in customer retention and increasing sales revenue.

A CRM "system" is a software application that manages a company's interactions with current and future customers and involves using technology to organize, automate, and synchronize sales, marketing, customer service, and technical support. This includes the management of business contacts, clients, contract wins, and sales leads within the sales function, sometimes referred to as "sales force automation" (SFA) software. The four largest vendors of CRM systems are salesforce.com, Microsoft, SAP, and Oracle. There are also many other smaller CRM vendors that are popular among small- to mid-market businesses.

Perhaps the biggest benefit to most businesses when moving to a CRM system comes from having all your business data stored and accessed from a single location, whereas before CRM systems, customer data was spread out over office productivity suite documents, e-mail systems, mobile phone data and even paper note cards and rolodex™ entries in various departments.

Order Fulfillment Systems for Efficiency and Effectiveness

The order-to-cash cycle is a critical lean measurement, and as a result, improving the order fulfillment process is key to shortening this cycle. That can include administrative functions, such as order management, or warehouse and transportation planning and operations.

At least at a macro level, order fulfillment is made up of four stages: order placement, order processing, order preparation and loading and order delivery (Figure 9.6).

So, if we look at these four processes, it becomes easier to see how lean principles and tools can improve the fulfillment process. These tools may include standardized work, layout more conducive to improving flow, visual workplace, 5S-workplace organization, value stream mapping, team building, kaizen, problem-solving and error proofing, pull systems utilizing kanbans, line balancing and cellular applications, and general waste reduction.

Order Placement

Order placement is the series of events that occur between when a customer places or sends an order and the time the seller receives the order. There are a variety of methods of order placement including in person, mail, telephone, Fax, or electronically via EDI (electronic data interchange) or the internet. Electronic means such as EDI or via the internet offer a distinct advantage in terms of timeliness and accuracy which can significantly reduce cycle times and errors.

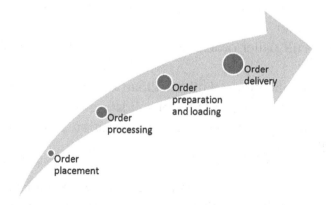

Figure 9.6   Order fulfillment process.

Order Processing

Order processing refers to the time from when the seller receives an order until an appropriate location (i.e., warehouse) is authorized to fill the order. Order processing may include the following steps:

- Check for completeness and accuracy.
- Customer credit check.
- Order entry into the computer system (manually or electronically).
- The marketing department will credit the salesperson.
- The accounting department will record the transaction.
- The inventory department locates the nearest warehouse to the customer and advises them to pick the order (again, manually or transmitted electronically depending on the company's technological capabilities).
- The transportation department arranges for shipment of the order.

Factors that may affect order processing time include:

- Processing priorities – Similar to short-term scheduling, priorities can be first come first served, shortest lead time, etc. This varies based on an individual organization's strategy and policies.
- Order-filling accuracy – The more accurately the order is received from the customer and input by customer service, the less time is spent correcting it.
- Order batching – It may be more efficient to batch orders for picking in a warehouse. An example of a batching method is known as "wave picking" where orders are assigned into groupings or waves and released together.
- Lot sizing – Full pallet orders may be processed faster than case or unit pick.
- Shipment consolidation – Full truckload orders will be delivered faster than less-than-truckload (LTL). Consolidating small orders going to the same area can not only decrease transportation costs but speed delivery as well.

Value stream mapping order processing can identify significant lean opportunities by reducing the dwell time of orders between steps such as order entry, credit checking, reconciliation, and confirmation/acknowledgment.

For example, using the concept of creating a work cell for this process with cross trained employees may cut cycle time along with reducing batch sizes and setup time.

OMS and CRM systems greatly assist in both order entry and order preparation and loading since they ensure that all current information and requirements of the customer are factored into the fulfillment process, thereby reducing the chance for errors and subsequent rework and returns.

Order Preparation and Loading

Order preparation and loading includes all activities from when an appropriate location is authorized to fill the order until goods are loaded aboard an outbound carrier.

In many cases, this can be one of the best places to improve the effectiveness and efficiency of an order cycle and can account for most of a facility's operating costs and time. Technology such as handheld scanners, handheld computers, RFID, voice-based order picking, and pick-to-light systems can be used to speed up the process. Of course, WMS software helps to make this process in the warehouse or distribution center more efficient.

Order Delivery

Order delivery is the time from when a carrier picks up the shipment until it is received by the customer. It is important to closely coordinate picking and staging of orders with carrier arrival as docks and yards can get congested very easily and charges apply when carriers are made to wait too long before loading.

Most consumer goods are delivered either from a point of production (factory or farm) in the case of larger or expedited shipments or more typically through one or more points of storage (i.e., manufacturer, field warehouse, wholesaler/distributor, and/or retail warehouses) to a point of sale (i.e., retail store), where the consumer buys the good to consume there or to take home.

There are many variations on this model for specific types of goods and modes of sale. Products sold via catalog or the internet may be delivered directly from the manufacturer or field warehouse to the consumer's home. In some cases, manufacturers may have factory outlets which serve as both a warehouse and a retail store.

While all processes in the supply chain in general, and order management specifically, are subject to measurement, this is where the "rubber meets the road" so to speak and is probably one of the most critical points for success or failure in the supply chain. This is because delivery, which in many cases may be performed by a third party, is the last point of physical contact with the customer (except in the case of returns or service).

TMS systems, discussed earlier in this chapter, assist in making this critical process more efficient.

Faster Fulfillment

We hear about companies like Amazon using technology such as kiva robots and drones to speed processing and delivery, but this goes well beyond e-commerce, where distributors, wholesalers, and "brick and mortar" retailers are moving to replenish their stores faster, keep less inventory at each retail location, and cut inventory across their entire network.

For example, many retail stores now receive cartons and mixed cartons several times a week and pallets and mixed pallets less frequently resulting in increasing their in-stock position from 90% to more than 97% while decreasing inventory by as much as 25%.

Faster fulfillment is a trade-off between three components of an order: the order receipt, processing, and delivery cycle times (see Figure 9.6)

Shortening the order processing cycle allows a company to move the order cut-off time to the right as shown in Figure 9.7 resulting in better service to its customers and/or the ability to move the delivery cut-off time to the left allowing access to a larger market or instead reduce current transportation costs.

Filling e-commerce orders as a part of an omni-channel marketing and distribution strategy, while convenient for the customer, can be costly for

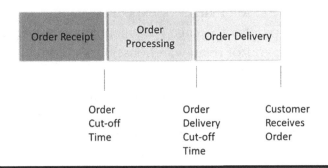

Figure 9.7 Faster fulfillment and trade-offs.

retailers that decide to outsource their fulfillment (up to 25% of sales for some), and retailers such as Kohl's, Walmart, Target, and Best Buy have seen reduced margins on e-commerce sales. To make this new reality work, many are rethinking their network, transportation, and distribution center operations strategies (Meller, 2015).

Order Fulfillment Systems Cases

How do they work to manage these trade-offs? What follows are some cases where technology has played a big part in this transformation.

Case #1 – Regional Pharmaceutical Distributor Requires Next-Day Delivery

Challenge

Customers of a regional pharmaceutical distributor with a single distribution center located in the central USA require next-day delivery, with most hospitals requiring that their orders arrive by 6 a.m. the next day. They had an order cut-off time of 7 p.m. This short transportation window gave them a range, or market size, of approximately 350 miles around their distribution center.

Approach

They carefully analyzed their situation and decided to invest in distribution center automation to shrink their order processing window by implementing two different automated solutions for their fast-movers and slow-movers. This allowed them to process many small orders at a low operating cost.

They also decided to split the distribution center into zones, rather than have a single tote travel the length of the building. Items in each zone were picked at the same time with the totes being combined into a complete order at the end of the process.

They chose to use the processing time reduction from the above changes (two-and-a-half-hour savings) by making their order cut-off time one hour later, putting them more in line with their competition.

Results

The new automation technology in their DC allowed them to process over 2,400 orders an hour, which was a large improvement over their previous manual picking process.

The combination of changes reduced their order processing window by two and a half hours, from four hours down to one and a half hours. This allowed them to increase their transportation window by 90 minutes, giving them an additional 75 miles to increase the size of the market they served by nearly 50%, eventually bringing them additional customers and increasing revenue by over $100 million per year (Meller, 2015).

Case #2 – Whirlpool Spins Optimized Supply Chain with Help from Manhattan Associates

Challenge

Whirlpool Corporation is the world's leading manufacturer and marketer of major home appliances with more than 40 manufacturing facilities sourced from approximately 7,000 different suppliers. They typically have from 2.2 to 2.5 million units in inventory delivered to about 30,000 retailers worldwide through a distribution network consisting of 15 factory DCs, 10 regional DCs, and 85 local DCs.

During their integration with Maytag, Whirlpool took its number of major manufacturing facilities from 47 down to 25.

With that in mind, Whirlpool felt that it needed a supply chain with flexibility, scalability, and agility for the various requirements going across multiple channels.

Furthermore, they realized that they would first have to address these challenges:

- Having a new standard of getting products to customers within 48–72 hours, the company realized that it had to move to a segmented inventory strategy supported by leaner processes.
- Since they were a U.S.-based manufacturer, they needed to lower production and distribution costs as they couldn't obtain the labor savings their competitors had because of overseas manufacturing.

Approach

After the consolidation, Whirlpool needed to restructure their warehouses and deploy the proper picking technologies to cut down on the number of miles that workers traveled inside the facilities. They also wanted to standardize processes and technologies across the entire network. So, they selected Manhattan Associates, who conducted a detailed needs assessment to understand the problems and challenges to assist with the integration.

Results

Utilizing a combination of innovative solutions from Manhattan Associates, including warehouse management, slotting optimization, and labor management Whirlpool has:

- Eliminated 40 million travel miles between facilities, reducing fuel costs and environmental impact.
- Reduced the time associated with the picking process by 50%, thereby speeding up pick rates.
- Cut damage to products by 50%.
- Improved warehouse uptime to more than 90% toward the established goal of 99.9%.
- Seamlessly integrated two competing supply chains (i.e., Whirlpool and Maytag) without customer or trading partner interruptions.
- Built a more exact, real-time view of inventory inside the warehouses which increased inventory accuracy.
- Gained warehouse efficiencies through integration of pick-pack logic and process with more exact inventory counts.
- Improved order-to-delivery time (www.manh.com, 2016).

Case #3 – TAGG Logistics Combines Cadence WMS and ADSI Ship-IT for Real-Time Supply Chain Execution System

Challenge

TAGG Logistics is an order fulfillment and third-party logistics (3PL) provider operating out of St. Louis, Missouri, and Reno, Nevada. They have a client base of manufacturers, wholesalers, and retailers that ship to their customers throughout North America and the world.

Founded in 2006, they were quickly outgrowing their legacy warehouse system.

Approach

TAGG required a new WMS and TMS to do the following:

- Operate in a high volume and diverse order fulfillment environment.
- Enable them to streamline and accelerate their shipment processing speeds and picking processes for both domestic and export shipments.
- Provide flexible product and shipment tracking.
- Provide least cost routing for small parcels and less-than-truckload (LTL) shipments.
- Automatically capture order handling and shipping details for billing.

They reviewed several WMS solutions before choosing the Cadence WMS by Cadre Technologies. They chose the Cadence WMS because it was designed for the 3PL industry, provided flexibility, and included an integrated billing solution.

Next, they replaced their TMS with ADSI's Ship-IT solution (tightly integrated with Cadence), with a single platform to manage all small parcels, LTL, USPS, and regional carrier shipping.

Results

Sales have increased 53% since 2007. At the same time, they have had:

- Faster pick rates – They can now configure how they group orders in waves, increasing the efficiency of their order processors.
- Improved inventory tracking – Helps them to better manage cycle counts, track products in the warehouse, and manage inventory. Inventory accuracy is now over 99.9%.
- Customer reporting – They can now customize and provide information to their clients.
- Integrated billing – It has enabled them to create a highly automated billing process that captures costs for all the value-added services they provide.

- Streamlined shipment processing – They now have a single system allowing them to perform least-cost routing for shipments, produce carrier labels, and upload the actual shipping costs back to the billing system.
- Customer-specific shipping programs – They can automatically send customer-specific shipping rules into Ship-IT.
- Paperless international shipping – Their staff no longer must interrupt their workflow to manually process international shipments. Now they are automatically processed in seconds (www.cadretech.com, 2023).

It would be nice if everything that was shipped through an order fulfillment system to the customer never came back. Unfortunately, that's not always the case, as most companies must deal with reverse logistics to some degree (especially e-commerce businesses), which is the topic of our next chapter.

Chapter 10

Supply Chain Software Systems: Return

Reverse logistics is a process that until recent times hasn't been put under the microscope, but once it has been, it can help companies significantly reduce waste and improve profits.

As the name implies, it is the reverse of what we've described so far in terms of plan, source, make, and deliver and can be defined as the process of planning, implementing, and controlling the efficient flow of recyclable and reusable materials, returns, and reworks from the point of consumption for the purpose of repair, remanufacturing, redistribution, or disposal.

Additionally, with today's environmental concerns, organizations need to try to integrate environment thinking into the entire supply chain process, forward and reverse. This includes product design, material sourcing and selection, manufacturing processes, delivery of the final product to the consumers, and "end-of-life" management of the product after its useful life.

In a perfect world, of course, there would be little need for much of the material handled in reverse logistics. However, the average retail total return rate for 2023 was 14.5% or $743 billion in merchandise (17.6% for online retailers, which has been exacerbated by the growth of e-commerce, and 10% for "brick and mortar" retailers), and it is clearly a major source of waste in the supply chain.

DOI: 10.4324/9781003372639-12

There are a variety of reasons for the reverse logistics process. They include:

- Processing returned merchandise including damaged, seasonal, restock, salvage, recall, or excess inventory.
- Green initiatives such as recycling packaging materials/containers.
- Reconditioning, refurbishing, and remanufacturing of returned products.
- Disposition of obsolete inventory.
- Hazardous materials recovery and electronic waste disposal.

So, depending on the specific reasons for the process existing in the first place within an organization, the reverse logistics network can be used for a variety of purposes such as refilling, repairs, refurbishing, remanufacturing, and so on, depending on the nature of the product, unit value, sales volume, and distribution channels.

Lean Reverse Logistics

There are five general steps to the product returns process, no matter what industry you are in:

1. Receive – Product returns are received at a centralized location, usually a warehouse or distribution center (usually after being gathered from retail locations or returned by the end user themselves). In many cases, the first step in this process is to provide a return acknowledgment.
2. Sort and stage – In this stage, returned products are received and sorted for further staging in the returns process.
3. Process – Returned products are then sub-sorted into items, based on their stock-keeping unit number. They can then be returned to inventory. If they are vendor returns, they are sorted by vendor.
4. Analyze – The value and subsequent status of the returned item is determined by trained employees.
5. Process – Returns in good condition such as back-to-stock or back-to-store items are returned to inventory. If the items require repair, refurbishment, or repackaging, then diagnostics, repairs, and assembly/disassembly operations are performed as needed. Items that have been repackaged, repaired, refurbished, or remanufactured are usually shipped to secondary markets.

How well these processes are planned and managed can go a long way toward minimizing waste.

Elements Key to a Lean and Agile Reverse Logistics Process

Rogers and Tibben-Lembke (1999) identified key reverse logistics management elements to help examine the return flow of product from a retailer back through the supply chain toward its original source, or to some other disposition (see Figure 10.1).

These elements, depending on how they are handled, can either positively or negatively impact a company's profitability. The elements are discussed next.

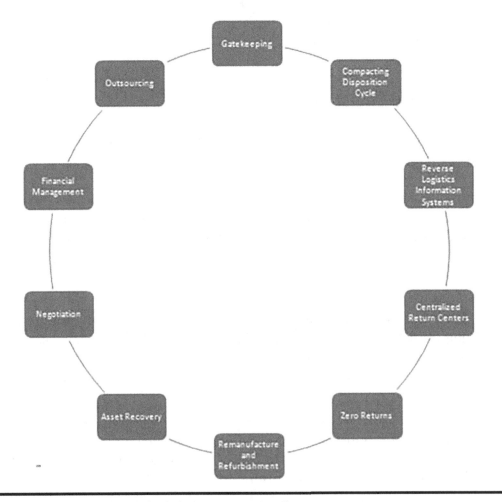

Figure 10.1 Key reverse logistics management elements.

Gatekeeping

Gatekeeping is the screening of defective or unwarranted returned merchandise at the beginning of the reverse logistics process.

It is the first critical factor to ensure that the entire reverse flow is both manageable and profitable. In the past, companies have put most resources into the forward logistics process and have given very little time and effort to the reverse process.

While liberal return policies, like those at L.L. Bean, Walmart, and Target, may draw customers, they can also encourage customer abuse such as the return of items lightly used for an event or one occasion.

So, it is important to have a solid gatekeeping process. For example, the electronic gaming company Nintendo will rebate retailers if they register the game player sold to the consumer at the point of sale. By doing this, Nintendo and retailers can determine if the product is under warranty, and if it is being returned inside the allowed time window. The impact of this new system on their bottom line was substantial: an 80% drop in return rates.

Compacting the Distribution Cycle Time

One of the major goals of the reverse logistics process once an item has entered it is to reduce the amount of time to figure out what to do with returned products once they arrive. This includes return product decisions, movement, and processing.

So, it is important to know beforehand what to do with returned goods. When material often comes back into a distribution center, it is not clear whether the items are: defective, can be reused, or refurbished, or need to be sent to a landfill. The challenge of running a distribution system in reverse is difficult … employees have difficulty making decisions when the decision rules are not clearly stated, and exceptions are often made.

Reverse Logistics Information Technology Systems

One of the most serious problems that companies face in the execution of reverse logistics is the scarcity of good information systems. To work well, a flexible reverse logistics information system is required.

The system should create a database at the store level so that the retailer can begin tracking returned products and follow it all the way back through the supply chain.

The information system should also include detailed information programs about important reverse logistics measurements, such as returns rates, recovery rates, and returns inventory turnover.

Useful tools such as radio frequency (RF) are helpful. Newer innovations such as two-dimensional barcodes and radio frequency identification license plates (RFID) may soon be in use extensively.

Some of the benefits of using reverse logistics technology include:

- Tracking goods as they travel through the returns process as poor product visibility in the reverse supply chain creates inefficiencies and allows for costly mistakes like the misplacement of a returned item.
- Complying with government environmental regulations around parts and product disposal will continue to tighten, especially in the area of recycling and disposal of e-waste.
- Reduced reverse logistics processing costs by eliminating manual processes through automation.
- Manage and improve inventory utilization by automating directed workflow processes such as return to stock or return to the supplier in the exchange and repair processes.
- Improved customer satisfaction by allowing them to return, exchange, or repair products anywhere, no matter what channel was used to originally purchase the product.
- Link multiple exchange or repair requests to their original sales orders enabling complete order lifecycle tracking.
- Integrate manufacturers, trading partners, logistics providers, and customers for efficient customer service.

At the end of the day, manufacturers, wholesalers/distributors, and retailers all can benefit from reverse logistics systems as U.S. companies spend more than $100 billion per year processing returns as well as the increased pressure from customers who are beginning to expect businesses to take back products regardless of the reason. In fact, research indicates that customers will stop shopping with retailers and manufacturers if the returns process is a hassle.

If reverse logistics software is fully integrated with a company's (and trading partner's) related processes and integrated with other systems such as CRM, they can significantly improve margin recovery by increasing the efficiency of returns processing, optimizing dispositions to enable maximum recoveries, and by providing timely and accurate compliance and reconciliation information through data accessibility and management tools.

Centralized Return Centers

Having centralized return centers (CRC) can offer many benefits to an organization, including:

- Consistency in disposition decisions and minimizes errors.
- A space saving advantage for retailers who want to dedicate as much of the shop floor to salable merchandise as possible.
- Labor cost reductions due to their specialization, as CRC employees can typically handle returns more efficiently than retail clerks can.
- Transportation cost reductions as empty truckloads returning from store deliveries are used to pick up returned merchandise.
- A convenient selling tool for the easy disposition of returned items. This can be an appealing service to retailers and may be a deal-maker for obtaining or retaining customers.
- Faster disposition times allow the company to obtain higher credits and refunds, as items stay idle for smaller periods of time, thus losing less value.
- Easier to identify trends in returns, which is an advantage to manufacturers who can detect and fix quality problems sooner than if these returns were handled entirely by customer service personnel.

Zero Returns

A company may have a program that does not accept returns from its customers. Rather, it gives the retailer an allowable return rate and proposes guidelines as to the proper disposition of the items. Such policies are usually accompanied by discounts for the retailer.

This type of policy passes the returns responsibility onto the retailer while reducing costs for the manufacturer or distributor.

The drawback is that the manufacturer loses some control over its merchandise.

Remanufacture and Refurbishment

The advantage of remanufacturing and refurbishment is using reworked parts resulting in cost savings.

There are five categories of remanufacture and refurbishment:

Make the product reusable for its intended purpose:

1) Repair
2) Refurbishing
3) Remanufacturing

Retrieve reusable parts from old or broken products:

4) Cannibalization

Reuse parts of products for different purposes:

5) Recycling

Asset Recovery

Asset recovery is the classification and disposition of returned goods, surplus, obsolete, scrap, waste and excess material products, and other assets. It tries to maximize returns to the owner while minimizing costs and liabilities for the dispositions.

The objective of asset recovery is to recover as much of the economic (and ecological) value as possible, thus reducing the final quantities of waste.

This can be a good cash generating opportunity for companies who can sell these goods that would otherwise end up in landfills.

Negotiation

Negotiation is a key element for all parties in the reverse logistics process. Because of the inherent lack of expertise on product returns, negotiations usually are informal and approached without formal pricing guidelines. Firms often do not maximize the residual value of returned products.

Financial Management

This is one of the most difficult parts of reverse logistics and also one of the most important.

Returns are sometimes charged against sales. Sales department personnel may tend to fight returns and delay them as much as possible. Accounts receivables are also impacted by returns.

Outsourcing

As mentioned previously, reverse logistics is usually not a core competency of the firm. In many cases, it may make more sense for the firm to outsource their reverse logistics functions than keep those in-house.

With all of this in mind, there are a variety of ways that technology can improve the reverse logistics process as seen in the cases below.

Reverse Logistics Technology Cases

Case #1 – RTL™ Adds up to Many Happy Returns for Philips

Challenge

Product returns cost Philips Consumer Lifestyle (part of Philips New Zealand Ltd.) hundreds of thousands of dollars each year just for the logistics, not to mention the cost of any subsequent repair and margin loss because of scrapping or selling the product as a second.

Approach

Although Philips had a very well-developed goods return authorization (GRA) policy, not everyone involved in the reverse logistics chain followed it. So, they started to look to reduce costs and increase efficiencies in their returns process. After a careful search, they went with RTL (Round Trip Logistics) with their innovative web-based GRA solution.

Results

Since implementing RTL, Philips has increased customer satisfaction, reduced call center costs, decreased staff training costs, and now has a standardized GRA process with minimal associated IT costs.

In fact, telephone and email GRA requests to Philips' internal call center have almost totally disappeared as customers can now obtain online authorization for returns as well as arranging for transportation on RTL. Estimated savings have been over $100,000/year.

The system prompts the retail returns clerk for all the pertinent information and won't allow them to proceed until all fields are filled in correctly, and as a result, the accuracy of their GRA forms is now approaching 100%.

Philips customers are happy as the decision-making process is immediate and any credit due is processed and applied to their account much faster. Philips staff are happier because RTL reduces the time they must spend on returns activities, which means more time being able to sell and they have also lowered their costs and increased efficiency of the return process.

Finally, the system offers online training for returns clerks and easily interfaces with a company's ERP or accounting systems (www.roundtriplogistics.com, 2023).

Case #2 – Nokia – Deployment of Global Service Strategy

Challenge

Historically the after-service repair landscape of many original equipment manufacturers (OEMs), including Nokia, the Finnish multinational communications and information technology company, was primarily nationally focused. Local organizations would typically oversee the contacts and contracts with local repair vendors that in most cases would offer a software solution with the capability to register and manage the reverse logistics and repair cycle. The repair vendor managed software would offer a local solution facilitating order entry, transportation management from retailers or even end-consumers to the repair center and vice versa, repair and swap solutions, track and trace, and local contact center support.

Approach

Nokia decided to move away from this local infrastructure and replace it with a global model. They decided to invest in their own global software solution to get full control and visibility over all their repair flows. By concentrating these flows to fewer repair vendors that focus purely on repair, costs could be saved.

Nokia partnered with ReturnPool, a global IT solutions provider, with expertise in the areas of business process optimization, rapid IT development, reverse logistics, and project management.

Results

In the new global process, Nokia connected its global system and the various parties involved in the reverse supply chain, took control over the reverse logistics flows, and created the ability to re-route repair volumes to different repair vendors when applicable for cost or quality reasons. In some geographical areas, logistics hubs were established with the ability to swap items when needed to meet the repair service license agreements (SLAs) promised to customers. In the new process, the repair SLA promised to customers could be managed separately from the SLAs agreed upon with the repair vendors if necessary.

The implementation of a global software solution wasn't as simple as just rolling it out. It required a change management approach where specific local requirements would be considered if needed while maintaining and safeguarding the global focus.

ReturnPool has positioned itself as an important partner to Nokia for the past decade to assist in the implementation of the global solution in over 30 countries. ReturnPool used a hands-on and global approach, making necessary adjustments to the software system as necessary in the ever-changing service landscape. Tools used included detailed process mapping, hands-on training, and on-site implementation (www.returnpool.com, 2012).

Case #3 – Return Central: Reconstructed Network Yields Big Efficiencies, Faster Processes

Challenge

A major national retailer of home improvement and construction products and services with over 2,000 stores nationwide had an inefficient reverse logistics process where products returned to vendors were controlled on an ad hoc basis by individual stores and regions, creating major disruptions in the reverse supply chain.

Furthermore, there were a significant number of do-it-yourself, non-conveyable commodities which created issues beyond the normal returns process, contributing to an even bigger waste stream.

Approach

GENCO, a major third-party logistics (3PL) company, developed a solution for the retailer that addressed five key areas: labor, salvage and liquidation of goods, the transportation network, visibility and management of return lanes, and recycling.

Significant resources were required to handle the retailers' returns, which was preventing them from their primary function of interfacing with customers to increase customer service and sales. By implementing standardization through GENCO's proprietary R-Log® software, automation-enabled teammates were redirected to customer service and sales.

With R-Log, the retailer can track the movement of goods through return channels in real time. R-Log also enabled the immediate application of vendor credits to the retailer's accounts payable system. In addition to removing the burden of returns management from customer service teammates, R-Log improved tracking and visibility for returned inventory.

Results

This case illustrates the synergistic power of lean supply chain techniques when combined with technology as GENCO implemented lean and kaizen events throughout the returns network to create a culture of continuous improvement. To support all these strategies, GENCO also designed and built a custom reverse logistics network for the retailer. Ultimately, a regional network of three U.S. locations was executed to facilitate returns management.

The retailer's new, centralized return system has been very successful. R-Log has delivered speed, efficiency, and automation throughout the complete returns process. The retailer has also had a significant reduction in the size of the workforce that were in returns management, enabling remaining employees to focus on other important areas of the business, such as improving the customer experience.

Furthermore, the implementation of lean processes in the three facilities has standardized process flows, improved productivity, eliminated wasteful steps, and streamlined sorting and palletizing.

The new process has reduced losses that the retailer was experiencing before engaging GENCO and using their reverse logistics technology, significantly increasing recovery and revenue (www.genco.com, 2023).

The Next Frontier in Retail

It's time for retailers (and manufacturers and distributors to some degree) to embrace a different approach, by predicting returns instead of trying to prevent them, so they can reduce return rates and improve customer satisfaction.

As stated earlier, as returns are basically a form of waste, it makes sense to focus on preventing returns from occurring in the first place, but you need to be careful as to the strategies employed to accomplish that. While policies like rigid return windows, restocking fees, and damage waivers may prevent some returns, they're ineffective in avoiding all returns (and not usually well received by customers).

Instead, retailers today can use data and technology to predict risks and identify customers more likely to return items.

By using predictive returns, you can generate:

Cost savings – Machine learning algorithms analyze customer data such as purchase history, product reviews, and shipping information to target the right shoppers and possibly avoid unnecessary returns and reduce shipping, restocking, and processing costs.

Enhanced customer experience – Retailers can reach out to customers who are at a higher risk of returning items, offering personalized solutions and addressing concerns before an issue arises. By engaging sooner and providing alternative options, businesses can improve the overall shopping experience and create customer loyalty.

Optimized reverse logistics – By pinpointing which items customers are most likely to return, retailers can also more efficiently manage storage, transportation, and disposal, as well as generally minimize costs, reduce waste, and streamline operations.

While predictive returns is still a relatively new field, it's growing rapidly. With the help of an abundance of data and technology, retailers can take a proactive approach to returns management.

The integration of AI-enabled supply chain management software yields remarkable improvements across logistics costs (15%), inventory levels (35%), and service levels (65%). When combined with supply chain and customer data, reverse logistics enables retailers to reduce returns, mitigate risks, lower costs, and enhance customer satisfaction.

Retailers who want to beat the competition must get their returns management in order. By shifting gears from preventing returns to predicting them, brands can provide great service, save money, and avoid headaches (Baror, 2023).

Up to this point in the book, we have covered the use of technology in the five major supply chain processes covered by the SCOR model (i.e., plan, source, make, deliver, and return).

We will now move on to the next section of this book where we will focus on the hardware currently available today, primarily in logistics facilities, which works in unison with much of the software systems mentioned in Chapters 6–10 to fully enable a lean, agile supply chain.

SUPPLY CHAIN EQUIPMENT

Chapter 11

Supply Chain Equipment: Distribution Centers and Warehousing

Modern order fulfillment depends on certain key pieces of software to keep the operation running smoothly and efficiently. For most warehouses and distribution centers, this will at a minimum include a warehouse management system (WMS) and enterprise resource planning (ERP) software which we previously discussed.

Of course, operations with a large amount of automation will also require software to manage that equipment, typically in the form of either a warehouse execution system (WES) or a warehouse control system (WCS).

Taken together, these four options, ERP, WMS, WCS, and WES, are the most common types of warehouse software that you are likely to come across in an operation (Figure 11.1).

So, while we have already discussed ERP and WMS software systems, the actual equipment used in a warehouse, discussed in this chapter, is usually directed and controlled by WCS and WES software.

Historically, typical warehouses or distribution centers had a variety of equipment to increase productivity and efficiency for storage systems (e.g., pallet racks, shelving, and specialty racks), material handling equipment (e.g., forklifts, conveyors, pallet jacks, and hand trucks), and packaging equipment (e.g., industrial scales, stretch wrap machines, and packing tables).

DOI: 10.4324/9781003372639-14

Figure 11.1 Warehouse software.

Today, many warehouses are moving toward fully automated warehouses, which are facilities that use automated, and in some cases autonomous, handling equipment and conveying systems to optimize the performance of operations, including truck loading and unloading. Automated warehouses don't need many, if any, standard forklifts and minimize the presence of operators inside them.

As companies seek to increase their competitiveness to become both lean and responsive, warehouse automation is a trend seen more and more in logistics nowadays. The goal is to gain efficiency and productivity, which only automated processes can ensure.

What Is a Fully Automated Warehouse?

A fully automated warehouse is a facility that uses automated logistics solutions to carry out all operations, from receiving goods to the processing of orders and their subsequent picking, staging, loading, and shipment.

They have minimal operator intervention in their logistics processes. There are even some facilities which are known as dark warehouses, which have no operators inside and don't need lighting.

An automated warehouse can be designed to handle different types of goods, and they are now common in e-commerce, automotive, and food industries, among others.

COVID-19 has accelerated the implementation of new technologies in the supply chain, and one area that has seen the most growth is warehouse automation as automated solutions make it possible to comply with all safety measures while maintaining production levels.

A study by McKinsey concluded that many operations could be automated by 2030, as artificial intelligence (AI) takes over the many repetitive activities that logistics companies perform. They expect to see fully automated high-rack warehouses, with autonomous vehicles navigating the aisles with managers wearing augmented-reality glasses to "see" the entire operation, helping them coordinate both people and robots (more on that in Chapter 16). They also felt that WMS would track inventory in real time.

Automating All Warehouse Operations

The main objective of installing automated systems is to optimize movements that take place in the facility, boost productivity, and limit errors. In a fully automated warehouse, all logistics operations have minimal human intervention. We will now discuss how it works in the operations below.

Automated Goods Receipt

In a logistics facility, the goods receiving process is critical for effective stock control. In this operation, the docks can be equipped with automatic truck loading and unloading systems.

To improve the movement of goods from the loading docks to the various storage and/or work zones, automated conveying systems such as pallet conveyors and roller conveyors for boxes, totes, and bins are installed. In automated facilities, this entire operation is controlled by warehouse management software that coordinates the automatic equipment to improve efficiency.

Automated Internal Transportation

Fully automated warehouses replace manual handling equipment (forklifts) with automated transportation systems that continuously supply the storage, order picking, and dispatch areas.

Examples of these are pallet or box conveyors which streamline the movement of goods to the different areas in the facility. An example of this is found at Zbyszko Company, a Polish drinks manufacturer that connects the storage and production zones in its new warehouse; it has incorporated a pallet conveyor system.

In the case of facilities with a low product density, manual handling equipment can be swapped with automated guided vehicles. Warehouses requiring several areas to be connected by means of a closed circuit can install electrified monorails. These transportation systems, which can be aerial or floor-mounted, have self-propelled trolleys that deliver the goods to the workstations.

Drones can be used to reduce inventory control costs and accuracy by flying mapped routes using an advanced AI-driven navigation system to capture images of barcodes, license plate numbers, and more. Then, each drone returns to its dock, where all the data can be securely uploaded to a warehouse or yard management system.

Storage of Goods with Stacker Cranes

The placement and removal of products on the racks is one of the most automated operations in a logistics facility. This is because automated solutions such as stacker cranes (automated storage and retrieval or AS/RS for pallets) and mini-load systems (AS/RS for boxes) ensure productivity in conjunction with a WMS.

One example of automation of product storage and retrieval from racks is BASF's rack-supported warehouse in Brazil where the facility is divided into two aisles served by stacker cranes for pallets. The WMS acts as the brain of the facility, ensuring efficiency in the storage of the goods.

Automated Order Picking and Dispatch

Order preparation is one of the most complex operations to automate, as processes are rarely constant or repetitive. However, there are solutions such as industrial robotic arms (supplied by conveyors), which increase picking throughput in a facility. Robotic arms can even handle multiple boxes simultaneously.

Order picking and dispatch can also be automated with solutions such as sorters, which divert products to the different workstations or shipping containers as well as solutions for automating value-added processes in order preparation and dispatch, such as stretch-wrapping and palletizing robots and labeling machines.

Software-Automated Warehouse Management

A fully automated warehouse requires software that coordinates the operations of the automated handling and transportation equipment in the facility. Typically, a WMS (previously discussed in Chapter 9) directs where each product should go and which operations to perform and interacts with the WCS, responsible for coordinating the movements of the machines (www. interlakemecalux.com, 2023).

Barcodes and more recently RFID tags are basically forms of data entry using various compatible hardware to read information to input into software systems such a WMS in a warehouse (thus their inclusion in this chapter). What follows is a discussion of both.

Barcodes

As you know and have seen, a barcode is a square or rectangle with a combination of vertical black lines of varying thickness and height, white space, and numbers that together identify specific products and their relevant information. Computers linked to scanners can read these codes and use a specific combination of bars, spaces, and numbers to retrieve the data for that product.

Although patented in 1949, barcodes didn't go into commercial use until 1979 (commercial testing started as early as 1971).

Today, barcodes are found on not only household items that come from supermarkets or retail stores but also licenses, rental cars, checked luggage, and hospital bands. In each case, they identify a product or person and encode important details.

Besides ease and speed to ring up items at a store or track inventory in a warehouse, barcodes' major business benefits include accuracy, inventory control, and cost savings.

Barcoding has a low barrier to entry, as all a business needs is a printer, scanner, and basic inventory management software.

There are many types of barcodes, but they all fall into two categories: linear codes, including widely used formats like UPC (universal product code) and EAN (European article number), both of which are one-dimensional (1D), and matrix codes, like QR (i.e., quick response) codes, which are two-dimensional (2D).

Most scanners can only read 1D, or linear, barcodes, and they remain the most popular format.

QR or 2D codes (see Figure 11.2) are usually read by an imaging device such as a camera and contain the data for a locator, an identifier, and for web-tracking.

Today barcodes come in many shapes and sizes and a wide range of designs, and many can even be read by mobile phones and other devices.

Figure 11.2   QR code example.

How Barcodes Work

The width of the black bars usually represents the numbers 0 or 1, while the sequence of those bars signifies a number between 0 and 9. A computer connected to the scanner has all the information on the item stored in a database of some kind that is associated with that unique combination of bars and spaces and may add, multiply, or divide those numbers to identify the correct product, which shows up on the screen.

In a warehouse (or a factory or retail location), the barcode might encode an item's size, color, and other attributes, as well as its location, so the company has a detailed view of current inventory and can quickly fulfill orders or conduct physical inventory and price that an associate needs to check out a customer.

Organizations also can use barcodes to track goods throughout their life cycle, from manufacture to distribution to purchase to service and repair.

Barcode Components

Barcodes (Figure 11.3) must be designed in a precise, uniform way so a scanner can read them and transmit the encoded data to a computer. Using various components, a barcode may also reveal the country of origin, product category, and manufacturer.

The diagram below shows the different elements of a UPC barcode. Basically, there is what is known as a "check" digit at the beginning and end (e.g., "5" and "7"). There are five digits (e.g., "12345") which represent

5 12345 00010 7

Figure 11.3   Barcode example.

the manufacturer's code followed by another five digits (e.g., "00010") representing the item number.

Business Benefits of Barcodes

The use of barcodes in the supply chain has taken off because they offer a clear and fast return on investment. They are used to label and track a variety of elements in a warehouse such as products and other assets (including cartons and skids), locations, packing materials, and picking totes. These labels dramatically speed up transactions, replacing manual, physical, or handwritten methods with a quick scan of a wireless device.

Below are some key benefits to businesses by using barcodes:

Accuracy – Barcodes eliminate manual entry of product information at receiving, resulting in fewer opportunities for error. Retail or warehouse associates simply swipe the barcode across the scanner.

Real-time data – When an employee scans a barcode, it immediately updates inventory and sales numbers in the company's ERP or business management system, giving a business constant access to up-to-date data, for current statistics such as inventory turns, recent sales by item, etc.

Reduced training – For the most part, barcodes and scanners are self-explanatory, so it doesn't take new employees long to become efficient at the checkout counter, and as a result, barcodes significantly reduce the need for training. At a grocery store, for example, the worker doesn't have to know the item codes to be productive.

Inventory control – Barcodes improve the speed and accuracy of inventory management and reduce excessive spending on products. As a result, employees can always find the most current information when reviewing inventory positions or trends in demand, which helps them to make better decisions around purchasing and discounting. This reduces inventory carrying costs, which increases long-term profitability.

Low cost – Barcodes are relatively inexpensive to set up and can be easy to implement. To implement, all you need are assigned barcodes, a barcode printer, a barcode scanner, and software to store your product details (which you probably already have in some form or another, such as a WMS, ERP, or just a basic inventory control system) (Wasp Bar Code, 2023).

Radio Frequency Device (RFID)

RFID is a wireless technology that uses radio frequency fields to transfer data. RFID has been available commercially since the 1970s and is used in many aspects of daily life, including car keys, employee identification, medical history and billing, highway toll tags, and security access cards.

When used within the supply chain, RFID gives businesses the ability to track and identify inventory in real time so management can always know where inventory is located.

RFID Warehouse Tracking System

RFID tracking in a warehouse environment works as follows:

A shipment arrives at the warehouse receiving dock and is unloaded from the truck.

An RFID tag is then attached to the items (or entire pallet) in that shipment. There are two main types of RFID tags:

Active RFID – An active RFID tag has its own power source, often a battery.

Passive RFID – A passive RFID tag receives its power from the reading antenna, whose electromagnetic wave induces a current in the RFID tag's antenna.

Each tag has an internal memory on which an item's information is stored and modified as it moves through different processes in the warehouse.

The RFID tag transmits the shipment or item's information to a central database via an electromagnetic signal.

A WMS analyzes and updates the data as the item progresses through the warehouse system.

Unlike the old barcode system that used to be standard in the warehousing industry, RFID tags don't require line-of-sight scanners and reading equipment. Workers don't need to be within inches of a box to scan it manually.

With an RFID warehouse tracking system, items can be scanned and cataloged from anywhere, even when they're hidden behind boxes or pallets.

RFID tags can also be detected and read remotely and simultaneously. With this kind of functionality, multiple tags can be read at once, unlike barcodes which need to be scanned one at a time.

How RFID Improves Warehouse Operations

RFID when used in a warehouse delivers benefits such as:

Accuracy – As it is highly accurate, it eliminates the risk of human error and saves time with automated processes that communicate with warehouse software. For example, when an item arrives or leaves the warehouse, the RFID tag automatically documents its arrival and exit.

Location – Workers can save a lot of time and increase productivity because RFID makes it possible to find the exact location of any item instantly for service activities such as pick and pack.

Integration – When RFID technology is integrated into a WMS, warehouse operating costs are reduced and accuracy and efficiency are increased.

Ultimately, RIFD makes for a more efficient warehouse and improved customer service (ProLogis, 2023).

In summary, thanks to the technology that has been discussed in this chapter, all movements in the fully automated warehouse are optimized, and errors are prevented in processes as complex as goods receipt and multi-SKU order picking.

Warehouse automation provides complete control over stock in a facility while improving an organization's performance and reliability with enhanced safety and accuracy.

Next, we will move on to discuss transportation-related hardware that helps to enable a smart supply chain.

Chapter 12

Supply Chain Equipment: Transportation

As the saying goes, "a chain is only as strong as its weakest link". In the case of the supply chain, the "link", between your facilities or "nodes" is your transportation system and its strength can mean the difference between the success and failure of your business.

To be successful, the transportation system used to connect your supply chain must be managed and controlled properly with complete visibility and great communication between partners. Transportation and logistics costs (mainly warehouse operations) can account for as much as 7–14% of sales depending on the industry you are in. Transportation costs alone comprise the majority of these expenses for most companies. Best-in-class companies have transportation and logistics related costs in a range of 4–7% depending on the industry sector. So, it's not hard to see how both operationally and financially important transportation is to a successful business.

The primary modes of transportation are truck/motor carrier, rail, air, water, intermodal transportation, and pipeline.

Transportation Industry Trends

There are a lot of technological advancements happening in the transportation industry. Many are in integration and collaboration utilizing technologies such as artificial intelligence (AI), the internet of things (IoT), etc. which will be discussed in Part IV of this book.

DOI: 10.4324/9781003372639-15

However, there is also a lot going on with the vehicles themselves which, while we may not see them in our everyday lives, are impactful.

These vehicles are discussed next.

Autonomous Vehicles

As transport vehicles account for significant pollution and traffic congestion, especially in big cities, one solution to these issues is the adoption of autonomous transportation systems.

Self-driving vehicles use sensors referred to as "Light Detection and Ranging" or LIDAR (an active remote sensing system that can be used to measure vegetation height across wide areas) and automated safety features to navigate roads. They also have cameras to read road signs and see them in high resolution and use AI algorithms to recognize objects on roads, which help guide the vehicles on how to perceive their environment. As a result, it is thought that autonomous vehicles increase road safety and reduce harmful emissions.

Another related transportation trend includes the commercialization of air and land delivery drones (*discussed in more detail in the next section*), which are useful to transport medical supplies, food packets, and more directly to even remote locations, or even to assist the elderly and enable rapid emergency response. Driverless trucks can also bring greater efficiency to the trucking market and help with current (and predicted, future) driver shortage challenges.

It's still not clear if self-driving trucks are ready to take to the roads in a critical mass. As mentioned earlier, one of the biggest drivers for self-driving trucks is the driver shortage which continues to grow every year, but it appears that autonomous trucks are not a quick solution to the driver shortage. Like autonomous robots within the warehouse, it appears that autonomous trucks are not necessarily here to replace human drivers, but more to collaborate with drivers to make the job easier.

The idea of platooning may be where autonomous trucks could first make an impact. In this scenario, a lead truck is equipped with technology while a follower truck operates in tandem through a fully autonomous system. The vehicles move in a group or platoon with the trucks driven by smart technology and communicate with each other. Each truck still has a driver onboard for safety and for taking over when exiting the freeway, which allows the follower driver to log off and rest while the truck is in motion. This allows drivers of the platooned trucks to drive twice as far while ensuring they don't exceed hours of service regulations.

Autonomous Last-Mile Deliveries

Last-mile which includes home delivery is one of the most difficult and expensive aspects of the supply chain. From a customer experience standpoint, it is also the most memorable and possibly important. As e-commerce continues to grow, autonomous last-mile deliveries are becoming more of a "high profile" issue.

The increase in driverless technology has at least been partially driven by the pandemic, a rise in e-commerce and omni channel retail, and a personnel shortage for delivery services, as well as advances in AI and other technologies.

As a result, many enterprises have invested or plan to invest in technologies such as autonomous and "semi-autonomous" (some human monitoring may be required) trucks, delivery air drones, and land-based bots.

Although many companies have been testing drone deliveries in recent years, the use of last-mile drones is still challenging for a variety of reasons including FAA regulations, public perception, and the technology itself. However, many companies such as Wing, Amazon, UPS, Matternet, Flytrex, and Zipline are looking at the use of last-mile drones, with hopes of reducing the cost of deliveries while improving customer service. These companies have completed drone deliveries of small packages while it still seems that the use of drones to deliver medical supplies and prescriptions has been the most effective of technology.

Many companies have also begun testing autonomous mobile delivery bots in cities and on college campuses. However, the term "autonomous" may be a little bit misleading as there is a team of humans that are tracking the vehicle throughout its journey. For the most part, humans mostly monitor the robot, but if it runs into trouble, they can use a remote control to drive or troubleshoot the vehicle. If the robot becomes unable to complete the delivery, the workers can then make the delivery themselves. Recently, there have been several companies such as Starship Technologies, Nuro, and FedEx that have completed pilot programs with delivery bots.

Driverless last-mile delivery faces challenges, however, due to infrastructure limitations and government regulations. Underdeveloped infrastructure and weak internet connectivity can delay delivery time or lead to delivery to the wrong locations. So, in the foreseeable future, the growth of autonomous last-mile delivery by air drones may be limited to less congested areas and by land robots to urban areas and campus environments. These factors may reduce the success rate of autonomous delivery mechanisms, leading to a lower market growth rate.

If these limitations can be resolved or minimized, the cost benefits are potentially immense – it is estimated that land delivery robots can reduce delivery costs by up to 80–90%, as well as significantly reduce carbon footprints.

This is especially important as last-mile delivery makes up more than 50% of the total cost of shipping and is the least efficient part of the shipping system.

Before the growth in single package deliveries – primarily due to e-commerce – everything was transported in bulk, allowing for costs shared across all packages. The last-mile single package makes up most delivery costs as there are few packages to share the fees.

With global small package deliveries increasing, costs will continue to increase, stressing the shipping industry and the consumer.

With that in mind, it's not surprising that investors have put more than $8 billion into autonomous delivery companies in recent years. The jury is still out as to the public perception of autonomous delivery vehicles, but as their use becomes more commonplace, the use of this technology will become more normalized.

Electric Transportation

Electrification is a major trend in the transportation industry. Electric vehicles (EVs) emit fewer greenhouse gases (GHGs) and air pollutants as compared to gasoline or diesel cars. Since EVs require electricity to recharge batteries, they eliminate dependence on conventional fossil fuels (although to varying degrees, fossil fuels are used to generate electricity at power plants). Furthermore, EVs offer better performance due to electric motor efficiency with less noise production. Due to the increased adoption of electric cars, startups are now working on improving the charging infrastructure.

A combination of new technologies such as vehicle-to-grid (V2G), fast charging, mobile charging, new battery innovations, and many more such solutions are being created and launched to facilitate the wider acceptance of EVs in everyday commute and delivery operations. Air transportation is also witnessing an increase in electrification via electric vertical take-off and landing (eVTOL) aircraft, electric air taxis, and drones. Other startups are also working toward reducing the negative impact of air travel on the environment (Banker, 2022).

Enabling Equipment

Telematics is a term that combines the words telecommunications and informatics to describe the use of communications and IT to transmit, store, and receive information from devices to remote objects over a network.

Vehicle telematics combines GPS systems, onboard vehicle diagnostics, wireless telematics devices, and black box technologies to record and transmit vehicle data, such as speed, location, maintenance requirements, and servicing, and cross-reference this data with the vehicle's internal behavior.

Telematics devices collect then transmit GPS and vehicle-specific data via General Packet Radio Service (or "GPRS", *which is a wireless communication protocol that uses packet switching to transfer data on cellular networks*), 4G and cellular networks, or satellite communication to a centralized server, where the data is categorized, interpreted, and optimized for consumer user interfaces.

Modern commercial vehicle manufacturers typically embed automotive telematics technology directly into fleet vehicles.

In general, telematics is a method of monitoring cars, trucks, equipment, and other assets using GPS technology and onboard diagnostics (OBD) to plot the asset movements on a computerized map.

Vehicle Telematics Usage

Vehicle telematics applications include:

Telematics vehicle tracking – In telematics vehicle tracking systems, GPS and an onboard GPRS modem communicate with the user and web-based software. Transmitted vehicle data is then transformed into information with management reporting tools and mapping software.

Trailer/container tracking – GPS devices communicate their location via mobile phone or satellite communication.

Fleet vehicle telematics management – Commercial vehicle telematics involves the management of a company's fleet of vehicles. This includes vehicle scheduling, financing, maintenance, onboard diagnostics, driver, fuel, health, and improved safety management. It helps to reduce costs, improve productivity, minimize vehicle investment risks, and maintain compliance requirements.

Telematics standards – Vehicle telematics providers must adhere to standards developed by the Association of Equipment Management Professionals (AEMP), which enables the delivery of telematics data in a standardized XML format.

Wireless vehicle safety communications – Sensors are sometimes found in electronic sub-systems installed in vehicles and in fixed locations, such as call boxes and near traffic signals. They can transmit important safety information via wider networks to driver displays. This is useful for optimizing routes and fuel usage in company vehicle telematics.

Emergency warning systems – Vehicle telematics architectures have generally been developed with the idea to blend warning information with vehicles in the vicinity. Telematics emergency warning systems can produce instantaneous autonomous warning notifications in real-time using computerized systems that update information in real time, which is particularly useful for intelligent vehicle technologies.

Engine immobilization - Advanced systems can remotely disable the engine if a theft is detected. Carsharing – Vehicle telematics services can enable the tracking of members' usage for pay-as-you-drive billing, tracking of available vehicles, and using GPS tracking to outline a predefined geofence for available vehicles.

Insurance – Insurance companies use driver behavior data to make risk assessments and adjust customers' premiums based on that information. Higher risk behavior, such as speeding and not obeying road signals, will result in higher premiums (www.heavy.ai, 2023).

RFID Technology – What Are Its Uses in the Transportation Industry?

Radio-Frequency Identification (RFID) technology is currently making a huge difference in the transportation sector due to its ability to support an incredibly versatile range of applications. Why is RFID being used so much in this sector, and how could you make the most of it?

What Is RFID Technology?

RFID is a technology that enables data to be transmitted securely at very fast speeds. It also doesn't require a line of sight like barcodes do, which means that it is more user-friendly and able to be used in a wide variety of settings.

Data relating to an object is stored on an RFID tag which can be added to an item. The tag carries this data in a small but powerful chip and operates in a variety of radio frequencies. An RFID reader is used in conjunction with the chip to transmit the data securely, and in that way, you can rely on the safe communication of information across your business! Businesses across the world use this technology, but how about the transportation sector in particular?

RFID Technology in Transport

One common reason you'll find businesses using RFID is to make labor-intensive tasks automated, saving them money on wages and staffing requirements while also making all their practices more streamlined. It's also a very popular way to gain a better insight into the status of tasks, for example, seeing where stock is or who is on a site at any given time.

RFID Tags on Vehicles

This method is often used to track when vehicles arrive back at the depot, and this then accurately keeps a record of the available vehicles at any given time. Other applications include vehicle identification when arriving at a site. These two ways of using RFID greatly contribute to faster business processes, planning, and in turn the overall success of the whole transportation company.

Leased Equipment

If your company offers equipment lease or rental to customers, equipping the assets with RFID tags can help to reduce the possibility of losses and theft. Tagging the equipment and having it actively scanned along their journey will help you to keep full control of things like the location and use times.

Shipping Containment Tracking

Perhaps one of the most common uses of RFID technology is to track shipping containers as they move along the shipping process. A container can be scanned at the port and then again once it arrives at the right destination, giving a live feed of where the container is up to in its journey. This gives you more control and a more detailed view of your assets (www. ussmartcards.com, 2023).

Now that we've reviewed the most common types of software and hardware technologies used in the supply chain today, it's time to discuss how they all work together to benefit your business as well as your customers, suppliers, and other partners.

INTEGRATION OF TECHNOLOGY

Chapter 13

Integration and Collaboration

By integrating and collaborating with partners, suppliers upstream and customers downstream as part of a lean, smart strategy for your supply chain, you can open a window into your future – and even your past. It's like having the ability to time travel.

But before we travel through time, we will need to define the subtle differences between integration and collaboration.

In general, integration in a supply chain is bringing together people, processes, and systems into one common platform. Integration is the starting point in a collaborative supply chain.

Supply chain collaboration, on the other hand, is when two or more businesses work together to plan and execute supply chain operations to achieve shared goals such as improved customer service, reduced costs, or optimized supply chain performance.

In a sense, you need at least some collaboration to integrate with supply chain partners, but little or no integration to collaborate with them (at least at the start).

Integration of supply chain components started in the 1970s when electronic data interchange (EDI), and later XML using the internet, created a business-to-business communications method and standard.

Software developers raced to provide better systems for supply chain management, and by the late 1980s, the first modern enterprise resource planning (ERP) systems automated supply chains. ERP systems centralized many business processes into a single suite of software, integrating supply chain management with other business functions. It allowed businesses to manage their costs and operations in a harmonic way.

DOI: 10.4324/9781003372639-17

Today, many supply chains are managed by ERP systems, many of which have moved to the cloud and added technologies such as artificial intelligence, machine learning, and predictive analytics. These AI-powered systems make it possible for businesses to oversee supply chains with little human oversight, and they'll likely become the nerve centers of tomorrow's autonomous supply chains.

Robotics and self-driving vehicles have crept toward widespread adoption in supply chains worldwide. Some warehouses, such as Amazon's, already make use of robots to prepare products for shipment.

However, true supply chain collaboration is more than just integrating information among business functions and partners. It is both companies working together to improve data sharing and an interactive process that results in joint decisions and activities – often in multi-company teams from various disciplines in each organization.

Furthermore, supply chain collaboration is not easy to accomplish for many reasons, including a tendency to rely too much on one technology, failure to understand when and with whom to collaborate, and a propensity for distrust among partners.

In fact, many collaborative attempts through the years have failed (as many as 8 in 10 can fail). Reasons range from lack of commitment from senior management, failure to provide collaboration efforts with sufficient resources to make them work, or limited resources spread too thinly over many initiatives. Not to mention the fact that the initiatives are spread over two different organizations.

However, collaboration is well worth the effort as it can result in reductions in inventories and costs, along with improvements in speed, service levels, and customer satisfaction.

Now that we're clearer about supply chain integration versus collaboration, let's talk time travel.

Integration versus Collaboration

Collaborative programs, such as quick response (QR), efficient consumer response (ECR), vendor managed inventory (VMI), and the most recent iterations of collaborative planning, forecasting, and replenishment (CPFR; described later in this chapter), have been around since the late 1980s. They all involve getting a more accurate downstream picture of the supply chain, using information such as point-of-sale data, retail store and distribution center inventory balances and withdrawals, and current and future events such as promotions, discounts, or advertising.

These types of solutions reduce the bullwhip effect – progressively larger inventory swings in response to changes in customer demand – the result of which is supply chain volatility, inefficiency, and waste.

Through a structured integration and collaboration process, it is possible for manufacturers and distributors, in essence, to time travel and see potential causes of future disruptions before they occur. While an initial investment in resources may be required, opportunities for fewer stockouts on store shelves, up-selling, and cross-selling may be worth it.

The 80/20 Rule

The initial investment often causes companies to shy away from integration and collaboration programs without looking at the big picture. One way to justify the investment is via the Pareto Principle (also known as the "80/20 rule"). The rule states that, in business, there is a natural tendency for a small number of items to generate a disproportionately large portion of sales and/or profits.

The 80/20 rule also applies to an organization's customer base, focusing on integration and collaboration efforts with larger customers who make up a greater portion of sales. Companies can use the advanced information gained through this process to significantly improve forecasts, thus boosting service levels, reducing inventory costs, and removing other types of additional waste in the supply chain (Myerson, 2014).

The Future of the Supply Chain Is Cloudy

We hear a lot about "the cloud" these days. The cloud (public or private) refers to software and services that run on the internet instead of locally on your computer. There is a good chance that most business data will eventually reside in the cloud.

There are three main types of cloud computing:

- Infrastructure as a service (IaaS)
- Platform as a service (PaaS)
- Software as a service (SaaS)

The cloud is the backbone of a "smart" supply chain – referred to as "Supply Chain 4.0" – because it contains the necessary data and interchanges.

To take advantage of all the Supply Chain 4.0 technologies now and in the foreseeable future, the cloud will be integral. Blockchain, the internet of things (IoT), artificial intelligence, and the digital supply chain will all require cloud computing (to be discussed in more detail in the following chapters).

The cloud centralizes data and then offers access to your extended supply chain network, which decreases costs, speeds velocity, scale, and visibility and enhances data security. The cloud also helps companies predict market changes and risks across their supply network.

An added benefit: The cloud enables innovation with affordable access to leading-edge technologies and capabilities.

A recent Accenture survey supports these benefits, finding that executives attribute their cloud use to a 26% increase in demand forecast accuracy, a 16% reduction in supply chain operating costs, and a 5% increase in revenue growth and profitability.

Call for Security

There is one major disadvantage to consider and attempt to minimize: cloud security issues can put your software supply chain at risk.

To reduce security risks, understand your cloud environment by learning what runs where. Consider a hybrid cloud architecture approach where sensitive data is kept on-premises. Also, consider spreading your workloads across different cloud accounts to reduce the impact of any potential breaches.

Finally, stay on top of cloud security issues by following the news and your cloud provider's security blog.

While traditional on-premises enterprise software or legacy solutions – either custom-built or packaged software – provide a powerful solution with robust features, they are difficult and expensive to acquire, install, and maintain and don't always keep pace with business demand. They also often require custom programming.

It's estimated that the global cloud supply chain management market will grow an average of 11% through 2028. The market has been segmented based on solutions, services, deployment models, organization sizes, verticals, and regions.

Many companies already leverage the cloud for supply chain applications including:

Forecasting and planning – They use the cloud to collect and unify information from customers, retailers, wholesalers, and manufacturers.

Logistics – The cloud helps companies provide and share tracking operations, automatic inventory management, and route optimization.

Service and spare parts management – The cloud makes servicing schedules more efficient, which reduces downtime, while RFID and IoT can help track inventory locations quickly.

Procurement – The cloud can serve as a master supplier database and automatically order when inventory reaches a set minimum level. It can also be a platform for contract development and maintenance.

To survive today's volatile global environment with a lean and agile smart supply chain, businesses must start moving to the cloud (Myerson, 2022).

Throughout most of this book, we have concentrated more on technology and systems that help with internal integration and collaboration. In this chapter, we will look more at external integration and collaboration with customers and suppliers/partners to truly enable a lean and smart global supply chain.

Collaboration for a Smarter, Leaner Supply Chain

In today's global economy with shorter lead times, product life cycles, and volatile demand, it is especially critical that we have timely visibility both downstream and upstream in our supply chain to be flexible and agile.

In general, collaboration enables you and your supply chain partners to:

- Improve forecast accuracy by getting closer to the points of demand and supply.
- Strengthen strategic supply chain relationships and profitability.
- Enhance sales and operations planning (S&OP) to achieve corporate goals.
- Accelerate and manage demand plans, direct material procurement and fulfillment throughout the supply chain.
- Manage supply chain processes on an exception basis.
- Resolve critical supply chain events through automated monitoring and alerts.

Collaboration with customers and suppliers accelerates S&OP, as well as strategic trading partner relationships to manage demand plans, direct material procurement, fulfillment, and financial goals to increase profitability and improve service.

Customer Collaboration

Customer collaboration (usually referring to downstream from manufacturers) involves receiving demand signals and automatically replenishing the customer's inventory based on actual demand. This is seen primarily in consumer products and other industries that have downstream distribution systems that extend to retailers.

This type of integration and collaborative effort enables manufacturers to shift from a "push" system to a demand "pull" supply chain while combining both forecasts and actual customer demand.

Collaborative continuous replenishment processes such as "quick response" and "efficient consumer response" are more responsive than purely forecast-based processes and they are driven largely by actual customer demand and provide visibility in out-of-stock situations so that manufacturers and retailers can react more quickly. Point-of-sale (POS) information can add visibility across the entire supply chain as well when included in a collaborative replenishment process.

Another type of customer collaboration which focuses on forecasts is known as collaborative planning, forecasting, and replenishment (or "CPFR", which is a trademark of the Voluntary Inter-Industry Commerce Standard Association or VICS). It is an outgrowth from some of the earlier customer replenishment initiatives such as QR and ECR.

In general, CPFR is an attempt to reduce supply chain costs by promoting greater integration, visibility, and cooperation between trading partners' supply chains. It combines the intelligence of multiple trading partners in the planning and fulfillment of customer demand.

Figure 13.1 shows collaborative or VMI configurations in terms of the level of sophistication or complexity. Levels 1 and 2 have been implemented in various industries and would include programs such as QR and ECR. Levels 3 and 4 are more advanced and would include CPFR-like programs.

Supplier Collaboration

Some of the types of supplier collaboration (usually referring to upstream replenishment for manufacturers) include:

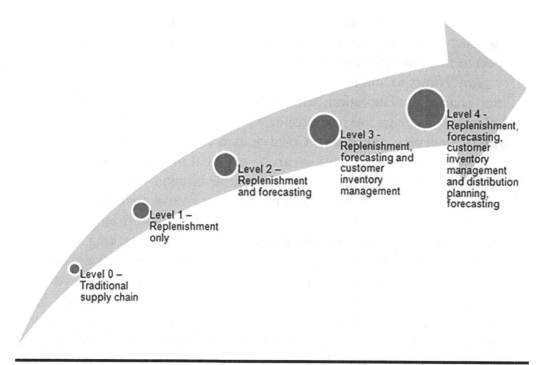

Figure 13.1 Types of collaborative or vendor managed inventory in supply chains.

Kanban – A signal-based replenishment process used in lean or just-in-time (JIT) production that uses cards or other visual signals such as a line on a wall to signal the need for replenishment of an item.

Using collaborative technologies, the kanban process allows customers to electronically issue the kanban replenishment signals to their suppliers who can then determine requirements and see exceptions.

Dynamic replenishment – This is a process where suppliers compare customer forecasts or production schedules with their own production plans to match supply and demand. It allows suppliers to adjust to changes in customer requirements or supply shortages.

Invoicing processes – Automating invoicing and related processes gives visibility to the vendor for the entire supply side including purchase orders, releases, supplier managed inventory, kanbans, and dynamic replenishment.

Outsourced manufacturer collaboration – When managing outsourced manufacturing relationships or contract manufacturers, you must shift your focus from owning and organizing assets to working collaboratively with partners.

The collaborative efforts should help simplify processes such as product development, reduce manufacturing costs, and improve reaction to response to customer demand.

Any efforts to automate these processes should support information sharing, collaboration, and monitoring activities that are needed to effectively manage the relationship with a contract manufacturer.

Logistics service partners – Collaboration can increase the effectiveness of any partnership, but it can be essential in maintaining an effective distribution network. Outsourced transportation, warehouse, and third-party logistics companies have become an essential part of many firms' supply chains. This involves sharing information from an assortment of transactional functions including contracting, tracking, tracking, billing, auditing freight bills, etc. and, more strategically, sharing and collaboration to support the planning and execution side for improved customer service, flexibility, agility, and cost reduction. Technology has increased the ease with which companies can monitor the supply chain. However, increased focus on social platforms can improve the communication between businesses and their logistics partners, making distribution networks faster and more responsive. This will be looked at in more detail in chapter 15.

Integrated and Collaborative Technology for a Lean Smarter Supply Chain

Many of the systems discussed throughout this book such as ERP, forecasting, and DRP systems, while traditionally viewed as internal integration and collaboration tools, in many cases can also help with external supply chain integration and collaboration.

An example of this is the use of a combination of EDI/internet, forecasting, and DRP software in an ECR program for a manufacturer that also imports customer data such as POS at the retail level and on-hand inventory, shipments, and open purchase orders at the retailers' distribution center locations. All of this helps to ensure that the company's products are always available at the retail locations.

Some technologies such as EDI can be used with an unlimited number of partners as they are more transaction based and automated, whereas others, such as forecasting and inventory planning, require a more strategic and selective approach as they require more of a commitment of resources (i.e., the 80/20 rule mentioned at the beginning of the chapter).

Collaborative software helps bring previously disconnected entities onto the same page, especially with the increasing use of cloud computing. Vendors are developing solutions that help optimize logistics and procurement, enable the exchange of data, and encourage collaboration among business partners. This has enabled many global manufacturers, distributors, suppliers, and retailers to be on the same page, in real-time, and at any given time.

In fact, research by the University of Tennessee's (UT) Global Supply Chain Institute (www.sdcexec.com, 2016) found that

> organizations today are investing in business-to-business electronic integration (B2Bi) to cut costs and increase business flow efficiency. Of those surveyed, 94% saw significant improvement in their electronic connectivity capabilities and 68% reported that their clients said they were easier to do business with after using cloud-based B2Bi managed services.
>
> Another major finding suggests that the opportunities for streamlining processes are richer than the resources to achieve it, as increased pressures on internal IT departments to meet core business objectives can lead to potential gaps in knowledge and technology.
>
> Ninety-six percent of those surveyed said they are linked electronically in some way with at least one of their trading partners, yet the average organization spends just over 5% of its IT budget on electronic connections. Electronic connections are expected to increase more than 20% over the next three years and 69% of those surveyed said that they intend to increase the number of customers they trade with electronically.
>
> The study presents several examples of successful collaborations that achieved impressive results. For instance, an office supplies retailer surveyed for the study invested time and technology to collaborate more effectively with a major supplier, and as a result, in-stock fill rates rose significantly to nearly 99% from below 95%. Lead times were reduced by nearly 60%. Forecast accuracy improved by more than 30% and inventory turnover increased 9%.

The Increased Importance of Collaboration and Visibility (and Technology) to the Omni Channel Retail Supply Chain

The emergence of omni channel retail, the integration of all physical channels (offline) and digital channels (online) to offer a unified customer experience, has put a great deal of focus and investment on engaging consumers, which has changed consumer expectations for delivery and service.

As omni channel retail continues to grow and evolve, we are seeing a broadening in focus to include the back-end supply chain to enable and support those new expectations. The supply chain is at the very heart of profitability and service.

The key to enabling omni channel retail is a supply chain that provides complete visibility into all inventory and investments, including goods that are found across all channels, in transit, or at consolidation points.

Retailers need to be lean and agile enough to identify all goods throughout the entire supply chain that are available to expedite, reroute, or allocate to consumers while simultaneously understanding the cost and value of these decisions. This affects their processes, systems, and organizational structure.

However, in many ways, accomplishing this task profitably is easier said than done.

Omni Channel Growth Will Dilute Margins Unless the Supply Chain Changes

Omni channel can be a drag on profits according to an EY survey (2015), where only 38% said their omni channel initiatives enhanced profits, while the rest said it either reduced profits or at best was neutral.

Therefore, where omni channel drives growth but isn't profitable, margins are reduced, so it is critical that companies transform their operating models to make omni channel effective for both the consumer and financial performance.

There are many reasons why companies have a hard time making omni channel profitable. The pace of change and urgency to sell products online has resulted in some bad decisions such as accepting poor terms, high transportation costs, little or no visibility of how products are sold, and limited collaboration between manufacturers and retailers.

Additionally, to develop e-commerce capabilities, many companies have bolted on systems and processes without considering integration with traditional store fulfillment resulting in inefficient supply chains with a lack of visibility across different channels.

Integrating IT and Supply Chain for Seamless Fulfillment

Better integration between information technology (IT) and the supply chain is critical for omni channel success. However, according to a survey by EY (2015), only 26% of companies felt that they had effective IT systems and capabilities to enable seamless visibility and fulfillment to end consumers.

Even though lead times are constantly shortening, consumers expect the same level of inventory and service no matter the channel. So, companies must put in place an IT infrastructure that enables cross channel visibility and the free flow of information across functional boundaries. Information silos still exist today and must be eliminated for cross functional visibility and collaboration between product development, demand planning, logistics, and marketing.

It's hard to be agile if your ordering systems, for example, don't allow it. You need IT systems that support areas such as real-time predictive analytics, stock counting, and ordering and you need the technology to make that happen.

Reducing Fulfillment Costs

One key area to focus on in the omni channel world are delivery costs.

Amazon and other e-tailers and omni channel retailers have struggled to adjust to this new world. Amazon is experimenting with drones, a private fleet of planes and food delivery trucks, as well as Amazon Logistics, where independents sign up to buy their own vans and deliver Amazon products.

As a result of focusing on these costs, Amazon is reducing per-package and per-order transportation expenses every quarter of every year.

It has been estimated that up to 18 cents out of every dollar generated online goes to fulfillment costs (shipping and handling), driving e-commerce and omni channel retailers alike to reduce fulfillment costs in a variety of ways.

Non-Amazon omni channel retailers who can't buy their own fleet of planes or vans have had to turn to other options, such as minimum order sizes for free shipping, curbside/in-store/locker pickups, and even having employees drop off orders on their way home.

Walmart, for example, charges $5.99 for shipping and handling on orders of less than $35. Because shipping alone averages $2.99–$3.99, that is about the minimum a retailer can charge and break even. This charge varies based on each order's size, weight, and distance.

Last-mile delivery is a critical part of an organization's transportation network, as it can make up 28% of a shipment's total cost. Ways to reduce last-mile delivery costs include offering a range of shipping options, dropping off packages at access points such as lockers, limiting distance, and changing/optimizing box sizes.

Before delivering orders, you must process them. Fulfillment, which technically includes delivery, as well as receiving and processing of orders, is another area of focus.

Twenty-five years ago, it took 5 days to process an order for shipment from a warehouse. Today, orders typically are processed and shipped within 24 hours, sometimes on the same day.

To gain a competitive advantage in fulfillment, consider and understand your true fulfillment costs per order, necessary metrics and benchmarks (costs, productivity, service), picking and slotting efficiency, employee turnover, management experience and level of training/education, use of technology, outsourcing, facility size, location, and functionality (i.e., e-commerce only or a blend with retail replenishment).

In the long term, the e-commerce and omni channel retail winners will be those who master fulfillment and last-mile operations and costs (Myerson, 2021).

Differences between Omni Channel and Omni Channel 2.0

As opposed to the original definition of omni channel, "omni channel 2.0" is about bringing the entire enterprise together, not just enabling support within legacy systems for an omni channel approach. Retailers and supply chain leaders need to increase integration and visibility across all channels, engaging with consumers and personalizing the shopping experience. In omni channel 2.0, you know who the customer is throughout the process, you know what the customer is looking for, and what the next best action is for the customer.

What Is Omni Channel 2.0, and How Is It Different from the Original Omni Channel?

Traditional omni channel, also known as "original omni channel", is the combining of supply chain channels allowing customers to shop from any channel seamlessly.

This required supply chains to integrate storefronts, distribution centers, and online ordering processes into an overarching platform which hasn't always occurred, as disruptions in the customer experience continued to exist.

Instead of an overarching, flexible platform, many retailers have continued to use legacy systems through custom interfaces that lead to inefficiencies and integration problems.

Omni channel 2.0 refers to retailers and supply chain leaders increasing their proficiency across all channels (not just being "present"), engaging with consumers and personalizing the shopping experience enabling them to eliminate barriers to new technology implementation, offering better customer service, and being ready for the next innovation.

In summary, the goal of omni channel 2.0 is to break down silos and bring the entire enterprise together (i.e., people, process, and technology) through a more open platform approach, not just enabling support within legacy systems for an omni channel approach.

Benefits of Omni Channel 2.0

Omni channel 2.0 has many benefits for consumers and retailers, including flexible fulfillment options across multiple channels, end-to-end visibility, improved inventory management, fewer occurrences of overstocking and understocking, and improved IT processes and integration between systems.

How to Move toward Omni Channel 2.0

Retailers and warehouses must work to satisfy more and more customers, stay competitive, and create a unique customer experience.

If companies don't embrace omni channel 2.0, they risk losing any chance for a sustained competitive advantage with higher overhead and employee turnover rates.

Some ways to fully utilize omni channel 2.0 in retail include:

Integrate and increase vendor base – Supply chain executives should begin the process by integrating existing systems and expanding their vendor base, allowing companies to exploit the value of newer, more adaptable, and flexible supply chain systems.

Break omni channel 2.0 implementation into steps – As rapid change across an entire enterprise can lead to disruptions, rather than applying all omni channel 2.0 processes at once, supply chain leaders should focus on incremental changes.

Develop and maintain a customer-centric strategy – Customer-centricity is a foundation of omni channel 2.0. Using a high-cost model of trying to meet omni channel standards with legacy systems is a recipe for failure in the long run. As stated earlier, not many retailers can fulfill omni channel demand profitably, so investments into omni channel should focus on improving profitability and meeting growing customer demands.

Engage with customers to obtain feedback – Customer expectations, especially through feedback, will continue to evolve as retailers offer new, exciting services as part of the omni channel 2.0 development trend. This can allow a retailer to differentiate themselves by interacting with customers to find out what they can do better to provide a better customer experience.

Take Advantage of Omni Channel 2.0

Omni channel 2.0 is not just a "prediction"; it is the recipe for a sustained competitive advantage as retailers and their supply chains need to continuously improve as customers today want their products now, from any ordering portal, with the ability to pick up online orders from in-store locations, have another piece shipped to their home, while still having the option of getting notifications on their phones when they enter a store about items on sale.

This requires integrated comprehensive systems with increased flexibility and productivity with limited resources (Rosing, 2019).

As collaboration is a process relying more on systems integration than the various functional software that has been discussed here previously, let's look at some cases where it can specifically enhance a business's productivity and bottom line by finding creative ways to connect partners in a global supply chain.

Heading in the Right Direction

Retailers are investing a lot of money into new technology to gain visibility, manage data, and collaborate with their global trading partners.

One option available is to use a cloud-based system, where retailers can provide customers and themselves with a view into all inventory, no matter which channel is being used. An advantage of an integrated cloud system is that they can automatically allocate from a single pool of inventory when an order is made, regardless of where the customer is viewing the product.

Other goals offering potential competitive advantages of having an integrated omni channel platform (installed or cloud-based) are to:

- Gain visibility across the extended supply chain at the most granular level possible.
- Combine data from partners (ERP, factory, forwarder, carrier, bank).
- Gain inventory visibility and availability of item/SKU from production to consumer.
- Accurately promise delivery dates and respond to changing customer demand.

An omni channel platform solution should also be able to help you:

1. Collaborate with your supply chain partners to find in-transit inventory status.
2. Adjust volumes and dynamically allocate based on changing customer demand.
3. Adjust manufacturing to produce and deploy (or not) SKUs that are overselling or underselling.

Value Proposition

By viewing all inventory in one integrated platform, retailers can greatly improve customer service (Figure 13.2).

To recap, the benefits from improved omni channel visibility can help omni channel companies to:

1. Obtain higher fill rates and reduce stockouts by using accurate item-level details to locate items and create dynamic ETAs from shipment notifications and milestones and count in-transit inventory as on-hand for any channel.

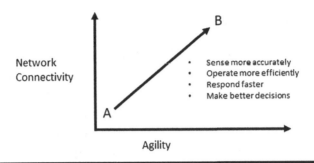

Figure 13.2   Omni channel and the networked company.

2. Reduce markdowns and the need for buffer inventory to increase margins by allocating to demand and lowering inventory costs.
3. Increase service levels and customer satisfaction by having your products in stock at the right place and right time.

In summary, to improve omni channel visibility, companies must transform themselves from silo-based, inward-facing corporate operators to interconnected, lean, and agile supply chain network collaborators (GTNEXUS, 2017).

Some cases follow showing how technology can assist in the collaboration process.

Supply Chain Collaboration Technology Examples

Case #1 – Agilent Technologies: Comprehensive Supply Chain Visibility Across a Multi-Enterprise Supply Chain

Challenge

Agilent is a test and measurement company that offers a broad range of innovative measurement solutions in the electronic test, life science, and chemical analysis markets.

Their products are high mix in a low volume environment, which creates a lot of variability in their plans. Products are typically configure-to-order along with many other options.

Outsourcing of manufacturing operations is also a key strategy for Agilent. This means they must make their way through demand and market volatility, while at the same time coordinating a virtual supply chain network made up of multiple suppliers and contract manufacturing (CM) partners. Therefore, Agilent requires visibility from the CM on everything from demand and supply to commit plans and delivery status.

Overall, Agilent requires accurate, synchronized, and timely information with a common view of themselves and all their supply chain customers, suppliers, and partners.

Approach

Agilent's existing requirement generation process took several weeks depending on how complex the relationship is. When there was a change, it had to flow through the same process which also took several weeks before the lowest level of the supply chain received it. So, by the time they responded, things had changed again.

Agilent's challenge was: how do you flow information down fast enough so that everyone can respond to the appropriate signal quickly?

To meet their challenges, in late 2010, Agilent began a supply chain improvement program where they created a vertically integrated planning process that would consolidate all its different MRP systems and those of its CMs, to create a single plan (via bill of material integration) with minimal data lag.

Agilent selected RapidResponse from Kinaxis as their platform to merge all their information systems and to provide the supporting capabilities to create and manage a single vertical supply chain.

Results

RapidResponse created a vertically integrated plan extending from top-level demand, exploded through the BOM and through all the sourcing. This allows them to see demand going through to the CM (and back through Agilent for inter-sourcing arrangements).

Agilent now has one common view where they can trace and facilitate information flow from top to bottom of the multi-enterprise supply chain all from within one system.

They now have:

- Integrated information with minimal delay, which has improved information flow and decision-making times.
- Complete information, fast and deep simulation capabilities, and a better understanding of all the interdependencies enabling better decision-making.

- More timely and accurate answers to provide to customers.
- Increased business opportunities while minimizing risks.
- Actions are now more aligned with corporate targets.

For example, Agilent was able to reduce their new order assessment and commitment process from 3 to 14 days with manually reconciled information to a day or two. They can now immediately assess the order and get it back to the customer with a commit date and production plan within 1–2 days (www.kinaxis.com, 2014).

Case #2 – Arrow Electronics Automates Replenishment Program with One Network's Real-Time Value Network

Challenge

Arrow Electronics is a $23 billion company that specializes in distribution and value-added services relating to electronic components and computer products.

Over the years, they have utilized their customer automated replenishment system (CARES) to monitor the inventory of components at customer sites. CARES was running on computers in each customer's manufacturing plant. Furthermore, the legacy CARES system didn't provide all the functions required by Arrow.

Their customers use CARES in connection with either a kanban or min/max replenishment policy where inventory falling below a minimum level triggers replenishment to the maximum level. It also no longer made sense to ask their customers to load the software on their own computers.

Arrow had considered building a new system in-house since they wanted to convert customers to a system where they could access over the internet so they could become more demand driven. They ultimately decided that they could reach their goals faster and cheaper if they used an external vendor.

Approach

Arrow selected One Network Enterprise's real-time value network. One Network has thousands of business partners and clients can build their own modules, use their existing legacy systems, or extend One's network to integrate to almost anything (e.g., SAP, Oracle, etc.) and unlock their legacy systems for collaboration with other organizations.

Most importantly, they chose One Network because of their focus on building networks to manage replenishment and other supply chain functions. They had created several electronic communities that successfully automated transactions and allowed collaboration among trading partners.

Results

Agilent went live with One Network in three months. It now gives all of their supply chain partners access to important information, such as inventory levels and actual demand at any time via the internet. Orders are automatically fed into Arrow's system upon receipt.

The system supports new functionality such as the ability to accommodate multiple manufacturing locations and multiple manufacturing cells within one location.

They have also gained more visibility into their supply chain to anticipate problems rather than waiting until a customer needs a part and then finding out they don't have it.

In the future with this network, Arrow will be able to see when customers sell end products that contain Arrow's components and gain visibility into how those components move and are stocked through manufacturing and logistics processes.

Arrow's network now accommodates hundreds of companies and about 60 original equipment manufacturers (OEM) and suppliers that serve those OEMs.

The more suppliers on One Network, the more value it has to the OEMs since all their suppliers are already on the network (www.onenetwork.com, 2011).

While the various technologies we have described throughout this book can be used to improve the efficiency and agility of a business's global supply chain network, it is evolving rapidly.

In our next chapter, we will discuss where and how emerging technologies such as the IoT and real-time visibility can work hand in hand with ever-changing processes driven in part by the continued growth of the internet, omni channel marketing (including e-commerce), and social media to achieve even greater process improvements.

Chapter 14

The Internet of Things (IoT) and Real-Time Visibility

In some ways, the supply chain of today is a living, breathing organism. It's not just links and nodes on a map, but a blend of digital and/or analog data, machines, and, yes, real people who are constantly moving and adapting.

The supply chain constantly changes and moves in an interconnected way, responding to external and internal influences.

The pandemic is the most recent of many external examples. As we saw during and after the pandemic, supply chains can become unhealthy and shut down completely when core processes fail, while minor damage can be addressed and minimized when treated quickly.

At the same time, old legacy systems are rapidly becoming obsolete as they are too slow to adapt. They can't support complex supply chains that change with increasing speed.

Moving to Real Time

In the past, it was sufficient (and to be honest, we only had the capabilities) to update information in batches, sometimes overnight only. As time went on and technologies advanced, we were able to move some processes to real time where it made sense. Digitalization has made supply chains faster, more flexible, more accurate, and more efficient.

 DOI: 10.4324/9781003372639-18

Today, thanks to how quickly technology is being developed, we have tools that allow organizations access to real-time visibility of delivery activities. We can access relevant information on one platform throughout the day, keeping all stakeholders current.

Examples of these tools include SAP HANA and Amazon Web Services. These platforms in the cloud offer supply chain resiliency and visibility, often in real time with a unified view.

They use tools such as advanced artificial intelligence (AI) and machine learning algorithms to identify dependencies, correlations, and current trends, as well as to suggest improvements and compute risks to mitigate and limit the impact of most supply chain disruptions.

Real-time visibility uses technology to track detailed information as raw materials and finished goods move through all stages of the supply chain. It allows you to know what is happening, so you can fix the problem by understanding the situation and finding the best solution, sometimes reducing or minimizing costs.

In the supply chain, real-time visibility refers to logistics activities that track and trace, in real time, the movement of goods and packages from suppliers, manufacturers, warehouses, and hubs to the end customer.

A lack of real-time visibility into your supply chain can result in negative consequences such as lost sales, inaccurate measurements, delayed deliveries, and increased costs.

On the flip side, if you do invest in real-time visibility, you can benefit from a general decrease in the dreaded bullwhip effect, where, through lack of visibility, small fluctuations in demand at the retail level can cause progressively larger fluctuations in demand at the wholesale, distributor, manufacturer, and raw material supplier levels.

Other benefits include better cost effectiveness, greater customer satisfaction, and lower supply chain risks.

It's time for all of us to finally "get real" time (Myerson, 2023).

The Internet of Things to Come

The "internet of things" (IoT) allows users to collect and make data visible at key points, improving customer satisfaction and optimizing supply chain responsiveness. It can also offer greater differentiation and innovation, leading to a competitive advantage.

IoT is widely discussed, but what does it refer to and how does it relate to the lean supply chain? Simply put, IoT is the interconnection – via the internet – of computing devices embedded in everyday objects, enabling them to send and receive data. By 2020, there were more than 26 billion of these connected devices, according to Gartner.

Searching for Increased Visibility

There are a variety of applications for IoT in the supply chain to help gain better visibility and control including:

- Sensors
- Communication devices
- Servers
- Analytics engines
- Decision-making aids

The areas of focus with the most potential in the supply chain are visibility, replenishment, and maintenance. Specific examples include the following:

Asset tracking – RFID and GPS (a satellite-based radio navigation system) sensors can track products in manufacturing, distribution, and retail facilities.

Supplier relationships – IoT enables better communication with vendors, which helps improve quality and performance.

Inventory accuracy and replenishment forecasting – Using IoT, you can substitute (and communicate) more timely and accurate information for the excess inventory you hold just in case. It also allows more automated timely replenishment through machine-to-machine communications.

Fleet management and maintenance – Applying IoT to planning, routing, and tracking containers and vehicles gets products to the customer faster. Installing sensors on plant and warehouse equipment and on vehicles improves performance and scheduled maintenance.

The supply chain has many moving and somewhat disconnected parts. Therefore, the successful application of IoT in your supply chain may not be as simple as it might sound. Improvements in sensors, communications, and cloud computing have made IoT adoption more realistic in recent years.

Facilitating and Enabling a Lean, Smart Supply Chain

To link the physical and digital in a more universal way requires the further development of standards, common architectures, and interfaces to integrate the information into current systems.

Of course, as always, technology can only enable a lean supply chain. So, it is important to first make sure that your existing supply chain is integrated and efficient internally, and at least to some degree externally.

Then you need to develop a strategy for where and how to leverage specific IoT technology – and how you will analyze all that data – as all companies are dealing with limited resources.

By starting down the IoT road now you will have a better chance of giving your company a competitive advantage in the long term (Myerson, 2018).

Supply Chain Visibility

Tools such as the IoT enable supply chain visibility (SCV), which is the knowledge and understanding of operations throughout an entire supply chain (including all stages and operational processes). This allows companies to better manage the flow of products and components through each step of the supply chain.

SCV helps ensure suppliers meet all necessary regulations and reduce risks and disruptions within your supply chain and it also can help increase customer satisfaction, productivity, and profits.

"Real-time" SCV is one of three common types of SCV, along with "multi-tier" (this refers to attaining visibility into each level of a supply chain from the most proximate level all the way to tier 3+ suppliers) and "end-to-end".

Real-time SCV refers specifically to attaining live information, or data, on what is happening in your supply chain.

What Is Meant by "Real-Time" Supply Chain Visibility?

Real-time SCV refers to current knowledge and understanding of what is happening at this exact moment in your supply chain. It most commonly shows you the tracking of products between each stage of production, the technical status of machines, and the location of goods traveling from manufacturers to end consumers.

Gathering real-time information on your supply chain enables managers to react quickly to disruptions and better predict problems in the future, leading to a reduction in costs, fewer disruptions, and a competitive advantage.

Benefits of Real-Time Supply Chain Visibility

Today, it is estimated that only 30% of companies frequently use real-time data. However, real-time SCV is becoming increasingly popular. Companies having real-time SCV benefit from the enhanced predictive abilities, reactivity, and agility that real-time information provides (Figure 14.1). Real-time data allows you to adjust to market trends or potential disruptions faster than competitors as documented below, providing a major competitive advantage to companies that utilize a strong real-time data strategy.

Reduced Disruptions

Real-time SCV helps you detect potential issues faster. Live information gives your organization faster response times and better information for decision-making, which helps you mitigate risk across the extended supply chain.

For example, one of the most common applications of real-time SCV is production and shipment tracking in real time. This can help to avoid late deliveries that can cause disruptions throughout the supply chain and/or result in customer complaints.

Figure 14.1   **Benefits of real-time supply chain visibility.**

Reduced Costs

Understanding current developments in the supply chain allows you to make decisions based on real-time information, rather than predictions, helping you to reduce waste and increase efficiency.

More specifically, real-time SCV helps you reduce costs associated with:

Wasted time – Reduce equipment and employee downtime by having a more accurate schedule.

Inventory levels – Make more accurate predictions on when and where inventory is needed, and how much inventory should be stored to meet customer demand.

Transportation – Create more efficient routes and avoid obstacles.

Inaccurate amounts of raw materials – Source specific materials as they are needed "just-in-time", not "just-in-case".

Unexpected market disruptions – Anticipate and avoid disruptions caused by events such as geopolitical unrest, natural disasters, or pandemics.

One example of how real-time SCV can reduce various costs is where it can provide early warning of variables that impact transportation, such as traffic or weather. Companies can use this information to re-evaluate their shipping route, which can save fuel, avoid damaged goods, and avoid wasting employee time taking reroutes or waiting for late deliveries.

Improved Product Quality

Real-time SCV is a crucial aspect of quality control monitoring and allows you to detect and solve quality issues faster using real-time data to improve product quality.

Customer Satisfaction

As we shift to a more "on-demand economy", customer expectations around delivery time and product quality continue to increase. Real-time tracking of all supply chain operations helps you to meet these expectations to ensure that customers have a great experience with your products.

Regulatory Compliance

Real-time SCV helps ensure compliance with regulatory requirements throughout the supply chain, such as import and export requirements, environmental regulations, and requirements for worker safety. Knowing how and when things are happening allows you to fix potential compliance issues before they cause disruptions, recalls, or even legal actions. Real-time SCV also enables you to track changes in regulatory requirements and adapt your supply chain in a timely manner.

How to Increase Real-Time Supply Chain Visibility

Increasing real-time SCV can be challenging, but the benefits it provides make the effort required worth it. What follows is a methodology to follow to increase real-time visibility in your supply chain (Figure 14.2).

Map Your Supply Chain

Start by creating a map of each supplier and process in your supply chain to identify gaps in information and challenges/issues in your supply chain.

A detailed "current state" map allows you to understand how information is currently being gathered, and where more visibility and timeliness are needed. This will help you to identify areas for improvement to create a "future state" map to plan, implement, and measure progress in the future.

Leverage Technology

Leading businesses today are relying more and more on digital technologies to increase visibility and enhance agility and resilience in their supply chain. Technology has many benefits, from turning large amounts of data into useful insights to automating processes within manufacturing and the supply chain.

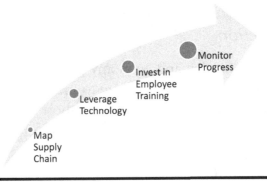

Figure 14.2 How to increase real-time supply chain visibility.

Supply chain technologies that increase real-time visibility include:

- Collaborative dashboards are used to analyze, monitor, and standardize reporting on a single platform and to share information across the supply chain.
- AI is used to create accurate plans and models, anticipate risk, and interpret data.
- Process automation, which can automate supply chain processes.
- IoT is used to monitor and exchange many types of data, ranging from shipment status to storage conditions.
- Cloud computing is used to store, manage, and process data securely.

All these technologies described above also help you make faster, more informed decisions that rely on accurate, thoroughly analyzed data.

Invest in Employee and Factory Worker Training

Technology and process improvement alone are not sufficient to truly maximize the benefits of real-time SCV. It is also very important to provide in-depth training for your employees on how to make the most of new technologies, improved processes, and increased information. Businesses that ensure communication and collaboration throughout the supply chain increase their productivity and resiliency, and ultimately, increase profits.

Monitor Progress

Increasing real-time SCV is an ongoing process with opportunities for continuous improvement. To ensure that progress toward your goals is accomplished, it must be monitored carefully, using specific metrics to measure growth.

Key Takeaways

Real-time SCV provides supply chain managers with live insight into what is happening at each stage of the supply chain and improves your ability to react quickly to disruptions or defects and fix the issue before it becomes a major problem. This leads to fewer disruptions, increased product quality and customer satisfaction, reduced costs, and regulatory compliance throughout the supply chain.

While real-time data isn't always a necessity, it is useful in many cases in the supply chain, such as inventory tracking to ensure efficient delivery (QIMAone, 2023).

The View from the Control Tower

Real-time SCV is a great help when an organization uses a relatively high-level strategic tool known as "integrated business planning" (IBP), which is a process that uses "outside-in" thinking by integrating demand forecasts, supply plans, inventory projections, and financial plans into one medium-term strategic model.

But the leading-edge way to manage your short- to mid-term global supply chain in real time (or close to it) is through a control tower that utilizes technology, organization, and processes that capture product movement visibility (especially real time) from the supplier all the way to the customer.

The control tower creates an overview of total supply chain performance using key performance indicator (KPI) dashboards. It resolves problems with management functions to deliver visibility and provide capabilities such as collaboration with trading partners and functionality enabling supply chain planners to automate processes and controls.

Types of Control Towers

Currently, software vendors offer two general types of operational control tower systems:

1. Transportation control towers are mainly focused on inbound and outbound transportation. They are usually offered as a module in a transportation management system (TMS).
2. Supply chain control towers typically focus on the multi-enterprise supply chain, ensuring visibility and control across internal as well as external supply chain processes and milestones. These control towers enable end-to-end visibility and control across your entire supply chain network and include real-time collaboration with suppliers and partners.

Moving Beyond Decision Support

Until recently, supply chain control towers have been largely about providing visibility to your immediate trading partners. But with the development of multi-party, consumer-driven networks, advanced control towers now provide real-time visibility, collaboration, analytics, and AI capabilities to move beyond decision support to decision-making and autonomous control.

Leading technology vendors allow users to set parameters to supply chain elements such as inventory levels and replenishment plans, and then leave the tool to adjust when issues arise.

Additionally, vendors are providing capabilities that help enterprises work with multiple tiers of trading partners, manufacturers, transportation and logistics providers, and customers to better coordinate their operations. If designed and managed properly, a supply chain control tower can increase inventory turns and significantly reduce safety stocks, stockouts, and expediting costs.

Supporting a Lean and Smart Supply Chain

A lean philosophy and culture are compatible with a control tower system. While a control tower helps to plan and control a more reliable supply chain, a lean philosophy helps achieve that goal. The end-to-end SCV and transparency a control tower provides, combined with a lean culture of continuous improvement, can produce coordinated, sustainable execution processes allowing companies to successfully manage the complexities of today's supply chains and gain a competitive advantage.

It's one thing to envision having a lean and agile supply chain, but another thing to see one in action, which is very "smart". Like sales and operations planning and IBP, control towers can be a critical component in achieving the goal of a lean, agile, and smart supply chain (Myerson, 2019).

Once integration exists in your extended supply chain, businesses need to take advantage of this plethora of information through supply chain decision support systems and analytics tools that are available today, which is the topic of our next chapter.

SUPPLY CHAIN ANALYTICS, DECISION SUPPORT SYSTEMS, AND OTHER LEADING-EDGE TECHNOLOGIES

V

Chapter 15

Decision Support Systems and Supply Chain Analytics

Decision support systems (DSS) are interactive software-based systems intended to help managers in decision-making by accessing large volumes of information generated from various related information systems involved in organizational business processes, such as office automation system, transaction processing system, etc.

A decision support system provides data, analysis, and insights to businesses, to help direct their decision-making process. In general, DSS integrate information from various sources, apply analytics and modeling techniques, and present the data in a user-friendly way.

Most DSS platforms include features such as data visualization, advanced analytics, and collaboration capabilities, which allow organizations to get a deeper look at the data, identify patterns, and gain actionable insights. By adding automated analysis and utilizing technologies such as AI and machine learning (covered more in the next chapter), decision support systems provide decision-makers with current information necessary to support their strategic, tactical, and operational decisions.

Within the supply chain, DSS can be used to optimize operations by analyzing data on demand, inventory, and other factors. By analyzing this data, manufacturers can make more informed decisions about production schedules, inventory levels, and other supply chain operations.

DOI: 10.4324/9781003372639-20

For example, a DSS will show real-time updates regarding delays, weather, and traffic activity. This information allows organizations to adjust their delivery schedules or change routes to avoid unnecessary delays.

In the end, the primary goal of a decision support system is to provide actionable insights that aid management to make better decisions for their business and as a result DSS can ensure that the lean supply chain that you designed will be run and controlled properly.

Characteristics of a Decision Support System

Regardless of the industry or functional area, a decision support system needs to have the following attributes:

Data integration – The system must integrate data from various internal and external sources to offer a thorough overview of the decision context. It combines structured and unstructured data to support analysis and decision-making.

Analytical capabilities – The DSS takes the data and incorporates advanced analytical techniques, such as statistical analysis, data mining, simulation, and optimization, to extract insights from data. This enables organizations to analyze complex scenarios, assess risks, and evaluate alternative options in real-time.

User-friendly interface – To avoid having a complex user interface, most DSS use data visualization, interactive reports, and graphical representations, so anyone can quickly understand the data and make the right decision quickly.

Flexibility and adaptability – A flexible and adaptable platform allows organizations to customize models, parameters, and reports based on specific requirements and in different decision contexts and, as a result, can adapt to the organization's specific business conditions.

Decision collaboration – Today's DSS platforms need to support collaborative efforts by sharing the data among all relevant stakeholders, internally and externally.

Integration with existing systems – DSS integrate with existing systems and data sources within an organization to leverage data assets and ensure data accuracy and can be implemented into existing workflows via APIs (application programming interface) (Windward, 2024).

Synergy between Supply Chain Data Analytics and DSS

Supply chain (and all) data analytics and DSS complement each other seamlessly. While supply chain analytics is focused on processing and extracting insights from data, DSS takes these insights and translates them into actionable decisions.

Here's how the synergy between the two works:

Data preparation – Data analytics processes like cleansing, integration, and transformation prepare raw data for analysis. DSS relies on this clean and well-organized data to generate meaningful reports and insights.

Insight generation – Data analytics identifies patterns and trends in data. DSS uses these insights to provide decision-makers with a clear understanding of the current situation and potential scenarios.

Decision-making – Decision-makers can use the information provided by DSS to evaluate options, assess risks, and make informed decisions.

Monitoring and feedback – DSS often include monitoring features that track the impact of decisions. This data is then fed back into the analytics process to refine future decision-making.

What Is Data Analytics?

Most companies are collecting lots of data all the time, but in its raw form, this data doesn't really mean anything, which is where data analytics comes in. Data analytics is the process of analyzing raw data to gain meaningful, actionable insights, which can then be utilized to drive smart business decisions.

The full process entails a data analyst extracting raw data, organizing it, and then analyzing it, which transforms it from just numbers into coherent, intelligible information. After interpreting the data, the data analyst can then pass on their findings in the form of suggestions or recommendations about what the company's next steps should be.

Data analytics is really a form of business intelligence, used to solve specific problems and challenges within an organization. It involves finding patterns in a dataset which can tell you something useful and relevant about a particular area of the business, such as how certain customer groups behave, for example, or how employees engage with a particular tool.

Data analytics helps you to make sense of the past and predict future trends and behaviors. Instead of basing your decisions and strategies on a guess, you're making informed choices based on what the data is telling you.

Supply Chain Analytics

As most of us already know, data analytics is a hot topic these days, especially when applied in the supply chain (and supply chain professionals have been using analytical tools for 40+ years in areas such as demand forecasting, supply chain network optimization, etc.).

Supply chain analytics examines raw supply chain data, reaching conclusions or making predictions with the information. Its growth is being pushed by the rise in computing capabilities and big data with huge volumes of data being generated in business organizations including retail, healthcare, manufacturing, and electronics.

As previously mentioned, data analytics is the science of examining raw data to help draw conclusions about information. When applied to the supply chain, it allows companies to drive insight, make better business decisions, and verify or disprove existing models or theories.

Supply Chain Data Analytics Categories

Data analytics breaks out into the following categories:

Descriptive analytics – In the supply chain, descriptive analytics helps companies better understand historical demand patterns, how product flows through the supply chain, and when a shipment might be late.

Diagnostic analytics – Once supply chain problems occur, you need to analyze the source. Often this can involve analyzing data in the systems to see why a company was missing certain components or what went wrong that caused the problem.

Predictive analytics – In the supply chain, predictive analytics could be used to forecast future demand or the price of a product.

Prescriptive analytics – In the supply chain, you might use prescriptive analytics to determine the optimal number and location of distribution centers, set inventory levels, or schedule production.

Cognitive analytics (a potential subset of any of the above) – This helps an organization answer complex questions in natural language in the way a person or team might respond to a question. It helps companies think through a complex problem or issue such as, "How might we improve or optimize x?"

As a result, supply chain analytics are also the foundation for applying cognitive technologies, such as artificial intelligence, to the supply chain process. Cognitive technologies understand, reason, learn, and interact like humans, but at enormous capacity and speed.

Using these categories of analytics can give you a leg up on the competition as traditional measures tend to be based on historical data and not focused on the future. They don't relate to strategic, non-financial performance goals such as customer service and product quality or are directly tied to operational effectiveness and efficiency.

Other useful applications for analytic techniques include:

Evaluating disaster risk – Supply chain disruptions can come in many forms. To evaluate the risk to a supply chain, you can classify events that cause disruptions into two types: super events (disrupting all suppliers simultaneously) and unique events (disrupting only one supplier).

Managing the bullwhip effect – This phenomenon describes the tendency for larger order size fluctuations as orders are relayed up the supply chain (toward suppliers).

Supplier selection analysis – Suppliers are often evaluated on far more than simply the price offered.

Transportation mode analysis – A faster shipping method is usually more expensive but saves pipeline inventory costs. This is the core trade-off in transportation mode analysis. Other important considerations could include on-time as opposed to fast delivery, coordinating shipments to maintain a schedule, and keeping a customer happy.

Warehouse storage – Placement decisions within huge warehouses with dozens of trucking docks and thousands of items can be complicated.

With the power of analytics, companies can fine-tune their supply chains in ways that weren't possible in the past. If your supply chain management models are based only on past demand, supply, and business cycles, you could be missing opportunities to use analytics to achieve a competitive advantage (Myerson, 2019).

Benefits of Supply Chain Analytics

It is now common for companies to use supply chain analysts to collect, manage, and extract insights from their supply chain. Supply chain managers use these insights to make informed decisions about planning, streamlining operations, and risk reduction daily. The three main benefits of utilizing supply chain data are discussed next.

Cost Reduction

Supply chain managers can increase their margins by making their supply chains more efficient by using insights from proper data analytics to help them make decisions about how and when to best utilize resources. It can allow them to see how even minor adjustments can result in large cost savings over time.

Risk Reduction

Accurate, timely data can help catch potential quality, compliance, and supplier issues in their early stages. Supplier performance data, for example, can help a supply chain manager see suppliers that are improving or declining in performance and recognize warnings that may lead to more serious problems. By identifying and fixing these potential issues early, you can prevent a manageable supplier issue from developing into a supply chain crisis.

Increased Effectiveness

Along with reducing cost, a more effective supply chain using a process of collecting and organizing the right data can help a company be more competitive by improving quality, more accurately forecasting consumer demands, and getting the products to market faster than competitors.

What Are the Main Areas to Collect Data?

Supply chain professionals can collect and utilize data throughout each step of their supply chain, giving them the visibility they need to adjust in each area. Some of the biggest data sources are from raw materials suppliers, manufacturing audits and inspections, logistics, inventory, export and import trends, retail sales and returns, and market trends (more on that in the next main section below).

These data sources can provide valuable information about opportunities to streamline processes and reduce risks. However, it is important that the data is collected, stored, and processed in a usable format.

What Type of Data Should Be Collected?

The typical approach to collecting data is getting as much data as possible, then finding a way to utilize it. Supply chain data falls into two categories: structured and unstructured.

Structured data is organized, quantitative information that, with minimal manipulation, can be entered into a spreadsheet or database. This is the type of data most of us are familiar with.

Unstructured data is unorganized, qualitative information that cannot be processed or organized like structured data. This type of data usually comes from text sources like written reports or social media or can be unorganized data from a sensor, for example, a smart tracking or IoT tag on a retail item.

Both forms of data are valuable, but depending on your needs and data processing capabilities, unstructured data may not be applicable. For companies in the early stages of collecting and analyzing supply chain data, harvesting structured data to help improve a specific area of your supply chain is the best place to start (QIMAone, 2023).

Data Sources for Supply Chain Analytics

Now let's take a bit of a "deeper dive" into possible internal and external data sources for supply chain analytics.

Traditionally, business management systems such as enterprise resource planning (ERP) or customer relationship management (CRM) software were the main source of data for making decisions. These days, the variety of data sources used by organizations to make better decisions is growing as was mentioned previously.

Not to mention that use of the cloud enables supply chain managers to automate these and other functions and leverage data analytics from a variety of sources (many in real-time) and locations to make more informed decisions.

Some common data sources are listed below.

Internal Data

Internal data is captured by your organizational processes. It can be transactional data such as inventory, sales, orders, shipments, returns, costs, quality, etc. from ERP, CRM, WMS, and other internal systems.

Your organization might also have machine-generated data from sensors or devices used to manufacture a product or recorded by the product itself (e.g., smartphones or IoT devices).

Finally, you might capture engagement data from your customers or clients. Examples of this include:

- Email marketing metrics (email opens, click-through rates).
- Information in customer profiles.
- Records of customer interactions (email queries, support calls, etc.).
- Online activity (e.g., placing items in an online shopping cart).

You'll typically find this data stored in databases, operational systems (e.g., CRM, ERP), or system log files.

Internal data is essential for supply chain analytics because it helps you monitor and improve your own operations, identify and solve problems, and benchmark your performance against your goals.

Using internal data has advantages such as:

- It's already there (and free!), so you can get started right away, so you might not need to request its use (i.e., no restrictions for use in your organization).
- You can talk to the people who gathered the data.
- It might already be in the right format for you (i.e., same code, software, using the same standards and formats), which can save a lot of time.

External Data

External data can range from historical demographic data to market prices, from weather conditions to social-media trends. Businesses use external data to analyze and model economic, political, social, or environmental factors that influence their business.

External data can be derived from a variety of sources. There are open initiatives (e.g., data.gov), social-media services (e.g., Twitter or LinkedIn), and paid services (e.g., Thompson Reuters and various third-party analytics providers).

Third-Party Analytics Providers

Third-party analytics are useful if you don't have the capacity to capture and process the data.

The use of high-quality third-party data in supply chain analytics means faster assessment of potential supply chain risks and a greater ability to assess challenges in the future.

While internal data analytics have their merits, supplementing these efforts with third-party data analytics from trusted providers can bridge the gap between expectations and outcomes in supply chain operations. The combination of comprehensive data access, specialized expertise, advanced tools, and cost efficiencies positions companies for enhanced competitiveness and sustainable growth in today's dynamic business environment.

Some of the benefits of using third-party supply chain analytics providers include having or developing:

- A wide range of data sources, including industry benchmarks, market trends, and competitor analysis. This breadth of data enables more robust and insightful analytics, leading to better-informed decision-making.
- Specialized expertise in logistics and supply chain analytics, which surpasses the capabilities of in-house teams. With a dedicated focus on analyzing shipping, freight, and logistics data, they can uncover nuanced insights and optimization opportunities that might be overlooked internally.
- Access to advanced analytics tools and technologies specifically tailored for supply chain operations. These tools go beyond basic data reporting, offering predictive analytics, real-time monitoring, and scenario modeling capabilities. Such advanced functionalities empower supply chain executives to proactively address challenges and seize opportunities.

- Robust internal analytics capabilities which can be costly and resource-intensive, especially for smaller or mid-sized companies. However, by leveraging third-party analytics services, organizations can achieve cost efficiencies through shared infrastructure, scalable solutions, and access to cutting-edge technologies without heavy up-front investments.

Open Data

Open data is accessible to everyone and is free to use. However, if it's high-level data, or it's heavily summarized and aggregated, it might not be very relevant to you. It might also not be in the format you need, or it might be very difficult for you to make sense of, which can require a lot of time to make the data usable.

Open data sources include:

- Government data – data.gov (US), data.gov.uk (UK), data.gov.au (AUS)
- Health and scientific data – World Health Organization (WHO), Nature.com scientific data, Open Science Data Cloud (OSCDC), Center for Open Science
- Social media – Google Trends (look at national trends on search terms), Yahoo Finance (great for stock market information), Twitter (allows you to search by tags and users, which can be downloaded by using Twitter APIs).

Accessing Data through APIs

APIs technically aren't a source of data, but they provide a way to share data, where you can take it from one app to another and prepare it for use. APIs can be used for a range of applications, from social (e.g., Twitter, Facebook), to utilities (e.g., Dropbox), and to commerce (e.g., Mailchimp, Slack), to name a few.

Today, data is everywhere, the challenge is to convert it into useful information for decision-making. To do so requires an analyst's intuition and a subject matter expert's input to gather the right data from the right sources to help solve your business analytics challenges (www.futurelearn.com, 2023).

While other technologies for supporting, making, and executing decisions such as AI and robotics have been awhile a long time, it looks like their time has finally come as we will detail in the next chapter.

Chapter 16

Artificial Intelligence (AI), Machine Learning (ML), Blockchain, and Robotics

How Is the Modern Supply Chain Evolving?

Technologies like artificial intelligence (AI), robotics, and blockchain are being incorporated into the digital supply network, combining data and information from various sources to distribute goods and services along the supply chain.

Supply chain infrastructure develops from physical, functional systems to a linked network of assets, data, and activities. For example, by utilizing AI algorithms, businesses may extract insights from large data sets to proactively manage inventory, automate warehouse processes, optimize important sourcing connections, enhance delivery times, and develop unique customer experiences that raise customer satisfaction and increase sales.

Additionally, AI-powered robots help automate various human operated manual tasks, such as order picking and packing processes, delivering raw material and manufactured goods, moving items during storage and distribution, and scanning and boxing items. At Amazon, for example, robotic systems in its fulfillment centers help employees move products more efficiently and safely and can also reduce costs and improve the customer experience.

Furthermore, as blockchain is unchanging in nature, it can be utilized to track and trace the source of products and identify counterfeit items and fraud within the value chain.

DOI: 10.4324/9781003372639-21

For example, if a business is transporting perishables like fish, they must be always maintained a specific temperature. The company transporting the fish can determine whether the temperature has risen beyond the permitted threshold during the journey, enabling them to minimize problems with food quality.

Supply Chain AI: This Time It's for Real

Data analytics and AI are both hot topics these days, especially in supply chain circles.

As discussed in the previous chapter, data analytics is the science of examining raw data to help draw conclusions about information. Predictive analytics uses data to foresee trends and patterns.

AI is a catch-all term for computer software that mimics human cognition to perform complex tasks and learn from them. Machine learning (ML), on the other hand, is a subfield of AI that uses algorithms trained on data to produce adaptable models that can perform a variety of complex tasks.

AI is a continuation of the concepts around predictive analytics, with one major difference: an AI system can make assumptions, and test and learn autonomously. Then it applies ML, deep learning, and other techniques to solve actual problems.

AI technology has been with us for a long time. What has changed recently is the power of computing, cloud-based service options, and the applicability of AI to supply chain and logistics.

AI at Work

In general, AI can be used in two ways. First, it can assist people in their day-to-day tasks, personally or commercially, without having complete control of the output. It can also reduce errors, for example, using a virtual assistant and in data analysis. Second, AI can help automate processes by functioning without the need for any human intervention – for example, robots performing process steps in a fulfillment center.

Using AI to assist people and automate processes helps the top and bottom line because companies waste a lot of time and money on having humans perform basic supply chain tasks.

Companies can significantly improve network, capacity, and demand-planning decisions with AI predictive capabilities using big data. Big data insights, along with AI, can improve supply chain transparency and optimization and can potentially revolutionize the agility and efficiency of supply chain decision-making.

On a more tactical and operational level, companies are using AI in robotics and automated vehicles to track, locate, and move inventory within warehouses. While totally autonomous vehicles might not happen for a while, we already see technology such as assisted braking, lane-assist, and highway autopilot.

Streamlining procurement-related tasks can happen through the automation and augmentation of chatbot capabilities, which require access to robust and intelligent data sets. This can allow for automating actions such as placing purchasing requests, researching and answering internal questions regarding procurement functionalities, or receiving, filing, and documenting invoices and payment/order requests.

Improved Customer Service

AI can also personalize relationships between logistics providers and customers. A logistics provider can now enable a customer to query Amazon's Alexa to track a shipment. If there is a problem with the shipment, Echo users can ask for assistance and be directed to the logistics company's customer assistance department.

Using predictive analytics for supplier selection and supplier relationship management with data generated from supplier assessments, audits, and credit scoring could provide a basis for decisions regarding supplier selection and risk management. The supplier relationship would be more predictive and intelligent.

There is no doubt that the potential of AI and ML will finally be achieved in the supply chain, enabling companies to eliminate waste, in many cases before it even occurs. Now that's real (artificial) intelligence (Myerson, 2020).

Machine Learning

The ML era is upon us, with affordable processing power, in-memory storage, and an abundance of data driving mainstream adoption. One of the most important factors behind this ML revolution may be the business need. In today's supply chain, escalating supply, distribution, sales channels, and demand complexity make it increasingly difficult to plan accurately.

At the same time, industry professionals are grappling with relatively new phenomena that create variability, including fast fashion and other types of hyper-seasonality, shorter product introduction cycles, and the impact of social media. Not to mention extreme weather, stock market fluctuations, and socioeconomic volatility which add to the challenges. ML is of great assistance in alleviating the challenges caused by the abovementioned factors in many key supply chain processes.

Strategies for ML Implementation Success

The following are some ways supply chain professionals can ensure ML drives desired business benefits.

Set clear objectives – The scientific and iterative nature of ML calls for it to be implemented methodically. Create a clear charter of what you want to accomplish and why. This should include establishing baseline metrics so you can track how your ML application is performing.

Gather the necessary data to compare previous results to those enhanced by ML – This is the best way to gain confidence in your initiative. Since ML systems get smarter over time, having a consistent measurement method is essential to tracking return on investment and outcomes. Consider making this a part of your sales and operations planning (S&OP) process.

Embrace probability forecasting – To build a solid foundation for a successful and sustainable initiative, probability forecasting is most compatible with ML because it enables planners to forecast at the most granular level, on different time horizons, and to understand the range of possibilities of demand in the forecast.

This method is ideal for supply chains that face demand variability and uncertainty. Using this approach, you still get one number that's associated with the most probable outcome, but also banded around this number is a range of other possible outcomes, each with a different probability.

Walk before you run – A phased approach helps ensure a sustainable ML solution that meets business objectives today and needs change. It starts with establishing an adaptive, probability-based model for demand forecasting using existing historical data, then layering in more sophisticated ML using external data sources. A reliable demand forecast is critical to success with advanced ML and provides significant benefits on its own.

Below is a typical progression of the phases a company goes through in modeling and applying data:

Phase one involves the organization building a self-adaptive model for probability forecasting, considering trends, seasonality, calendars, and daily sales patterns to create a baseline self-learning model for probability forecasting using historical demand history.

In phase two, the impact of marketing activities such as trade promotions, media events, product introductions, and so on is factored in. This improves the baseline probability forecast by applying ML technology to existing historical data.

In this external demand-sensing step, the business looks for additional correlations by introducing external data sources, such as weather, point-of-sale information, social media, and machine-generated data.

In phase three, specialized business knowledge is introduced from subject matter experts across sales, marketing, and operations (and often emerges through the S&OP process). This is also a good time to introduce external market intelligence into the model.

The described iterative approach is the best way to determine which data is meaningful and to what degree. It also gives you the opportunity to change course based on what you learn along the way, looking for correlations with each step.

During ML implementation, it is critical to remember the four dimensions of data:

1. Data volume – It is essential to have the right amount of data to draw upon, from which the model can derive statistical significance (ML is compatible with big data), and also don't overlook "small data" related to historic demand.
2. Data granularity – ML is perfect for data granularity, examining that noise and using it to find correlations that train the model and make it more powerful.
3. Data quality – While ML can determine if a specific data stream has a correlative significance, it cannot tell whether that data is reliable. So, ML projects should include governance programs to clean, filter, and maintain information quality through the data life cycle.
4. Data variety – The more types of data sources you use, the more robust and accurate the planning outcomes can be.

Additionally, you should operationalize your ML tool as businesses tend to build an ML solution to tackle a one-off business challenge without considering its long-term worth. So, for sustainable business value, you should operationalize your results.

To achieve the stability and adaptability required for operational use, it is important to use models that are self-adaptive and do not require continuous tuning by experts due to changing business environments which can make them unreliable.

This is pretty common with traditional demand planning processes that use multiple forecasting algorithms assigned to each item or location according to the demand behavior. The forecast generated by these algorithms tends to become less accurate as the demand patterns evolve over time.

Discrete selection and tuning of algorithms require human skills that most businesses can't afford, and as a result, there is a tendency to create (or license) "black boxes" that only the developer can understand and support. This can leave users skeptical, and, if the developer or expert user leaves the company, these models can be shelved or discarded altogether.

"One-off" type ML projects also require continual manual work to refresh the model when business needs change, so the better method uses a self-adaptive model as part of a fully integrated solution, with frequent models updated automatically to react to changes.

ML, if implemented properly, can free up planners to do more value-added, strategic work. As your business changes over time, you will need to adjust your existing models so that they remain accurate and usable. One of the many reasons that it's critical to understand the needed skills and resources before kicking off the project.

Human Machine Interactions

ML can only do so much; business knowledge and process expertise are required to fine-tune models and maximize results. The system will get smarter over time as it factors in human input, and humans will get smarter by learning from the success rate of the probability forecasts. This enables employees to focus on service, work on strategic projects, and add their business insights to the system.

Three Real-World Machine Learning Applications

Lennox Industries

Lennox industries, a large heating and cooling systems provider, faced the challenge of managing a North American distribution network enlargement while also moving to a hub-and-spoke model with 55 shipping and 161 selling locations.

Management wanted to both improve service levels and optimize inventories to reallocate working capital and balance inventory in the changing network. However, the supply chain environment was very challenging, with a multi-echelon distribution network about to grow by 250%, 450,000 stock-keeping unit (SKU) locations, many slow movers, and new product introductions.

Lennox implemented a supply chain planning solution to rationalize the inventory mix and design an operational plan that sets inventory stocking targets and balances service levels with inventory cost. ML enabled the business to reliably model highly variable seasonal demand patterns as it sifts through hundreds of thousands of SKU locations to identify clusters of similar seasonality profiles.

This substantially increased forecast accuracy during peak periods. In addition, service levels have improved by 16%, inventory turns have increased by 26%, and Lennox is now able to support significant growth in both sales and market share.

Granarolo

The Italian dairy producer **Granarolo** runs thousands of promotions annually, producing 34,000 item-promotion forecasting combinations and causing demand peaks of up to 30 times baseline sales.

Dairy industry supply chain planning can be extra difficult because products have short shelf lives and demand varies greatly in response to promotions. Its supply chain environment consists of eight production plants, six logistics technology platforms, 35 transit depots holding inventory, a large fleet of refrigerated vehicles, and about 750 merchandisers servicing daily sales with a network of 100 wholesale distributors covering other local markets.

Granarolo uses advanced planning software with ML to optimize the demand plan for perishable products which also identifies exceptions and optimizes inventory and logistics to meet demand and minimize waste. Average forecast reliability has grown from 80% to 85%, peaking at 95% for fresh milk and cream and 88% for yogurt and dessert products. As a result, inventory levels and delivery times have been cut in half, resulting in fresher products and less waste, with Granarolo also having significantly better customer service levels and lower transportation costs.

British Luxury Car Manufacturer

New demands for a British luxury car manufacturer's client base prompted its board to raise targets for first-time availability (FTA) by 2% without increasing inventory. They also wanted to achieve FTA parity across all three of its car categories: heritage (pre-1997), recent production (mid-1990s forward, but no longer in production), and current (today's models).

They used advanced ML to analyze historical data on consumer behavior to better anticipate customer needs. The tool used the company's historical data and found eight completely new categories of behavior, which the software then uses to generate a more accurate forecast. Each day, the ML engine tunes the safety stock for 80,000 SKUs, automatically reducing inventory before creating a replenishment plan to deliver the demanding new target service levels.

After two months, the car manufacturer reduced the inventory value of its safety stock on the clustered items by 18% and raised FTA service levels to 97.1%. The results have continued trending toward further improvements in both service levels and reduced inventory (Kaufholz, 2020).

Building a Transparent Supply Chain with Blockchain

Blockchain, the digital record-keeping technology behind bitcoin and other cryptocurrency networks, also holds great promise in supply chain management. Blockchain can improve supply chains by enabling faster and more cost-efficient delivery of products, enhancing products' traceability, improving coordination between partners, and aiding access to financing.

A blockchain is a decentralized ledger, a digital system for recording transactions among multiple parties in a verifiable, tamperproof way. The ledger itself can also be programmed to trigger transactions automatically. For cryptocurrency networks that are designed to replace existing currencies, the main function of blockchain is to enable an unlimited number of anonymous parties to transact privately and securely with one another without a central intermediary. For supply chains, it is to allow a limited number of known parties to protect their business operations against malicious actors while supporting better performance. Successful blockchain applications for supply chains will require new permissioned blockchains, new standards for representing transactions on a block, and new rules to govern the system (all are currently in various stages of development).

The Advantages of Blockchain

Thanks to companies such as Walmart and Procter & Gamble using enterprise resource planning (ERP) systems, advancement in supply chain information sharing has taken place since the 1990s (as described in Chapter 13). However, visibility, detailed in Chapter 14, remains a challenge in large supply chains involving complex transactions.

To illustrate the limitations of the current world of financial-ledger entries and ERP systems, along with the potential benefits of blockchain, consider a simple transaction involving a retailer that sources a product from a supplier, and a bank that provides the working capital the supplier needs to fill the order.

The transaction involves information flows, inventory flows, and financial flows. However, a given flow does not result in financial-ledger entries at all three parties involved, and individual ERP systems, manual audits, and inspections can't necessarily connect the three flows, which makes it hard to eliminate execution errors, improve decision-making, and resolve supply chain conflicts.

Capturing the Details of a Simple Transaction: Conventional vs. Blockchain Systems

The financial ledgers and ERP systems currently used don't reliably allow the three parties involved in a basic supply chain transaction to see all the meaningful flows of information, inventory, and money. A blockchain system can effectively eliminate the blind spots which can often be caused by execution errors and complexity.

Execution errors – These can include mistakes in inventory data, missing shipments, and duplicate payments which can be nearly impossible to identify in real-time, and even when a problem is discovered after the fact, it is difficult and expensive to pinpoint its source or fix it by tracing the sequence of activities recorded in available ledger entries and documents. While ERP systems capture most types of flows, it can be tough to assess which journal entries (accounts receivable, payments, credits for returns, etc.) correspond to which inventory transaction, which is especially true for companies engaged in thousands of transactions each day across a large network of supply chain partners and products.

Supply chain activities are often extremely complicated – Orders, shipments, and payments may not line up neatly, because an order may be split into several shipments and corresponding invoices, or multiple orders may be combined into a single shipment.

One common approach to improving supply chain execution is to verify transactions through audits. Auditing is necessary for ensuring compliance with contracts, but it's of limited help in improving decision-making to address operational deficiencies. Audits can reveal the number of expired items in retail, for example, but it won't explain the causes. Those can include glitches in any part of the supply chain, such as inefficient inventory management upstream, suboptimal allocation of products to stores, weak or sporadic demand, and inadequate shelf rotation (failure to put older products in front of newer ones). A record of all those activities can help reduce expirations.

Another way to strengthen supply chain operations would be to mark inventory with either RFID tags or electronic product codes that adhere to GS1 standards (globally accepted rules for handling supply chain data) and then integrate a company's ERP systems with those of its suppliers to construct a complete record of transactions. This would eliminate execution errors and improve traceability. However, integrating ERP systems is expensive and time-consuming and large organizations may have multiple legacy

ERP systems because of organizational changes, mergers, and acquisitions over time. Those systems often do not easily communicate with one another and may even differ in how they define data fields.

When blockchain is used for record keeping, assets such as units of inventory, orders, loans, and bills of lading are given unique identifiers, which serve as digital tokens (like bitcoins). Participants in the blockchain are also given unique identifiers, or digital signatures, which they use to sign the blocks they add to the blockchain. Every step of the transaction is then recorded on the blockchain as a transfer of the corresponding token from one participant to another.

Each block is encrypted and distributed to all participants, who maintain their own copies of the blockchain. Thus, the blockchain provides a complete, trustworthy, and tamperproof audit trail of activities in the supply chain.

Blockchain greatly reduces, if not eliminates, execution, traceability, and coordination problems. As participants have their own individual copies of the blockchain, each party can review the status of a transaction, identify errors, and hold counterparties responsible for their actions. No participant can overwrite past data because doing so would entail having to rewrite all subsequent blocks on all shared copies of the blockchain.

Additionally, many of these functions can be automated through smart contracts, in which lines of computer code use data from the blockchain to verify when contractual obligations have been met and payments can be issued. Smart contracts can also be programmed to assess the status of a transaction and automatically take actions such as releasing a payment, recording ledger entries, and flagging exceptions in need of manual intervention.

It is important to realize that a blockchain would not replace the broad range of transaction-processing, accounting, and management-control functions performed by ERP systems, such as invoicing, payment, and reporting. Each participant company would generate blocks of transactions from its internal ERP system and add them to the blockchain. This makes it easier to integrate various flows of transactions across firms.

The Applications

Let's now take an in-depth look at how companies are applying blockchain to tackle needs that current technologies and methods can't address.

Enhancing Traceability

The U.S. Drug Supply Chain Security Act of 2013 requires pharmaceutical companies to identify and trace prescription drugs to protect consumers from counterfeit, stolen, or harmful products. As a result, some pharmaceutical companies collaborate with their supply chain partners to use blockchain for this purpose. Drug inventory is tagged with electronic product codes that adhere to GS1 standards. As each unit of inventory flows from one firm to another, its tag is scanned and recorded on the blockchain, creating a history of each item all the way through the supply chain, from its source to the end consumer.

Others are working on a similar effort to create a safer food supply chain by using blockchain for tracing fresh produce and other food products.

These kinds of applications require minimal sharing of information as purchase orders, invoices, and payments do not need to be included on the same blockchain. As a result, companies that are hesitant to share competitive data are more willing to participate on the platform.

There are several benefits to using blockchain for traceability. They include:

1. Quality issues – If a company discovers a faulty product, the blockchain enables the firm and its supply chain partners to trace the product, identify all suppliers involved with it, identify production and shipment batches associated with it, and efficiently recall it.
2. Perishable products (such as fresh produce and certain drugs) – The blockchain lets participating companies monitor quality automatically: For example, a refrigerated container equipped with an internet of things (IoT) device to monitor the temperature can record any unsafe fluctuations on the blockchain.
3. Authenticity – The blockchain can allay concerns about the authenticity of a product because counterfeit goods would not have a verification history on the blockchain.

Thanks to these types of benefits, many organizations are looking into this application of blockchain. They are motivated either by regulations requiring them to demonstrate the provenance of their products or by customers seeking the capability to trace component inventory.

Increasing Efficiency and Speed and Reducing Disruptions

Blockchain can help to increase supply chain speed and efficiency and reduce disruptions.

For example, Hayward, a multinational manufacturer of swimming pool equipment, feels that it is possible to treat finished goods, process capacity, work-in-process inventory, and raw materials like digital currency. If you do, machine time and inventory at various stages can be reliably assigned to customer orders. Blockchain makes this possible to avoid the erroneous allocation of the same unit of capacity or inventory to two different orders.

Walmart Canada has already begun using blockchain with the trucking companies that transport its inventory. A shared blockchain makes it possible to synchronize logistics data, track shipments, and automate payments without requiring significant changes to the trucking firms' internal processes or information technology systems.

One major reason it is so appealing to use blockchain to enhance supply chain efficiency and speed is that these applications, much like those for improving traceability, require participating companies to share only limited data, such as inventory or shipment data, and these applications are useful even within large organizations with multiple ERP systems.

Improving Financing, Contracting, and International Transactions

Sharing inventory, information, and financial flows among firms through a blockchain can result in significant gains in supply chain financing, contracting, and doing business internationally.

Banks that provide working capital and trade credit to firms face a problem known as information asymmetry regarding a borrower firm's business, the quality of its assets, and its liabilities where, for example, a company might borrow money from several banks against the same asset or request a loan for one purpose and then use it for another. Banks design their processes to control such risks, which increases transaction costs, slows down access to capital, and reduces the capital available to small firms.

Another area where it is useful is in accounts payable management. Even though ERP systems have automated many of the steps involved (i.e., invoicing, reconciling invoices against purchase orders, keeping track of terms and payments, and conducting reviews and approvals), considerable manual intervention is still needed. And since neither of the transacting parties has complete information, conflicts can often come up.

A Counterfeit Can Be Traced to Its Source Using the Blockchain Trail

A third area of opportunity is cross-border trade, which involves manual processes, physical documents, many intermediaries, and multiple checks and verifications at ports of entry and exit. Transactions are slow and costly, with low visibility as to the status of shipments.

By connecting inventory, information, and financial flows and sharing them with all transacting parties, a blockchain enables companies to reconcile purchase orders, invoices, and payments much more easily and to track the progress of a transaction.

When the supplier receives an order, a bank with access to the blockchain can immediately provide the supplier with working capital, and when merchandise is delivered to the buyer, the bank can promptly obtain payments. As there is a readily available audit trail and reconciliations can be automated, using applications that rely on the blockchain data, conflicts between the bank and the borrowing firm are eliminated.

Creating a Workable Technology

The companies using blockchain in supply chain management will require the creation of new rules because the needs of supply chains differ from those of cryptocurrency networks in important ways. The blockchain protocol for the bitcoin network is a system that provides a secure, irrevocable record of financial transactions, and provides proof of ownership of a digital coin, without relying on a centralized authority while allowing participants to remain anonymous and enter and exit the network freely. However, to do this, the bitcoin network sacrifices speed, consumes a large amount of energy to mine bitcoins, and has some vulnerability to hacking.

Supply chains do not need to make the same trade-offs because they operate in a different way and have different characteristics. Let's now look at some of those characteristics.

Known Participants

Supply chains require private blockchains among known parties, not open blockchains among anonymous users. This enables members of a supply chain to determine the source and quality of their inventory, each unit of it must be firmly coupled with the identity of its owner at every step along the way. As a result, only known parties can be allowed to participate in such a blockchain, which means that companies must receive permission to join the system.

Moreover, permission must be granted selectively. For security reasons, therefore, the blockchain participants need to be vetted and approved.

Building a trusted group of partners with which to share data on a blockchain entails overcoming several challenges.

One is the need for a governance mechanism to determine the rules of the system (e.g., who can be invited to join the network, what data is shared, how it is encrypted, who has access, how disputes will be resolved, and what the scope is for the use of IoT and smart contracts).

Another challenge is to address the impact that blockchain could have on pricing and inventory-allocation decisions by making information about the quantity or age of products in the supply chain more transparent. It's not easy to predict where in the supply chain the costs and benefits of this transparency will fall.

Simpler Consensus Protocols

Blockchain requires a consensus protocol (i.e., a mechanism for maintaining a single version of the history of transactions that is agreed to by everyone). Since cryptocurrency networks are peer-to-peer without a central authority, they use a complex method called proof of work, ensuring that all transactions on the network are accepted by most participants. However, it is too slow to handle the speed and volume of transactions in supply chains.

Luckily, if a blockchain is "permissioned" and private, the proof-of-work method is not necessary to establish consensus. Simpler methods can be used to determine who has the right to add the next block to the blockchain.

One method is a round-robin protocol, where the right to add a block rotates among the participants in a fixed order. Since all participants are known, a bad actor would be discovered if it used its turn to modify the chain in a harmful or illegitimate way. As a result, disputes can be resolved easily by participants' validating previous blocks.

Security of Physical Assets

Even when a blockchain record is secure, there is still the danger that a contaminated or counterfeit product might be introduced into the supply chain, either in error or by a corrupt actor. There is also the possibility that inaccurate inventory data from mistakes in scanning, tagging, and data entry can enter the supply chain.

Companies address these risks in three ways.

1. They conduct physical audits when products first enter the supply chain to ensure that shipments match blockchain records.
2. They build distributed applications, called dApps, that track products throughout the supply chain, check data integrity, and communicate with the blockchain to prevent errors and deception. If a counterfeit or an error is detected, it can be traced to its source using the blockchain trail of the transactions for that asset.
3. Companies are making the blockchain more robust by using IoT devices and sensors to automatically scan products and add records to the blockchain without human intervention.

Conclusion

There is considerable room to improve supply chains in terms of end-to-end traceability, speed of product delivery, coordination, and financing. Blockchain can be a powerful tool for addressing these deficiencies.

It is time for supply chain managers who are standing on the sidelines to assess the potential of blockchain for their businesses. They need to join the efforts to develop new rules, experiment with different technologies, conduct pilots with various blockchain platforms, and build an ecosystem with other firms. This will require a large commitment of resources, but the investment promises to be well worth it (Gaur, 2020).

Robotic Applications in Supply Chain and Logistics

Robotics is playing an increasingly important role in logistics and shipping as they can improve efficiency and safety by automating repetitive and physically demanding tasks while reducing costs. Robots can be used for a range of activities such as loading and unloading goods from vehicles, sorting and assembling products, and packing and unpacking boxes as well as being used to monitor inventory levels and track shipments. It is quite possible that, in the future, robotics may also be used widely to deliver goods directly to customers.

Loading and Unloading Cargo

Robotics can be used to load and unload cargo from vehicles in several ways. The first way is to use them to load the goods onto the vehicle, which can be done by using a robotic arm to pick up the goods and load them onto the vehicle. Another way is to use robotics to unload the goods from the vehicle which can be done by using a robotic arm to unload the goods from the vehicle and then place them onto a conveyor belt.

Sorting and Assembling Products

Robotics has been used in logistics for many years to help sort and assemble products, which is one of the most used applications for robotics in business.

There are many reasons why robotics is such a good fit for logistics such as:

- They are very good at repetitive tasks and can be programmed to sort products by type, size, or other criteria and assemble them in the correct order. This can help improve the assembly line's efficiency and reduce the number of errors.
- Robots can work 24/7 and do not need breaks, which can help increase productivity.
- Finally, robots can be used in hazardous or difficult environments, such as in warehouses where there is a lot of dust or factories with dangerous goods or chemicals, meaning that humans do not need to be put in danger to do these jobs.

Packing and Unpacking Boxes

Robotics can significantly improve efficiency in the logistics industry, particularly in the packing and unpacking of boxes. By automating these tasks, robots can significantly improve the speed and accuracy with which boxes are packed and unpacked, leading to potential cost savings for logistics companies. They can also reduce the likelihood of errors and improve safety in the cargo packaging process.

Monitoring Inventory Levels

Robotics can play a vital role in inventory planning and monitoring by automating the inventory management process, so businesses can track their stock levels and ensure there are never shortages.

This is accomplished with robots equipped with sensors that can track inventory levels and report back to a central database where reports are generated that can help businesses make informed decisions about their stock levels.

Additionally, robots can also be used to physically count stock levels and report back discrepancies which can help businesses keep an accurate and up-to-date inventory record, saving them significant time and money in the long run.

Tracking Shipments in Real-Time

Robots are increasingly being used to track shipments in the freight industry as they can:

- Quickly and accurately scan and track shipments in real-time as they move through the supply chain – The information can then be used to optimize the route and ensure that shipments arrive on time.
- Help to reduce labor costs associated with tracking shipments – By automating the tracking process, companies can reduce labor costs.
- Improve the accuracy of tracking data – Robots can provide more accurate and up-to-date information about shipments using sensors and other data-gathering technologies than human workers. The information can be used to improve the shipping process's efficiency and ensure that shipments arrive at their destination safely and on time.

Automating Equipment Maintenance

Robotics can be used to automate the maintenance of equipment in the logistics and freight industries which would reduce the downtime of equipment and allow it to be used more efficiently.

Robotics can also be used to inspect equipment for wear and tear and to identify and diagnose problems.

It can also carry out routine maintenance tasks such as lubrication and cleaning, reducing the need for human workers to carry out these tasks, allowing them to be carried out more frequently and with greater precision.

Finally, robotics can be used to monitor equipment performance and provide operator feedback, allowing for detecting problems early and implementing corrective measures.

Delivering Goods to Customers

As mentioned in Chapter 12, using drones (essentially a flying robot) to deliver goods directly to customers' doors is becoming increasingly popular as it is a fast and efficient way to get goods to customers at their homes without having to go to a store to pick up their items. This is useful for people who live in remote areas, who do not have access to a car, or people who cannot leave their homes, such as the elderly or those with disabilities.

Several companies are now using drones to deliver goods. For example, Amazon has been using drones to deliver packages to customers in the United States since 2016. In 2017, they delivered over 10,000 packages to customers using drones and over 20,000 packages in 2018. They are also increasing the range of products they can deliver using drones. Walmart is also using drones to deliver goods, working with a company called SkyDrop (formerly Flirtey) to deliver groceries and other items to customers' homes. They have completed over 1,000 deliveries since 2016.

In conclusion, there are many benefits to using drone delivery such as it is a fast and efficient way to get goods to customers, customers do not have to leave their homes to pick up their items, it can be used to deliver goods to people who cannot leave their homes, and it is an environmentally friendly way to deliver goods, contributing to greener logistics and supply chain sustainability (DFreight, 2022).

Product Storage

One of the most common robotics applications in logistics facilities is the warehousing of goods where cutting-edge technologies are used to execute movements in the facility.

Stacker cranes, for both pallets and boxes, are a type of automatic handling equipment that replaces forklifts. They can insert unit loads in their locations quickly and autonomously and pick up products on one end of the storage aisle and move them to a new position. Conversely, they can retrieve materials from the racks and transport them to a pick and deposit (P&D) station or an outgoing conveyor, as directed by the warehouse management system (WMS).

Storage robots can assist in running 24/7 operations, are capable of a higher number of goods-in/goods-out cycles per hour, and make fewer errors in product slotting and retrieval. By automating storage tasks with storage robots, all product movements are computerized, so you'll know the status of available merchandise and of goods entering and exiting a facility.

Internal Transport of Materials

Another valuable robotics application for high-throughput facilities is the automation of internal product movements. On-site transport systems such as pallet conveyors, electrified monorails, automated guided vehicles, and autonomous mobile robots (AMRs) can move large volumes of goods.

Pallet and box conveyors are the most widespread for this category in warehousing as they're used in distribution centers to move items between the areas of the facility, reducing costs and making faster deliveries.

One of the conveyance systems with the most potential is AMRs which can perform tasks and move around the warehouse without the need for human guidance. According to the consulting firm Grand View Research, the global AMR market size "is expected to expand at a compound annual growth rate (CAGR) of 15.5% from 2023 to 2030". These robots connect the different zones of a warehouse, logistics facility, or production center, moving goods to the working areas as required by the operations.

Order Picking

Order processing is one of the costliest and most complicated operations in any warehouse and robotics facilitates and streamlines picking through the goods-to-person method. In this case, automated systems bring the products to the operators so that they can put together orders without having to travel.

One of the most effective goods-to-person robotics applications is the "shuttle system" where transfer cars, lifts, and conveyors are all integrated into an automated storage and retrieval system (AS/RS) to fill boxes to supply workstations with the merchandise required to fill orders.

Companies with large numbers of orders can also rely on robotic arms, programmable devices that simulate or replace human arms during production and logistics operations as these arms can handle heavier loads faster and without tiring. As they operate with full autonomy, these robots are well suited for use in temperature-controlled facilities (Mecalux, 2023).

Final Words

These are just some of the many ways robotics is used in supply chain and logistics areas. As technology continues to evolve, we can expect to see even more and more robotics applications in these industries. By using AI, big data, and ML in conjunction with robotics in logistics, robotics can provide customers with a high level of service.

Now it's time to wrap things up (for now) and "put a bow on it" with a look at what the future holds for the even smarter supply chain of tomorrow!

THE SMART(ER), LIVING SUPPLY CHAIN THAT IS YET TO COME

Chapter 17

Emerging Technologies and Their Impact on the Extended Supply Chain in the Coming Years

In the "Future of Supply Chain", consultant EY research concluded that the future of supply chain is both digital and autonomous and that the pandemic has accelerated many preexisting trends, and the supply chain is no exception (EY.com, 2023).

However, simply utilizing digital technologies does not equate to creating a digitized, autonomous supply chain – it also needs connected supply chain technologies across planning, procurement, manufacturing, and logistics that work beyond the organization's four walls.

Autonomous operations in organizations use artificial intelligence (AI) technologies across the end-to-end supply chain to help make predictive and prescriptive decisions. An example is responding to a change in customer demand, seen instantly by the entire value chain (the organization, its suppliers, and their suppliers' suppliers) so they can collectively adjust supply plans and production schedules immediately.

Ultimately, digital and autonomous technologies will help make people's jobs easier and the supply chain more efficient and optimized.

DOI: 10.4324/9781003372639-23

The Supply Chain of the Future: Agile, Flexible, Efficient, Resilient, and Digitally Networked for Improved Visibility

So, organizations will need to:

- **Reimagine the strategic architecture of their supply chains** – Rapidly redefine their supply chain strategy and alter global trade flows, considering new trade agreements, country incentives, and omnichannel acceleration. Reimagine their supply chain operating model – what work should get done locally, regionally, and globally, including warehouses and manufacturing sites. There are considerable tax implications here, and a new model can also help you prepare for future disruption.
- **Build transparency and resiliency** – Improve disruption response with real-time visibility and monitoring of your end-to-end supply chain, as well as performing scenario planning and simulations. Review your supply chain footprint. Do you have alternate sources of supply established? Are you ensuring you do not have vendor or geographic concentration?
- **Extract cash and cost from your supply chain** – Drive a step change in your supply chain cost structure and working capital profile by focusing on SKU rationalization, procurement spend reduction, logistics and warehouse optimization, and manufacturing productivity. Reduce working capital via supply chain segmentation, refreshed inventory planning parameters, and changes in payment terms.
- **Create a competitive advantage with sustainability** – The future is a circular economy where there is no waste in your products or manufacturing. Explore ways to redesign and engineer new products to achieve this circular economy and monitor third-party risk with supplier sustainability assessments across tiers 1–3.
- **Drive agility and opportunities for growth through a digital supply chain** – Work toward implementing the digital and end-to-end supply chain across planning, procurement, manufacturing, and logistics. This can drive efficiencies and open new revenue streams. Realize that companies are using supply chains as an engine for growth and a key differentiator versus competitors.

A Digital Supply Chain Drives Dynamic Product Integration through an Autonomous Value Chain while Integrating with Operational Excellence

A digitalization strategy allows supply chains to move from a reactive mode to a state of proactive self-correcting ecosystems that create competitive agility and craft new value for enterprises. It can enable and drive revenue, enhance brand perception, and foster greater innovation while mitigating risk and helping businesses realize step change cost reduction. The risk of inaction is considerable: falling behind in automation, visibility, and integration translates to a supply chain that will underperform in the areas of service, supply, and cost.

People, Process, and Technology: Synchronized for the Evolving Supply Chain Planning Strategy

Suffice it to say, a lean, agile, and resilient smart supply chain strategy can transform business operating models to deliver superior customer experiences, enable digital transformation, improve quality and visibility, and create additional value.

However, while organizations try to adapt to a digital world, the results may fall short without a strategy that considers your people, process, and technology (PPT).

Principles of a Supply Chain Strategy

Enabling a supply chain that is ready for the future requires new ways of thinking. Having new capabilities can increase the pace of innovation and allow organizations to react quickly to changing market conditions, trends, and customer expectations.

To help accomplish this in a productive way, it will be important to free up time for employees to focus on higher value work. Helping in this endeavor, a study from the consulting firm McKinsey (2019) suggests that almost half of routine tasks can be automated by current technology.

Today's supply chain operating model is more and more based on insights from real-time demand. As a result, leading organizations are increasing investments in emerging technologies that support real-time demand, planning, and fulfillment execution capabilities.

Driving this are principles that include:

- Organizations must manage global volatility and build a lean, agile, and resilient supply chain – one that can react to any shock such as the recent global pandemic as our world becomes more interconnected.
- The acceleration of omni channel networks requires more speed, complexity, and efficiency.
- Fast and decisive action is critical to supply chain management in any market condition, which requires total visibility across the supply chain.

These principles should help determine the right roadmap toward achieving the future-state an organization envisions.

Developing and Implementing a Future-State Vision

Building a strategic supply chain begins by assessing your organization's current state by identifying current pain points and limitations (using external and internal analysis, culminating in a "S.W.O.T." analysis is a useful methodology in this task).

You should then build a future-state vision of your organization, targeting future capabilities and key areas for investment.

From a technology standpoint, you should identify where data management and standardization solve pain points and align findings with the technology necessary to converge data silos. From this, you should be able to create a technology roadmap outlining the application of technology and data standardization, defining the processes to support innovation, and resolving any major pain points.

Implementing emerging technology isn't enough to compete in the future of tomorrow. It also requires that organizations adopt a "PPT" framework into their technology roadmap, since as supply chains evolve, so do the people and processes that work in and around them (Figure 17.1).

The success of realizing a future-state vision depends on identifying actionable insights, enabling a realistic technology roadmap, and integrating PPT to build a future-ready supply chain.

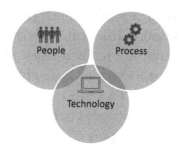

Figure 17.1 People, process, and technology (PPT) framework.

Leveraging the People, Process, and Technology Framework

PPT coordination is necessary for organizational transformation and management and to gain a competitive advantage. Organizations need to develop a "holistic" PPT methodology to balance and maintain good relationships among them to drive action.

This framework especially applies to organizations strategically using business intelligence (BI) through technology-enabled supply chain improvements.

To change supply chain performance, technology needs to be synchronized with people and processes, rather than against them.

To summarize, building a future-ready supply chain begins with four steps:

1. Assess your organization's current state
2. Build your future-state vision
3. Map your pragmatic technology roadmap
4. Adopt the PPT framework

While all organizations are adopting digital technologies, leading-edge supply chains recognize technology is only one component of a far more holistic effort (Nicholas, 2020).

Besides using a PPT framework, it will take a true visionary strategy to transform the supply chains of today into smart supply chains of the future, which we will discuss next.

The Smart Supply Chain of the Future

In recent years, global supply chains have been hit by a series of such black swan events (extremely disruptive outlier events that can't be anticipated scientifically): acts of terrorism, armed conflict, political upheaval, port strikes, rise in tariffs, intellectual property risks, and, of course, natural disasters.

During the Covid (although not really a black swan event as pandemics have been part of human history), large-scale shutdowns, mobility restrictions, and labor shortages created a serious supply chain crisis of increased demand (e.g., the panic-buying of toilet paper) and the inability of businesses to meet that demand (e.g., port congestion due to lack of labor).

Existing supply chains were not designed to deal with such disruptions in the first place. For the past 40+ years, most supply chain strategies have tried to run in a "just-in-time" mode to reduce operating costs and maximize efficiency by using information, planning, and forecasting systems to guide global supply chains and align resources with predicted demand signals. However, after living through recent shocks, many companies have started looking for a new way to operate. The traditional "just-in-time" approach for supply chain design may soon be giving way to "just-in-case" or even "just-in-worst-case". In other words, with the traditional model proving inadequate to withstand disruptive events, companies now want agile and resilient supply chains as has been stated throughout this book.

To accomplish this, organizations need to rethink the relationship between supply chain strategy, operations processes, people, and the currently available technology (i.e., the PPT framework previously discussed). Leveraging advanced digital technologies, which can now detect, analyze, predict, and provide prescriptive options in ways that legacy systems can't, will change how supply chains are planned and executed, and how organizations and roles are structured.

This vision will create a future where machines will perform the majority of the analysis, freeing up managers or other human workers to make strategic decisions, resulting in more agile and resilient supply chains. This will truly enable an "intelligent enterprise" that integrates an ecosystem-wide information layer with cutting-edge AI and machine learning (ML) algorithms to automate and optimize supply chain decisions.

Limitations of Legacy Systems

Global supply chains are under large pressure to be able to function in a complex world of increasing risk and uncertainty. Covid-19 showed how unprepared many organizations were in dealing with operational, structural, cultural, and data integration and flow constraints of the legacy information systems that global supply chains still rely on.

Legacy enterprise resource planning (ERP) legacy systems are not optimal in the unpredictable world of today. They were created to handle execution elements and connect data on basic transactions, and material and production capacity processes across functional areas such as manufacturing, finance, procurement, and order management. ERP systems effectively became the enterprise systems of record.

Over time, as supply chain management became more complex, core ERP functions were extended to advanced planning solutions (APS), which supported sales and operations planning (S&OP) processes. Many companies also extended S&OP to perform integrated business planning (and enterprise planning), which now connects operational planning decisions to commercial strategies and financial objectives. So today, the original idea of an ERP collecting and supporting most key business functions has resulted in a complicated web of processes and technologies addressing the complexities introduced by continuously evolving supply chain requirements.

By contrast, an agile response to supply chain disruptions is based on the idea that supply chain professionals with the right information in the right format can make faster, smarter decisions. Legacy systems lack this capability as these systems are often loosely coupled, with data flowing interdepartmentally in a cascading manner. As a result, data is either late, unintelligible, or wrong, leaving supply chain managers searching for insights to support decisions.

Recent disruptions have made supply unreliable and demand unpredictable and social-distancing mandates during Covid tended to keep customers away from physical stores which were often understocked due to supply issues. As a result customer preferences, changed overnight and curbside pickup service emerged as a major trend.

Opportunity: Evolving into the Intelligent Enterprise

It's now clear that legacy system driven supply chains will have a hard time tackling future disruptions as they aren't very good at handling exceptions.

On the other hand, it has been proven that advanced digital technologies can play a significant role in operational management. For instance, they can capture big data and use AI and ML to quickly identify critical information and offer prescriptive options, use the internet of things (IoT) to remotely manage automated factories, create digital twins to simulate functional operations, and have robots perform many of the most difficult operational functions efficiently.

With uncertainty becoming more and more common, organizations that will thrive will likely do so based upon their ability to adapt to the environment. Forward-thinking businesses are already implementing digital technologies to do more of the work that has been traditionally performed by legacy systems and human beings. But what is more challenging is the ability to create a governance and operational model that is aligned to leverage these new technological capabilities.

To get there, they need to develop digital models that can simulate how any change in supply networks, product design, sales opportunities, or customer mix would impact the entire enterprise. This new model will require that organizations operate using data models and digitally stored information from the cloud. After that, AI, ML, and other digital algorithms can help identify problems before they occur and run multiple simulations based on business objectives and priorities to determine potential consequences and trade-offs throughout the enterprise.

Future organizations will need to transform themselves into intelligent enterprises that adopt advanced digital technologies to create an agile supply chain model that is no longer defined by functional silos to be successful (Figure 17.2).

A successful intelligent enterprise will require the following components: an insights and decision platform, a digital organization, and a digital operating model as described below.

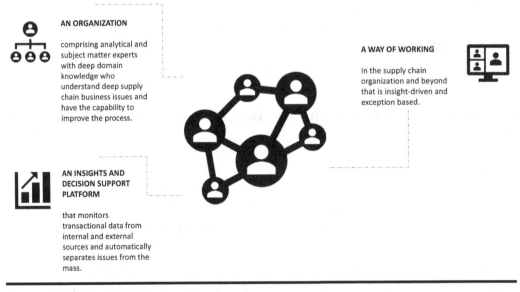

AN ORGANIZATION

comprising analytical and subject matter experts with deep domain knowledge who understand deep supply chain business issues and have the capability to improve the process.

A WAY OF WORKING

In the supply chain organization and beyond that is insight-driven and exception based.

AN INSIGHTS AND DECISION SUPPORT PLATFORM

that monitors transactional data from internal and external sources and automatically separates issues from the mass.

Figure 17.2   The intelligent enterprise.

An Insights and Decision Platform

To make intelligent decisions in large, complex supply chains, operators need to understand how their actions will impact the entire enterprise. Disruptions in one area could mean delayed or canceled orders in another, so accurate decisions that impact the production, sourcing, or routing of products must be based on data that is timely, accurate, pertinent, and holistic. The increasing use of business rules and algorithms will probably lead to more automated processes.

This will enable managers to make decisions based on rapid analysis of potential decision points and how those will impact the entire organization. This will require an insights and decision platform that must include the technology and tools necessary to access (in real-time) both internal and external data sources and organize it into a single data model, made available to supply chain operators through a rules-driven, cloud-based repository that covers the entire enterprise. AI/ML capabilities will subsequently be used to conduct this real-time analysis with the findings used to respond to supply chain exceptions and to guide the identification and automation of manual processes and non-value-added decisions.

A Digital Organization

The organization then needs to operate from one integrated data layer, gathering data into one dataset, accessible to the entire enterprise. AI and other analytics solutions can then expedite problem-solving.

This will allow for what would have previously taken days to perform manually within one department to now be executed in a matter of minutes using data from across the organization.

For example, if a manufacturer were utilizing 3D applications to render virtual representations of planned products, in the past, it would have used a process that required shipping product prototypes back and forth for approval, which was slow and cumbersome. The new 3D prototypes can be piloted internally and with customers with the resulting digital product development process getting products to market faster, while also speeding product life cycles in markets where consumer preferences change or require regional adjustment.

Free from legacy systems, organizations can construct a governance, technology, data, and operational model to support an agile business, where the company mission becomes customer-centric, and the business is restructured to provide the resources to efficiently pursue that mission.

Furthermore, organizations can be structured to prevent and address service failures by blending functional roles, such as planning and execution, which can improve collaboration and responsiveness when facing market fluctuations and disruptions. For example, positions such as a master planner, an inventory analyst, and a replenishment planner will be combined into one role. The combined function will utilize the same data, business rules, and policies to respond to demand changes and iteratively replan with the latest input from the market. This reduces the number of functional roles and systems involved and increases the organization's agility and decision-making speed.

A Digital Operating Model

A digital operating model can become operational through a series of business rules that will support a new customer-centric, fast approach with the goal of helping to identify and address the root cause of problems. This model basically assumes that supply chain disruption is an eventuality, rather than an exception.

The design of the digital operating model will assign decision-making authority based on information and analytics along with policies, procedures, and incentives as part of an integrated business planning process.

The technology layer provides a common, integrated data repository that will be accessed by roles across the organization for enterprise-wide impact using performance measurement and incentives using a common, holistic set of metrics. For example, a global manufacturer transitioning its supply chain planning processes to a digital platform would use it to help provide a single view of end-to-end supply chain operations across its global network.

New digital technologies will help automate routine, repetitive, transactional, and non-value-added work (e.g., manually manipulating spreadsheets to connect datasets or extracting data from siloed legacy systems).

New roles will be focused on capability rather than functional expertise. The work will now be more strategic since it is focused on data analysis, running scenario modeling, and debating the merits of various strategic choices amplified by new digital tools.

Moving Forward

Adequately handling disruptions requires the integration of all enterprise-wide variables including commercial strategies, production capabilities, financial impacts, inventory and supplier visibility, and order management capabilities tied directly to the customer.

Unfortunately, existing legacy operational models do not allow for necessary transformation. It is necessary to create objectives that will get the organization to cultivate a new customer-centric, extended enterprise–aware culture based upon questions such as "what kind of organization do you want to be?", "what is your identity?", and "who should be driving the final decisions?"

Organizations must figure out how human talent and digital technologies can work together (augmentation). Machines will do more of the work in the future, which can yield returns in the short run such as reduction in head count and fewer legacy systems to manage and provide significant benefits into the future including improved decision-making driving enterprise priorities and improved agility/resilience.

Once organizations have set their objectives, the next step will be to move toward a single system to collect data from all functions across the enterprise and consolidate it into one data source. This will require connecting internal and external data sources, which will likely be stored in the cloud.

Once this has been accomplished, organizations will be able to use advanced digital technologies to optimize decision-making. AI/ML capabilities can automate low-impact or time-consuming decision-making by learning from the impact of previous decisions, while simultaneously refining the algorithms. At the same time, staff can be reorganized to leverage analytics that will focus the enterprise on customer-centricity rather than functional silos.

Organizational change on this scale is not easy and there is no single right answer for how to end up with an intelligent enterprise. While some organizations have started on this transformation process, most are still focused on establishing the foundations.

For example, a global manufacturer would first launch its intelligent enterprise efforts by developing a new vision for better decision-making in an uncertain environment. The first step in that vision would be the modeling of decisions made across the entire enterprise from the factory to the store. To accomplish that, they need to first make data connections across the many functions of the enterprise, which will provide a holistic visibility into the supply chain. The resulting data will be used to build decision models, which will eventually be automated.

The next step would be to move the company culture to be in alignment with its technological and operational capabilities. Governance models will need to establish defined rules and roles to facilitate timely decision-making. Skill sets would need to be upgraded, and operations managers would then need to perform data-driven analysis for customer-centric decisions with enterprise-wide impact from a single set of data while building and analyzing simulated decision scenarios.

In closing, it is increasingly clear that for supply chains, both domestic and globally, more risks exist through black swan events and other forms of natural and man-made disruptions. This accelerates the need for organizations to transform and become intelligent enterprises.

Many companies have already begun laying foundational elements to create an intelligent enterprise supported by a smart supply chain. The race is on to improve operations, deliver better services, and offer improved value with agile and resilient supply chains (Calderon et al., 2022).

As the saying goes, "to be forewarned is to be forearmed", so be smart and get started transforming into an intelligent supply chain of the future, today.

Bibliography

Chapter 1

Myerson, Paul "Building the Smart Supply Chain", July 2022, *Inbound Logistics Magazine*.

Chapter 2

A Brief History of Supply Chain Technology, RTS Labs, June 4, 2020. Last accessed at www.rtslabs.com, 2024.

Bozarth, Cecil, Handfield, Robert *Introduction to Operations and Supply Chain Management*, Pearson, 5th Ed, 2018, pp. 516–518.

Cap Gemini Consulting "How Will Digital Impact SCM: Supply Chain Trends", September 9, 2014. Last accessed at: www.capgemini-consulting.com, 2023.

Council of Supply Chain Management Professionals (CSCMP). Last accessed at: www.cscmp.org, 2023.

"Current Trends in Supply Chain Management", Blog, CargoFlash, 2022. Last accessed at: www.cargoflash.com, 2023.

Fawcett, S. E., Magnan, G. M. "The Rhetoric and Reality of Supply Chain Integration", *International Journal of Physical Distribution & Logistics Management*, (2002), Vol. 32, No. 5, 339–361.

Simatupang, Togar M., Sridharan, R. *A Characterization of Information Sharing in Supply Chains*, Massey University, October 2001. Last accessed at: www.academia.edu, 2023.

"Software Market Insights: Logistics and Supply Chain Management (SCM)", Gartner Digital Markets, 2022. Last accessed: www.gartner.com, 2024.

"Supply Chain Management Software Market Chasing USD 35.3 Bn Mark by 2032, Due to The Ever-increasing Importance of Supply Chain Optimization", www.MarketResearch.biz, 2023.

Supply Chain Technology: History & Impact. Emma Shaffer, Nego Metrix (now Mercell), August 2, 2021. Last accessed at www.negometrix.com, 2023.

Trunick, Perry A., Inbound Logistics "Continuing Education – Making the Right Selection", February 2011. Last accessed at: www.inboundlogistics.com, 2023.

Chapter 3

Davydov, Roman "A Guide to Making Your Supply Chain Smart", itransition.com, April 20, 2022. Last accessed at: www.itransition.com, 2022.

"What is the Digital Supply Chain?", Supply Chain Game Changer, October 4, 2022. Last accessed at www.supplychaingamechanger.com, 2022.

Chapter 4

Martichenko, Robert "The Lean Supply Chain: A Field of Opportunity", January 2013, *Inbound Logistics Magazine*. Last accessed at: www.inboundlogistics.com, 2015.

Myerson, Paul "The Journey to Continuous Supply Chain Improvement", April 2012, *Inbound Logistics Magazine*.

Myerson, Paul "A Lean and Agile Supply Chain: Not an Option, But a Necessity", October 16, 2014, *Inbound Logistics Magazine*.

Myerson, Paul, "How to Cut Seven Non-Traditional Wastes", June 2015, *Inbound Logistics Magazine*.

Myerson, Paul "Lean Isn't Mean and Agile Isn't Cheap", May 2022, *Inbound Logistics Magazine*.

Salazar, Luis "Process Improvement: The Key to Effective Technology Implementation", www.LinkedIn.com, April 3, 2023.

Thompson, Richard, Mankrodt, Karl, Vitasek, Kate "Lean Practices in the Supply Chain", Jones Lang LaSalle, 2008. Last accessed at: www.joneslanglasalle.com, 2015.

Womack, James P., Jones, Daniel T. *Lean Thinking: Banish Waste and Create Wealth in Your Corporation*, Simon & Schuster, 2nd Ed, January, 1996.

Chapter 5

Bozarth, Cecil, Handfield, Robert *Introduction to Operations and Supply Chain Management*, Pearson, 2nd Ed, 2008, pp. 516–518.

Fortune Business Insights Market Research Report, June 2023. Last accessed at: www.fortunebusinessinsights.com, 2023.

Gartner.com (Press Release) "Gartner Says Worldwide Supply Chain Management Software Market Grew 7.1 Percent to Reach $8.3 Billion in 2012", 2013 www.gartner.com. Last accessed at: www.gartner.com, 2014.

Gilmore, Dan "Insight from the 2010 [2013] Gartner Supply Chain Study", Supply Chain Digest, June 8, 2010 and June 28, 2013. Last accessed at: www.scdigest.com, 2023.

Heizer, Jay, Render, Barry *Operations Management*, Pearson, 11th Ed, copyright 2013, pp. 60–64.

McDonnell, R., Sweeney, E., Kenny, J. "The Role of Information Technology in the Supply Chain", *Logistics Solutions*, (2004), Vol. 7, No.1, 13–16.

Simatupang, Togar M., Sridharan, R. *A Characterisation of Information Sharing in Supply Chains*, Massey University, October 2001.

Software as a Service (SaaS) Market Size, Share & Industry Analysis, Fortune Business Insights, October 21, 2024. Last accessed at www.fortunebusinessinsights.com, 2024.

"Supply Chain Management Software Market Chasing USD 35.3 Bn Mark by 2032, Due to The Ever-increasing Importance of Supply Chain Optimization", www.MarketResearch.biz, 2023.

"Supply Chain Management Software White Paper", www.erpsearch.com. Last accessed at: www.erpsearch.com, 2014.

Chapter 6

Bartholomew, Doug, "Can Lean and ERP Work Together?", April 12, 2012, *Industry Week Magazine*.

Case Study: Manufacturing Production Planning, Corporate Technologies. Last accessed at: www.cptech.com, 2023.

"Client Case Study – Global Network Design", White Paper, Establish Inc. Last accessed at: www.establishinc.com, 2023.

Continental Mills, Logility Voyager Solutions Case Study. Last accessed at: www.logility.com, 2023.

Cooke, James A. "Kimberly-Clark Connects Its Supply Chain to the Store Shelf". Quarter 1 2013 issue of CSCMP's Supply Chain Quarterly. Last accessed at: www.supplychainquarterly.com, 2015.

Dougherty, John, Gray, Christopher *Sales and Operations Planning – Best Practices*, Trafford Publishing, 2006. Last accessed at: www.grayresearch.com, 2023.

"Faribault Foods Plans with AI to Become More Agile", New Horizon, Case Study, September 29, 2021. Last accessed at: www.newhorizon.ai, 2024.

Harris, Daniel "Compare Demand Planning & Forecasting Software", November 15, 2015. Last accessed at: www.softwareadvice.com, 2023.

"How AI Saves Your S&OP Planning Process", Logility Blog. Last accessed at: www.logility.com, 2024.

"Infinite Possibilities: Infineon Technologies Takes Planning to the Next Level With JDA S&OP", Case Study, 2014. Last accessed at: www.jda.com, 2023.

"Introduction to Strategic Supply Chain Network Design, Perspectives and Methodologies to Tackle the Most Challenging Supply Chain Network Dilemmas", White Paper and Case. Last accessed at: www.spinnakermgmt. com, 2023.

Kahn, Kenneth B., Mello, John "Lean Forecasting begins with Lean Thinking – On The Demand Forecasting Process", *Journal of Business Forecasting*, (Winter 2004–05), Vol. 40, pp. 30–32.

Lance, Logility Voyager Solutions Case Study. Last accessed at: www.logility.com, 2023.

"Luxury Automaker Improves Forecasting Capabilities with AI", phData, Case Study. Last accessed at: www.phdata.io, 2024.

Po, Vincent, "Understanding the 3 Levels of Supply Chain Management", December 12, 2012, The Procurement Bulletin. Last accessed at: www. procurmentbulletin.com, 2023.

Production Planning Case Study, ORM Technologies. Last accessed at: www.orm-tech.com, 2023.

"Recipe for Success", Case Study, JDA Software. Last accessed at: www.jda.com, 2023.

Salman, Mustafa Ramzi, van der Krogt, Roman, Little, James, Geraghty, John, "Applying Lean Principles to Production Scheduling", *Journal of Scheduling*, (August 2010), www.springer.com

SAS "The Lean Approach to Business Forecasting – Eliminating Waste and Inefficiency from the Forecasting Process" White Paper, 2012. Last accessed at: www.sas.com, 2023.

"Techlogix Helps Nestlé Innovate in Milk Production Planning", Case Study, Techlogix. Last accessed at: www.techlogix.com, 2023.

Viswanthan, Nari "S&OP – Strategies for Managing Complexities with Global Supply Chains", Aberdeen Group, 2010. Last accessed at: www.aberdeen.com, 2023.

"What is AI Planning and Forecasting?", AI Planning and Forecasting, www.domo. com, 2023.

Chapter 7

"A Picture Perfect MRP Implementation Helps Traffic Enforcement Camera Maker to Profitability". Last accessed at: www.e-z-mrp.com, 2023.

"Clariant Cuts Costs with Ariba Solutions – Automating and Enhancing Procurement Processes", SAP Software Case Study. Last accessed at: www.sap. com, 2023.

Dominick, Charles "Ten Types of Procurement Software", July 1, 2015, College Planning and Management. Last accessed at: www.webcom.com, 2016.

"Enabling Online Supplier Collaboration at Toshiba Semiconductor Company", JDA Software Case Study. Last accessed at: www.jda.com, 2023.

Gables Engineering: Case Study, IFS Software. Last accessed at: www.top10erp.org, 2023.

Heizer, Jay, Render, Barry *Operations Management*, Prentice Hall, 12th Ed, 2020, p. 642.

"New Purchase-To-Pay System Allows Smarter Processes at Atea", Basware Software Case Study. Last accessed at: www.basware.com, 2023.

"Raytheon Streamlines and Automates its Material Requirement Planning Processes with Exostar's Supply Chain Platform", Exostar Raytheon Case Study. Last accessed at: www.exostar.com, 2023.

Chapter 8

"10 Ways to Use ERP to Lean the Manufacturing Supply Chain", IFS software White Paper, 2009. Last accessed at: www.ifsworld.com, 2023.

Allen-Bradley "Full Sail Brewing Taps Manufacturing Intelligence to Enhance Brewing Process", Rockwell Automation, White Paper, September 2011. Last accessed at: www.rockwellautomation.com, 2023.

"Auto Parts Manufacturer Chooses Asprova for Its Good User Interface Reduces Labor of Adjusting the Schedule", Case Study. Last accessed at: www.asprova.com, 2023.

Case Study: Flexpipe Systems Inc., IFS ERP Systems Software. Last accessed at: www.top10erp.org, 2023.

Case Study: Radio Flyer, Ultra Consultants. Last accessed at: www.ultraconsultants.com, 2023.

"CI Precision implements Asia/Pacific Region", CI Precision Case Study. Last accessed at: www.ciprecision.com, 2023.

Cottyn, Johannes, Van Landeghem, Hendrik, Stockman, Kurt, Derammelaere, Stijn "The Role of Change Management in a Manufacturing Execution System", *Proceedings of the 41st International Conference on Computers & Industrial Engineering* (2011), pp. 453–458. Last accessed at: www.usc.edu, 2023.

"EZ-MES Production Tracking System: Case Study", Eazy Works Case Study. Last accessed at: www.eazyworks.com, 2023.

Kreipl, Stephan, Pinedo, Michael "Planning and Scheduling in Supply Chains: An Overview of Issues in Practice", *Production and Operations Management Society (POMS)*, (Spring 2004), Vol. 13, No. 1, pp. 77–92.

"Mueller Stoves Reduces the Assembly Line Stops After Preactor Deployment", Case Study. Last accessed at: www.preactor.com, 2023.

Nissen Chemitec America – Leading Automotive Supplier Accelerates Lean Operations with IQMS ERP, IQMS Manufacturing ERP Case Study, 2015. Last accessed at: www.iqms.com, 2016.

Schiff, Jennifer Lonoff "9 Tips for Selecting and Implementing an ERP System", July 30, 2014, *CIO Magazine*. Last accessed at: www.cio.com, 2023.

Chapter 9

Banker, Steve "Return on Investment for Transportation Management Systems", ARC Strategies, November 2011. Last accessed at: www.leanlogistics.com, 2023.

"Everlast Builds a Championship Company with New Product Lines", Demand Solutions, *DS Magazine*, (Spring 2007), Vol. 7, No. 1, pp. 3–5.

"Leading Dairy Trims 18% from Transportation Costs Using Optimizer Software", Ultra Ship TMS Case Study, 2015. Last accessed at: www.ultrashiptms.com, 2016.

Martichenko, Robert "Lean Transportation Management: Creating Operational and Financial Stability", LeanCor, Supply Chain Group. Last accessed at: www.leancor.com, 2023.

Meller, Russ "Order Fulfillment as a Competitive Advantage", Supply Chain 247, March 5, 2015. Last accessed at: www.supplychain247.com, 2023.

"Miller Brands UK Uses Transwide TMS to Manage Growing Transport Volumes", Transwide TMS Case Study. Last accessed at: www.transwide.com, 2023.

Murphy, Jean V. "Canadian Tire Keeps Stores Rolling with Replenishment Program", Supply Chain Brain, October 1, 1999. Last accessed at: www.supplychainbrain.com, 2023.

"Papa on the Platform – Hold the Anchovies: Papa John's Pizza Orders Optimization Supreme with Manhattan's Supply Chain Process Platform", Manhattan Associates, Inc. Customer Case Study, 2013. Last accessed at: www.manh.com, 2013.

Partridge, Amy Roach "Auto Logistics: Revving Up Service Parts Logistics Operations", Inbound Logistics, January 2011.

"TAGG Logistics – Supply Chain Management & Order Fulfillment", Cadre Technologies Case Study. Last accessed at: www.cadretech.com, 2023.

Turbide, David "How Can Distribution Requirements Planning Help Inventory Management?", Tech Target. Last accessed at: www.searchmanufacturingerp.techtarget.com, 2023.

"Whirlpool Spins Optimized Supply Chain with Help from Manhattan Associates", Manhattan Associates, Inc. Customer Case Study, 2013. Last accessed at: www.manh.com, 2023.

Chapter 10

Baror, Yifat, "From Prevention to Prediction: Revolutionizing Returns Management in Retail", Supply Chain Brain, www.supplychainbrain.com, August 25, 2023.

Logistics Case Study: Return Central – Reconstructed Network Yields Big Efficiencies, Faster Processes, GENCO, a FedEx company. Last accessed at: www.genco.com, 2023.

Nokia – Deployment of Global Service Strategy, Return Pool Case Study, 2012. Last accessed at: www.returnpool.com, 2016.

Rogers, Dale, Tibben-Lembke, Ronald "Going Backwards: Reverse Logistics Trends and Practices", Reverse Logistics Council, 1999.

"RTL™ Adds Up to Many Happy Returns for Philips", Customer Case Study, RTL. Last accessed at: www.roundtriplogistics.com, 2023.

Chapter 11

"Barcode: The Ultimate Guide to Barcodes", Wasp Bar Code. Last accessed at: www.waspbarcode.com, 2023.

"Examining RFID Usage in Warehouses", Prologis. Last accessed at: www.prologis.com, 2023.

"Fully Automated Warehouse: A Snapshot", Interlake Mecalux, Blog – Logistics & Supply Chain Trends. Last accessed at: www.interlakemecalux.com, 2023.

Chapter 12

Banker, Steve, "Top 5 Transportation Technology Trends for 2023", Forbes, December 16, 2022.

"RFID Technology – What are its Uses in the Transportation Industry?", Universal Smart Cards. Last accessed at: www.usmartcards.com, 2023.

"Vehicle Telematics", Heavy AI. Last accessed at: www.heavy.ai, 2023.

Chapter 13

"Agilent Technologies: Comprehensive Supply Chain Visibility across a Multi-Enterprise SupplyChain", Kinaxis Customer Spotlight, 2014. Last accessed at: www.kinaxis.com, 2023.

"Arrow Electronics Automates Replenishment Program with One Network's Real Time Value Network", One Network Enterprises Case Study, 2011. Last accessed at: www.onenetwork.com, 2023.

Dittmann, Paul "Benefits of Collaboration Technology to Improve Supply Chain Efficiencies", www.sdcexec.com, April 22, 2016.

"Enhance Omnichannel Visibility – How to Gain Visibility Across the Extended Supply Chain", GTNEXUS, an Infor Company. A Strategic Imperative for Retailers White Paper, www.gtnexus.com, 2017.

Myerson, Paul "Supply Chain Integration + Collaboration = Time Travel?", December 2014, *Inbound Logistics Magazine*.

Myerson, Paul "Omnichannel Delivers, But at What Cost?", March 2021, *Inbound Logistics Magazine*.

Myerson, Paul "The Future of the Supply Chain is Cloudy", October 2022, *Inbound Logistics Magazine*.

"Re-engineering the Supply Chain for the Omni-channel of Tomorrow – Global Consumer Goods and Retail Omni-channel Supply Chain Survey", EY and the Consumer Goods Forum Supply Chain Committee, February 2015. Last accessed at: www.ey.com, 2019.

Rosing, Jason "Differences between Omnichannel & Omnichannel 2.0", Supply Chain 247, January 14, 2019. Last accessed at: www.supplychain247.com, 2019.

Chapter 14

Myerson, Paul "Internet of Things to Come", March 2018, *Inbound Logistics Magazine*.

Myerson, Paul "The View from the Control Tower", October 2019, *Inbound Logistics Magazine*.

Myerson, Paul "The Supply Chain: It's Alive! It's Alive!", January 2023, *Inbound Logistics Magazine*.

QIMAone "Real Time Visibility Series", QIMAone. Last accessed at: www.qimaone.com, 2023.

Chapter 15

Decision Support System: What is a Decision Support System?, Windward. Last accessed at: www.windward.ai, 2024.

"How to Perform Effective Supply Chain Data Analysis", QIMAone. Last accessed at: www.qimaone.com, 2023.

Myerson, Paul "Drilling Deeper Into Your Supply Chain", December 2019, *Inbound Logistics Magazine*.

"What Are the Common Data Sources?", Future Lean. Last accessed at: www.futurelearn.com, 2023.

Chapter 16

"5 Robotic Applications in Logistics", Mecalux, June 22, 2023. Last accessed at: www.mecalux.com, 2023.

Gaur, Vishal, "Building a Transparent Supply Chain: Blockchain Can Enhance Trust, Efficiency, and Speed", Harvard Business Review, 2020. Last accessed at: www.hbr.org, 2023.

Kaufholz, Robert "What Can Machine Learning Do for Your Supply Chain?", ASCM Insights, 2020. Last accessed at: www.ascm.org, 2023.

Myerson, Paul "Supply Chain AI: This Time It's for Real", February 2020, *Inbound Logistics Magazine.*

"Top Use Cases of Robotics in Logistics and Shipping", D Freight, October 10, 2022. Last accessed at www.dfreight.com, 2023.

Chapter 17

Brosseau, Daniel, Ebrahim, Sherina, Handscomb, Christopher, Thaker, Shail "The Journey to an Agile Organization", May 10, 2019. Last accessed at: www. McKinsey.com, 2024.

Calderon, Rafael, Lam, Bill, Entrup, Christopher "Intelligent Enterprise Fueling the Supply Chain of the Future – Advanced Digital Technologies Can Redefine How an Enterprise Operates to Create an Agile and Disruption-proof Supply Chain", Deloitte Insights, www.deloitte.com, November 28, 2022.

"Future of Supply Chain", EY. Last accessed at www.EY.com, 2023.

Nicholas, Clayton "Building a Future-Ready Supply Chain", Vibronyx.com, 2020. Last accessed at: www.vibronyx.com, 2022.

Index

Pages in *italics* refer to figures and pages in **bold** refer to tables.

Printed in the United States
by Baker & Taylor Publisher Services